"In *Toward Thriving Communities*, Brian Stiltner provides us with a splendid text that teaches us the viability of virtue in social contexts. This timely contribution captures the best that ethics offers us today: a character and growth formation ethics that can be cultivated in families, schools, work, and community service. In these fundamental settings, we can become virtuous, and Stiltner offers us concrete ways to see how this can happen. The book is a welcome dream for any teacher wanting to convey a living, social ethics."

—James F. Keenan, SJ
Canisius Professor
Boston College

"Virtue-based ethics can be found among the most ancient Eastern and Western philosophical traditions, yet it has been largely obscured in the past few hundred years by principle-based and consequentialist ethical systems. Brian Stiltner's *Toward Thriving Communities* effectively extends the recovery of virtue ethics to concrete moral situations we face in our everyday lives. Integrating theoretical analysis with case-based application, Stiltner's text illuminates the importance of virtue ethics in contemporary society: from parenting to politics, from being a good neighbor to being a conscientious global citizen. Stiltner's approach prompts us to engage in our own personal reflection on what sort of moral character we should strive to embody and also to inculcate in the next generation in accord with our best philosophical, anthropological, and sociological understanding of what it means to genuinely flourish as a human being. Going beyond the narrow confines of many introductory ethics texts, Stiltner's grounded elucidation of virtue theory—in contrast to other ethical approaches—will prove to be a useful guide for students and lay readers who haven't yet been introduced to this most classical and time-honored of approaches to moral living."

—Jason T. Eberl
Semler Endowed Chair for Medical Ethics
Marian University

"Eschewing hyperbolic lamentations over the challenges posed for the cultivation of virtue by deep pluralism and rampant materialism, *Toward Thriving Communities*, by Brian Stiltner, patiently attends to the ordinary communal contexts within which virtuous character is shaped and tested. In accessible, uncluttered prose, peppered with examples from daily life, Stiltner unpacks the interdependent character of personal and communal flourishing. Social contexts such as family, schools, workplaces, and volunteer organizations, he shows, have the potential either to help or to hinder the development of lives worth living, lives of virtuous activity directed toward the common good."

—Professor Jennifer Herdt
Yale Divinity School

D0022036

# Author Acknowledgments

I am grateful to the team at Anselm Academic for helping me bring this book from an initial big idea to final execution. Brad Harmon first excited me about working with Anselm. Maura Hagarty and Jerry Ruff believed in my idea and helped me focus it. Jerry and Beth Erickson were patient, diligent editors who read drafts multiple times, gave me excellent feedback, and kept me on track.

I am appreciative of support from Sacred Heart University (SHU) in the form of a sabbatical leave, a course release, and a URCG summer grant. The staff of the SHU library, directed by Peter Gavin Ferriby, has been of great assistance. Students in my virtue ethics courses gave me great insights as I tested out these ideas and some of the text with them.

Colleagues at SHU and elsewhere provided advice and answers to research questions. These colleagues include Jennie-Rebecca Falcetta, Andra Gumbus, Jennifer Herdt, Kendy Hess, Mary Latela, Dawn Melzer, Amanda Moras, and Phillip Stambovsky. Lesley DeNardis, Matthew Kaye, and Kirsten Nestro each gave great feedback on a chapter in an area of their expertise. I am blessed to have eleven good colleagues in philosophy, theology, and religious studies at SHU—among whom, for guidance on topics in the book, I thank Jesse Bailey, Chris Kelly, Ed Papa, Drew Pierce, Gordon Purves, and Mike Ventimiglia. Two other colleagues stand out: Steve Michels, a professor of political science at SHU, and Tim McCranor, a SHU alumnus now in doctoral studies at Boston College, each read many chapter drafts and advised me on everything from the fine points of Aristotle to making my prose clearer. Other colleagues and friends to whom I also owe deep thanks are Barbara Blodgett, David Clough, Frances Grodzinsky, and Paul Lauritzen.

Friends and family have helped me flourish in the work of writing this book. Those who gave substantial feedback include Mike Fazzino, Peter Kane, Rev. Matthew Richardson, Ed Wallace, Rev. John White, and Noka Zador. There are other friends and colleagues who have discussed the project with me—too numerous to name—but all are greatly appreciated. Special thanks to the Zador-Kane family and the Cumberbatch-Kaffman family for being steadfast friends, intellectual partners, parenting advisors, and promoters of the common good.

My brother, Jim Stiltner, gave feedback on chapter 5, and my wife Ann Stiltner, a special education teacher, did so on chapter 6. These family members—along with my brother Jeff and his family, my dad, my mom and her husband Bob, my father-in-law Hugh, my aunt Clare, and my extended family—have been my sure foundation. I am extremely grateful to Ann and our children, Brendan and Grace, for their patience with my working habits and, even more so, for their unmerited love. For me, they are virtue personified.

## Publisher Acknowledgments

Thank you to the following indivuduals who reviewed this work in progress:

William Frank, *University of Dallas, Texas*

Gina Messina-Dysart, *Ursuline College, Pepper Pike, Ohio*

Nancy M. Rourke, *Canisius College, Buffalo, New York*

# TOWARD THRIVING COMMUNITIES

*Virtue Ethics as Social Ethics*

## BRIAN STILTNER

ANSELM
ACADEMIC

Created by the publishing team of Anselm Academic.

The scriptural quotations in this book are from the *New American Bible*, revised edition © 2010, 1991, 1986, and 1970 by the Confraternity of Christian Doctrine, Inc., Washington, DC. Used by permission of the copyright owner. All rights reserved. No part of this work may be reproduced in any form without permission in writing from the copyright owner.

Cover image: ©UVAconcept / shutterstock

Printed in the United States of America

7073

ISBN 978-1-59982-689-9

# Contents

# Introduction

> Every state is a community of some kind, and every community is
> established with a view to some good; for everyone always acts in
> order to obtain that which they think good.
>
> —*Aristotle*[1]

The film *Please Give* is a character study of a family living in New York
City. Married couple Kate and Alex run an antique furniture store in the
same swanky neighborhood where they live. They have one child, a teen-
age daughter named Abby. The family is reasonably happy and free from major
crises. Yet the father, mother, and daughter deal with the ordinary stresses of
life and each, it seems, is trying to figure out why they don't feel happier with
the state of their lives. Their awkward searches for happiness and meaning are
the point of the film. Abby dislikes her acne and feels fat. Seeking to feel more
attractive, she wants her parents to buy her a $200 pair of jeans, which Kate
resists. Alex, trying to feel young again, stumbles into a brief affair with a young
day-spa worker. Driven by feelings of guilt mixed with compassion, Kate gives
money to homeless people.

In one scene, Kate and Abby pass a homeless man on the sidewalk. Kate
pulls out her wallet and, having only a five-dollar and twenty-dollar bill inside,
moves to give the twenty to the man. Abby snatches it and berates her mother
for giving so much. "Just give him the five," she yells. Kate says that it is her
money to do with as she wants. She orders Abby to pass along the twenty, which
Abby refuses to do. Shocked at her daughter and mortified in front of the man,
Kate gives him the five and then hurries away with her daughter. This tense
moment represents the characters' anxieties and the strains in their relationship.
Abby feels her mother is more generous toward strangers than toward her. Kate
feels she would be less of a good person for giving only five dollars to someone
in need. In addition, like most parents, she sometimes doesn't know how to deal
with the wildly emotional creature that is her teenager.

This scene is interesting because it invites the viewer to consider the complexity of everyday decisions. Is it good to give money to a homeless person? If
so, how much? There is no formula for deciding the right amount, although the

---

1. Aristotle, *The Politics*, 1.1 (1252a1), trans. Jonathan Barnes (New York: Cambridge University
Press, 1998), 1. In *Toward Thriving Communities*, classical works will be cited in the translation used
and according to their traditional divisions (usually books and chapters) and pagination. The current
citation, for instance, is to book 1, chapter 1 of *The Politics*. Advanced readers can use the parenthet-
ical number to find the specific location. Such numbers are printed in the margins of many editions
of Aristotle, Plato, and other classical authors.

context matters, as does the motivation with which one gives. Is it good to buy one's daughter a $200 pair of jeans? Will it boost her confidence, send her the wrong message about emphasizing her looks, or encourage her to become selfish? Outside of the context of the relationship, there is no way to know for certain. A mother or father has to make such decisions guided by parental wisdom, compassion for the child, and a sense of responsibility for the family's finances and the child's moral development. Yet, what is one's responsibility toward others who are struggling in society? The film's writer and director, Nicole Holofcener, commented,

> One of the great things about living in New York (if you have money) is being able to buy a beautiful place and fill it with beautiful things. But how do you do that and feel okay about it when there are hungry people right outside your (beautiful, newly stripped solid walnut) door? I've been struggling to forgive myself for those contradictions my whole life, and I think that's a struggle I heaped upon my characters, especially Kate.[2]

There are no formulaic answers to these questions, because the questions are not of the form, "What is the right action to do?" but of the form, "What is the best way to live?"

## Character and Community: Two Important Dimensions of Ethics

This book is about two dimensions of ethics, *character* and *community*, that go beyond questions of right action. Character requires reflection about the people who act, the make-up of their moral personalities, their abiding values, their moral traits and habits, and the story of their lives and relationships. This diverse list sets the context for human decisions. A character-based approach to ethics starts with *virtues*, which are character traits (including well-known qualities such as honesty, compassion, courage, and fairness) that lead to a happy and well-lived life—a state that virtue ethicists call *human flourishing*. Humans flourish when they live well and excellently as the rational, emotional, desiring, and social beings they are. When ethics is framed in terms of character and flourishing, then its subject matter expands to encompass decisions about whom to choose as friends, what career to seek, where to work, how to parent, when and where to volunteer, and so on. In Western culture, the theory of virtue ethics was first shaped by ancient Greek and Roman philosophers, such as Plato, Aristotle, and Seneca, who made "the shape of one's life" their preeminent philosophical

---

2. Nicole Holofcener, director's statement, *http://www.sonyclassics.com/pleasegive/presskit.pdf*.

concern. Since "How should I live?" is such an important ethical question, this book explores virtue ethics as an indispensable resource for addressing it. To be sure, "What is the right thing to do?" is also an important question. Virtue ethicists say, though, that questions of right action are often more effectively addressed within a wider exploration of the best way to live.

The community dimension requires attention to the interpersonal and social relationships that shape and inform an individual's moral actions. People live within many communities and institutions simultaneously—for example, one has a family, a neighborhood, a workplace, friends, social and civic clubs, and perhaps a religious community. These groups are the small and medium-sized communities to which people belong and in which they participate, enabling them to survive and thrive in many ways. Groups facilitate individuals' participation in the large structure known as *society*, the network of persons and groups held together by cultural, economic, geographical, legal, and political ties. Each community or society has a moral character—or ethos—constructed during a long span of time by the ethical characters and choices of its members. In turn, the ethos of each community and society contributes to the characters that its members develop. So, an ethical approach that is sensitive to the community dimension examines the complex influences of persons and communities on each other.

A community-oriented ethical approach further affirms that when individuals develop a robust understanding of human flourishing, they are more likely to appreciate that their well-being cannot be separated from the well-being of others or from the quality of the social fabric. When individuals have developed a range of virtues, they can better understand what an improved world might look like and can work collaboratively toward its improvement. A good example is Bead for Life, a nonprofit organization started by three U.S. women.[3] Torkin Wakefield, while doing aid work in Uganda, encountered a woman making beautiful beaded necklaces from scraps of paper. Wakefield brought some of the necklaces home to the United States as gifts. They were popular among her friends, many of who wanted to buy more. This experience inspired Wakefield, her mother, and a friend to recruit entrepreneurial Ugandan women, train them in bead making, sell the necklaces in the United States through parties, and give the proceeds to the Ugandans. The women who make the necklaces earn as much as $200 a month, which is deposited into savings accounts that they control. The fact that the women have protected financial assets wins them more respect from their husbands and communities. The women and their communities flourish because Bead for Life has a long-term plan for community development that includes helping the women start their own businesses.

This example illustrates that individuals with key virtues—such as the justice, compassion, and creativity of the program's founders and the

---

3. This example is drawn from Nicholas D. Kristof and Cheryl WuDunn, *A Path Appears: Transforming Lives, Creating Opportunity* (New York: Knopf, 2014), 30–32.

persistence and courage of the Ugandan women—can lead groups and communities toward a better future. The Ugandan participants flourish, as does their community. Those who volunteer with Bead for Life flourish, as does the organization itself. Entire societies—Uganda, the United States, and the international community—are positively influenced by such activities. The impact of one program on the global common good is tiny, but when many social movements and volunteer groups do similar work and share ideas, the effects multiply. From the work of people and communities pursuing their own flourishing, social change is born. Community-oriented ethics offers guidance for the combined pursuit of personal, communal, and social flourishing, since these are inextricably linked.

## Restoring the Connection between Virtue and the Common Good

Some books, especially those not written from a virtue perspective, give the misimpression that virtue ethics is limited to the personal level. Yet as theorists of virtue throughout history have appreciated, virtue ethics is valuable for articulating a vision of a good society and providing an ethical compass toward it. Aristotle's claim that "every community is established with a view to some good" indicates that this connection has been recognized from the beginning of the theory in fifth-century BCE Greece.[4] Aristotle described an ethical concept that came to be known as *the common good*.

The common good is the idea that the well-being of individuals and of society are interdependent. As an ethical principle, the common good requires that society create conditions that provide everyone with what they need to flourish. Government has a significant responsibility in promoting the common good, but the common good is about much more than government programs. Individuals, families, and civic groups of all sort—such as Bead for Life—are essential. The common good is a vibrant reality only when it includes everyone in a society. Achieving this requires that a critical mass of people and groups honor this principle in their words and deeds.[5]

A notion of the common good can be distilled from Aristotle's writings and the writings of most thinkers associated with virtue ethics. The ancient and medieval virtue thinkers believed that society inevitably shapes its individual

---

4. The roots of Greek philosophy start with the Pre-Socratics of the fifth century BCE. Aristotle, the most famous and influential of Plato's students and the tutor of Alexander the Great, lived in the fourth century.

5. Clearly, there need to be enough good people in a society to make the society good, but there is no way to specify how many or what proportion of people are needed. The factors for the common good are highly complex and variable; nevertheless, certain ethical baselines can be identified, and that is one of the purposes of this book.

members' characters, that society has a duty to try to educate people to have good character, that society may rightly expect its adult members to act with virtue, and that society cannot have a good ethos without its leaders and many of its citizens having good characters. But these long-held beliefs are debated in modern societies for many reasons, such as: the pluralism of worldviews, the separation of church and state, and the development of the rights of conscience and privacy. These developments are not bad, but they question old assumptions about who is a virtuous person and what a good society resembles. If the common good is an ideal that can appeal to contemporary people, it needs to be defined in light of contemporary realities, such as pluralism and democracy.

An updated understanding is possible. As Aristotle recognized, people want good things; hence, they want to live in a good society. Yet people do not agree on what those good things are and, therefore, do not agree on the way society should be arranged. This is a challenge, not an intractable problem. The methods of social ethics are designed to sharpen thinking about the goods people *in fact* want and that they *should* want, so they can get a clearer picture of how to live their lives, individually and collectively.

Members of a democratic society will never reach complete agreement on the complex issues facing them. Disagreement is part of human nature and free societies. Indeed, there is much that is good about disagreement, for it is a byproduct of political freedom. Despite the challenges of disagreement, citizens need to find ways to talk, listen, argue civilly, deliberate, and cooperate. To be capable of those activities, citizens must have characters that enable them to apply their virtues within social contexts. The intermediary groups examined in this book—families, schools, workplaces, and volunteer groups—are instrumental for the development of character that encourages people to contribute to the common good. While virtue ethics will not provide simple, indisputable answers, it recommends productive ways to think about social and political impasses and, just as importantly, civil ways to work on them.

## About This Book

This book differs from most books on ethical theory by presenting virtue ethics as a combined approach that offers guidance for individuals, groups, and society. A contemporary renewal of interest in the common good occurred at roughly the same time as a revival of virtue ethics—in the 1980s.[6] One might

---

6. A large wave of academic interest in virtue ethics followed the publication of Alasdair MacIntyre's book *After Virtue* (Notre Dame, IN: University of Notre Dame Press, 1981). A few years later, both academic and popular interest in the common good was stoked by the bestseller *Habits of the Heart* by Robert N. Bellah et al. (Berkeley: University of California Press, 1985). However, a number of otherwise very good philosophers of virtue ethics—such as Phillipa Foot, Rosalind Hursthouse, and Bernard Williams—did not pay much attention to MacIntyre or to works on the common good.

expect that virtue ethicists promoted this attention to the common good. Yet, especially among the philosophers of virtue, this was not the case, with a few exceptions. Theological virtue ethicists and the diverse group of sociologists, political scientists, and philosophers known as communitarians were the ones advocating for the common good and linking personal and social flourishing.[7] But since the connection of character and community is so long-standing, contemporary philosophers of virtue have many guideposts to point them toward a deeper inquiry.

The field has begun to respond with both theoretical and applied works. The theoretical contributions have been by authors following in the footsteps of Alasdair MacIntyre, whose 1981 book *After Virtue* was a trailblazer, not only for redirecting attention to the virtue tradition, but for powerfully arguing that virtue is a highly social reality. An example of applied work is a 2007 anthology titled *Working Virtue*. Its editors wrote that, even though the contemporary revival of interest in virtue had been happening for several decades, there was still "a relative paucity of writings that offer clear examples of virtue ethics actually at work in various practical fields."[8] With articles applying virtue ethics in such areas as medicine, psychiatry, education, law, business, race relations, and the environment, *Working Virtue* has helped fill the gap.

This book further contributes to advancing this new horizon for an ancient ethics by addressing both theoretical and practical tasks to give a comprehensive picture of the value of virtue ethics for social analysis. A work of applied ethics, this book examines how one who adopts the ethical theory of virtue might use it to analyze social problems and argue for practical responses to those problems. Many readers could benefit, including those new to philosophical ethics or theological ethics, those familiar with virtue ethics who would like to understand the theory's social implications, and those interested in one or more applied areas, such as business or education, who would like to understand what virtue ethics has to say about that area. *Toward Thriving Communities* helps readers reflect on two interconnected, fundamental human questions: What is the good life for me? What is the good life for society? Readers of this book can expect to do the following:

- understand more about virtue ethics in its classic formulation and its value as a resource for contemporary social ethics
- gain perspective on obstacles to human flourishing and resources for overcoming them

---

7. As a guide to some of this literature, see Brian Stiltner, *Religion and the Common Good: Catholic Contributions to Building Community in a Liberal Society* (Lanham, MD: Rowman and Littlefield, 1999).

8. Rebecca L. Walker and Philip J. Ivanhoe, eds., *Working Virtue: Virtue Ethics and Contemporary Moral Problems* (Oxford: Clarendon Press, 2007), 1.

• learn how to apply virtues to the pursuit of personal, communal, and social flourishing in several social contexts

Part 1, "Virtue Ethics as Personal, Communal, and Social Ethics," begins by framing virtue ethics within the context of two other ethical theories: deontology (based on duties) and consequentialism (based on consequences). While the ethics of duties and the ethics of consequences are both valuable methods for ethical analysis, chapter 1 argues that virtue ethics is particularly attractive for its holistic approach, including its ability to connect ethical concerns about personal flourishing to ethical concerns about communal and social flourishing. Ethical theories are complex. To make it easier to understand and compare ethical theories, chapter 1 introduces three features of moral experience to which every ethical theory pays attention:

• the guidelines by which people live and think they should live
• the purpose of human life in general, an individual's life in particular, and the lives of communities and societies
• the situational factors influencing the choices made by people and communities

Ethical theories address these features by proposing moral *norms*, giving accounts of moral *purpose*, and critically examining the *contexts* of moral living.

Chapters 2, 3, and 4 explain a virtue-ethical perspective on each of these features. These chapters develop important ethical tools, including the following:

• a list of virtues relevant to the needs of human beings, and particularly to their needs for communal and social living
• a specific account of what human flourishing means, so the well-being of persons, groups, and society can be assessed
• an understanding of how social capital is built or eroded in society through the activities of communal groups, so the health of a society's network of relationships can be assessed and its unhealthy elements targeted for improvement

The goal is to provide a roadmap for virtue ethics as a combined personal-communal-social ethic, so that ancient wisdom about character might help modern people live together in a just and flourishing manner.

Part 2, "The Pursuit of Flourishing in Social Contexts," shows how virtues enable people in groups to promote their own flourishing and that of society. The closer society comes to a mutually beneficial relationship among its members, the more it achieves the common good. In this part, four major groups are addressed: families, schools, workplaces, and volunteer organizations. These are neither the only groups involved in the promotion of character and flourishing, nor the only contexts where the common good is a major concern. As a result, these other groups figure in the discussion occasionally: friends, who are extremely important for individual well-being, and religious groups, which inculcate virtues in their members and influence society as communities of moral deliberation and philanthropic activity. Institutions of government also arise often in part 2, since public policies make a significant impact on the material resources that are part of personal and social flourishing. As for other, large contexts—such as international relations and the global environment—even these are amenable to improvement by the virtuous activity of groups. However, the challenges in these settings involve technical details that are beyond the scope of this book.

The strength of virtue ethics is that its norms, purpose, and appreciation of context enable people to pursue personal, communal, and social flourishing. Yet the entire picture of the interrelationships of persons, groups, and society, with implications for the character and flourishing of each, is complex. Thus each chapter in part 2 examines four main topics regarding the particular type of group being examined:

1. how the mutual relationships among a group and its members promote the character and flourishing of both
2. how the mutual relationships among a group and society promote the ethos and flourishing of both
3. ethical challenges encountered within a group, and how virtue ethics can be used to develop responses to those challenges
4. ethical challenges placed on a group by external social forces, and how virtue ethics can be used to develop the group's responses and society's obligations to assist that group

In short, what is the proper relationship among groups and society, such that the character and flourishing of each benefits the other?

For the sake of offering specific, useful examples, the context in part 2 will be U.S. society, that is, the United States as a cultural, geographic, economic, and political entity. To say that that the United States presents obstacles to the flourishing of the groups within it is not to make a negative judgment on the country overall. Rather, it is simply to acknowledge that U.S. society, like any society, both helps and hinders social flourishing. Civic-minded persons are concerned to know how they can improve their society. This book presumes, as Aristotle would, that the United States is organized with a view toward certain goods and that its citizens want to know how to live virtuously and promote the common good. Whether it is "most," "many," or "a few" who want to know does not matter; this book is written for those who *do* have such an interest. This approach follows the lead of Aristotle, who did not address his writings on ethics to those concerned only with satisfying their own wants. Aristotle said that other readers, "those who regulate their desires and actions by a rational principle," would greatly benefit from studying virtue ethics.[9]

For those interested in the journey toward the flourishing of individuals, groups, and societies, virtue ethics is an ethical compass for the voyage.[10] It is an approach both old and new—an ancient ethics that has remarkably much to say about contemporary concerns.

---

9. Aristotle, *Nicomachean Ethics*, 1.3 (1095a10), trans. Martin Ostwald (Englewood Cliffs, NJ: Prentice-Hall, 1962), 6. This work will be used extensively in this book. Usually, the translation will be from Terence Irwin but two other translations are occasionally used. After a first mention of the *Nicomachean Ethics* in each chapter, the subsequent references will be simply to the *Ethics*. (Aristotle also wrote a work called the *Eudemian Ethics*, which might have been compiled from his students' lecture notes. The content of the *Eudemian* is similar to the content of the *Nicomachean*, and the latter is believed, by most scholars, to be the superior work.)

10. The metaphor of a compass is suggested by Jim Wallis, *Rediscovering Values: A Moral Compass for a New Economy* (New York: Howard Books, 2010).

# PART

# Virtue Ethics as Personal, Communal, and Social Ethics

The first part of *Toward Thriving Communities* provides an in-depth summary of virtue ethics, with particular attention to the connections among its expressions at the personal, group, and social levels.

The background provided in chapter 1, "Approaches to Ethics," defines ethics and locates this book's analysis at the normative and applied levels. Virtue ethics is explained in relationship to two other ethical theories: deontology and consequentialism. Together these are applied to a case study of ethics in the workplace that illustrates similarities and differences among the theories. Virtue ethics is recommended for its realistic and holistic approach. All ethical theories attend to three important features of the moral life: norms, purpose, and context. The next three chapters take up each feature in turn and examine it from a virtue-ethical perspective.

Virtues display an individual's excellence of character and contribute to the flourishing of that person and others. Virtues help people live well—in their personal lives and in community. To better understand them, chapter 2, "Virtues: Norms for Acting and Living," precisely defines virtue, illustrates its definition through a school-shooting case study, and organizes virtues into categories.

Drawing on ancient and contemporary virtue theorists, chapter 3, "Human Flourishing: The Purpose of Life, the Purpose of Ethics," presents human flourishing as the best way to understand happiness. Flourishing is defined as doing good and living well in the domains of body, mind, character, and relationship to others—a status that requires sufficient material resources. This account of flourishing is a standard against which the well-being of persons can be measured, as illustrated by a case study comparing the lives of two schoolchildren.

The mutual influences among persons, groups, and society is the focus of chapter 4, "Communities: The Contexts for Becoming Good and Living Well." Social capital is built up or eroded in society through the activities of groups, so the health of a society's network of relationships can be assessed and its unhealthy elements targeted for improvement. As people and groups move their society toward improvement—toward social flourishing—the common good becomes an increasing reality. Intermediate social groups are instrumental in developing the personal and social virtues that tend to move society toward the common good.

# Approaches to Ethics

*Ethics has to do with things to be chosen or avoided, with different ways of life, and with the purpose of life.*

*—Epicurus (341–270 BCE), Greek philosopher*[1]

## Chapter Overview

- defines ethics and explains its personal and social dimensions
- summarizes three ethical theories—deontology, consequentialism, and virtue ethics—and applies these theories to a case study
- discusses three core elements of the moral life addressed by ethical theories

## Levels of Ethics

In a letter to a newspaper advice column called "The Ethicist," a college student named L. T. asks how to handle an everyday ethical dilemma. "At my university, many students use tests from previous quarters to study for exams. These old tests are available to about 75 percent of the students—fraternities and sororities and some dorms keep them on file—but not all. Every time I consider using one, I find myself in moral conflict. Is it ethical to use these tests?"[2] The column's author, Randy Cohen, begins his answer by focusing on the specific action involved—using an old test to study for exams: "As long as you're not using the actual test you'll be taking, and as long as your professors permit this

---

1. Epicurus's statements survive only in fragments; this one is from Diogenes Laertius, *Lives of Eminent Philosophers* 10.30, in Epicurus, *The Art of Happiness*, trans. George K. Strodach (New York: Penguin, 2012), 85.

2. The letter and the response appeared in the *New York Times Magazine* on September 14, 2003, and was reprinted in Randy Cohen, *Be Good: How to Navigate the Ethics of Everything* (San Francisco: Chronicle Books, 2012), 253–54.

practice—i.e., as long as you're not cheating—you're free to employ these old tests as review material." This answer is guided by the rules of a university community and the contracts between individual professors and their students.

But even an unambiguous, action-oriented question such as this has multiple dimensions. First, L. T. is probably thinking about more than a single action, as his[3] statement suggests, "Every time I consider using one, I find myself in moral conflict." The reference to "moral conflict" suggests the student is considering matters of character and conscience and whether or not, if he uses one of the old tests, he will be able "to look at himself in the mirror," as the saying goes. L. T. also is thinking about the possibility of gaining an unfair advantage over other students. The ethical question is, therefore, not simply about the personal dimension of L. T.'s discrete action, but about the fairness of a system that impacts many others. L. T. is not sure what, if anything, to do about the system. Before one can begin to address either the personal or the social dimension of the situation, however, it is helpful to understand exactly what is meant by "ethics."

L. T. asks, "Is it ethical to use these tests?" But it would have made just as much sense to ask, "Is it moral to use these tests?" *Ethical* and *moral* derive, respectively, from Greek and Latin words (*ethos* and *mores*) for the same concept: the character of individuals or groups. All English words based on these roots have something to do with the way people live by beliefs and values regarding right and wrong, and good and bad. The adjectives *ethical* and *moral* are used, usually interchangeably, to characterize ideas relating to how people should live. These terms do not need to be put together. It is redundant to say "an ethical and moral issue." However, there is a difference between the noun forms. *Ethics* is associated with formal analysis, academic study, and social and professional codes of conduct. *Morality*, on the other hand, is associated with one's personal living based upon values. As one author puts it, "'morality' is what we live, whereas 'ethics' is what we study."[4] This book often refers to ethics, since the overall topic is the academic theory of virtue as applied to social contexts. However, virtue ethics is a lived approach. One of its appealing features is that it is an ethics for regular people. People intuitively know what good character is. Therefore, one source for virtue ethics is the morality of ordinary people.

The investigations in this book are *normative* and *applied*. In normative inquiry, ethicists develop (or refine and comment on) theories that justify ethical *norms*, which are basic guidelines for ethical action in any context. These theories and their norms then can be applied to practical questions. In applied inquiries, ethicists analyze concrete problems encountered in jobs and careers

---

3. It is unknown whether L. T. is a male or female student. For the sake of simplicity in the retelling of this case study, a gender was assigned.

4. Vincent J. Genovesi, *In Pursuit of Love: Catholic Morality and Human Sexuality*, 2nd ed. (Collegeville, MN: Michael Glazier, 1996), 16.

(a subtype of ethics called *professional ethics*), in large social and political systems (a subtype called *social ethics*), and in technical fields such as medicine,
technology, law, and so on (these subtypes are called *applied ethics* or are named
according the context, such as *medical ethics, legal ethics,* etc.).[5] *Toward Thriving
Communities* draws upon the works of normative ethicists throughout the ages,
largely in the Western tradition and, above all, Aristotle and those influenced by
him. The Aristotelian tradition is prominent because this book advances virtue
ethics as the most helpful ethical theory for addressing the combination of the
personal and social dimensions of ethics. When this investigation turns to contemporary issues, the ideas of applied ethicists, especially those associated with
virtue theory, will be examined.

## A Definition of Ethics

As a field of study and a method of analysis, normative ethics can be defined
through four characteristics:

> Ethics is (1) reflection (2) on principles, consequences, and virtues
> (3) to determine what acts to do or avoid and what kind of person to
> be, (4) creating standards to which persons hold themselves and their
> communities.[6]

As each part of this definition is explained in more detail, keep the L. T. example
in mind.

## Ethics Is Reflection

Ethics is, first of all, reflective. To be ethical, one must consider one's actions and
be able to give reasons for one's moral viewpoint and behavior. Making an ethical argument is not the same as being argumentative; rather, it means making a
reasonable case so that, even if others do not agree, they at least understand one's
point of view. As a reflective process, ethics usually benefits from discussion
among reasonable and well-meaning people. Individual and group reflection are
strongest under conditions of freedom and knowledge, exercised by people using

---

5. Besides (a) normative ethics and (b) applied ethics, two other major types of ethics are
(c) descriptive/comparative ethics, which depicts, compares, and contrasts the moralities of groups
or cultures, and (d) metaethics, which analyzes the meaning and sources of ethical values. Reference
works and textbooks describe these main types of inquiry, although the exact terms may vary. For
further information, see an encyclopedia of ethics, such as *A Companion to Ethics*, ed. Peter Singer
(Malden, MA: Wiley-Blackwell, 1993); *Encyclopedia of Ethics*, ed. Lawrence and Charlotte Becker,
2nd ed., 3 vols. (New York: Routledge, 2001); and "Ethics," "Applied Ethics," and "Comparative
Philosophy," in *Internet Encyclopedia of Philosophy, http://www.iep.utm.edu.*

6. A version of this definition appears in David L. Clough and Brian Stiltner, *Faith and Force: A
Christian Debate about War* (Washington, DC: Georgetown University Press, 2007), 29.

sound reasoning and wise discernment.[7] A process of self-reflection is seen in L. T.'s letter: L. T. is thinking about what to do and knows that it is important to get advice from others. A process of reflective argument is seen in Cohen's response as well, when he shows a process for thinking through the nature of the action, the people affected, and the codes in force.

## Principles, Consequences, and Virtues

Ethics reflects upon three key resources:

- *Rules and principles*: specific and general guidelines to action, such as "do not misreport your finances on your tax return" (a rule) and "help a person who is in need" (a principle)[8]
- *Consequences*: the good results of actions balanced against the bad results, such as the well-being of a friend who is helped and the satisfaction felt by the one who helps balanced against the time taken to help and the possible neglect of another obligation
- *Virtues*: character traits of persons, such as friendliness and compassion[9]

The relevance of these key resources is seen in L. T.'s question and Cohen's response. L. T. and Cohen discuss principles of fairness and honesty. L. T. is concerned about consequences for students who do not get access to old tests and about his own character. Cohen appeals to the values and principles that bind a university community.

## Determining What Acts to Do or Avoid and What Kind of Person to Be

It has been said that ethics is about both "doing" and "being."[10] Ethical reflection leads one to determine appropriate actions. Ethical theories based on principles and consequences focus particularly on "doing." Ethics is also a framework for thinking about the shape of one's life. As was seen in the book's introduction, this "being" dimension of ethics was of particular interest to ancient philosophers, and it's the special concern of virtue ethicists, both ancient and modern.

---

7. See Michael R. Panicola et al., *Health Care Ethics: Theological Foundations, Contemporary Issues, and Controversial Cases*, 2nd ed. (Winona, MN: Anselm Academic, 2011), 5–7.

8. When describing guidelines for action, the key difference between a rule and a principle is that the former is specific about an action and a context while the later is a general guideline that applies in many areas of one's life.

9. Another resource that could be identified is *values*, which are desirable qualities in life, such as friendship, peace, and compassion. However, such values can be translated into the language of principles, consequences, or virtues, so it is not necessary to add an additional term.

10. Panicola et al., *Health Care Ethics*, 6.

Relating this third characteristic to the question about using old tests, one can see that Cohen's and L. T.'s interchange is focused mostly on what to do, but one can also sense that L. T. is concerned about his character.

## Creating Standards to Which Persons Hold Themselves and Their Communities

Ethics creates strong standards. To say, "Action X is the only ethical course of action" means "I (or we) should do X." Ethical duties are morally obligatory, not optional, so people hold themselves to ethical standards under pain of self-contradiction. One should not say, "I know that is the ethical thing to do, but I don't have to do it," or, "but I don't want to do it."[11] Of course, people can and do advocate or act contrary to ethical standards, but according to the moral point of view, one cannot *reasonably* behave this way. Philosophers call this feature of ethics *normativity*, which means that people discerning what is right or wrong will recognize a certain *norm* or accepted standard as decisive when weighing options. For instance, for L. T., it matters more whether using an old test counts as cheating than whether L. T. has time to study because a favorite television show is airing.

Similarly, it is a characteristic of normative ethics that a community or society recognizes its need for normative standards. The ethical standards for a society ultimately derive from reason. Members of the society can discuss and claim those standards through public conversation. For example, from colonial times to today, people in the United States have held political freedom dear. Therefore, respect for freedom operates as a cultural and legal norm in the United States, but it also operates as an ethical norm when people claim that freedom is just and liberty is a human right. When conflicts and new questions about freedom arise, and citizens use reasoned arguments to figure out the answers to these conflicts and questions, they engage in normative ethics. The determinations may be political, legal, or cultural, depending upon the situation, but in all cases, the deliberative process is guided by accepted normative standards.

## The Personal and Social Dimensions of Ethics

In his response to L. T., Cohen argues that professors should not remain blithely unaware of the widespread practice of circulating old tests. In fact, he puts the onus to take action on the professors.

---

11. Normative ethics stands against egoism (the claim that ethics should be based on what each individual wants) and relativism (the claim that ethical standards should vary according to the values of different people or different societies). See "Egoism" and "Moral Relativism," in *Internet Encyclopedia of Philosophy*, *http://www.iep.utm.edu*. Drew E. Hinderer and Sara R. Hinderer make arguments against egoism and relativism in the context of professional ethics in *A Multidisciplinary Approach to Health Care Ethics* (Mountain View, CA: Mayfield, 2001), chs. 2 and 4.

But while you [L. T.] are meeting your ethical obligations, your professors are not. If they regard these old tests as legit study aids, they must make them available to all (online? at the library? printed on pastries in the dining hall?). In other words, this situation demands not student abstinence but faculty action. What you might do is make sure that your professors are aware of the problem and that they are indeed resolving it.[12]

Cohen's response is a good example of connecting the personal and social levels of ethical concern. He says L. T. should act on his conscientious concern about fairness for others by proactively mentioning the situation to one or more professors. He says the professors should ensure that all of their students have the same study aids. (If one is worried that Cohen is not emphasizing the dimension of cheating in his response, Cohen might say, "If the professors do not want students to use old tests, that is fine, but they need to be clear. Instead of simply banning the use of old tests, which would be ineffectual in a large university, they must make the effort to change the tests yearly.")

Thus an important task of ethics is to examine, question, and try to change the social contexts that create or exacerbate today's major ethical challenges. "Every state is a community of some kind, and every community is established with a view to some good; for everyone always acts in order to obtain that which they think good," says Aristotle.[13] This claim seems like common sense—even today—especially regarding communities that people set up intentionally, for people would not go to the trouble of setting up a community for no reason, even if their reasoning was merely survival and basic safety. For Aristotle, this insight entails that every society and community has an ethos, a set of habits and practices that shape how the community lives toward its goals. In short, every society has ethics.

Yet if the society is large and complex—such as a modern, democratic society comprising subcommunities and people of diverse worldviews—is it possible to discuss its ethics? The answer is, "Yes," for this diversity simply means that a society's ethics are large and complex and influenced by the groups within it. A society's ethics or ethos is constituted by the values for which the society is established; how it incorporates and validates the ethics of its subcommunities; the values, virtues, and principles that guide its daily activities; and whether it shows relative consistency in its conduct. While there is danger in making generalizations about the ethos of a society, it is still a

---

12. Cohen, *Be Good*, 54.

13. Aristotle, *The Politics*, 1.1 (1252a1), trans. Jonathan Barnes (New York: Cambridge University Press, 1998), 1. This quotation is also discussed in the book's introduction.

valuable practice for understanding the context in which people live. If one does not discuss society's ethos, one cannot begin improving it. As with any large culture, American culture is marked by values that are somewhat contradictory. Americans are influenced by an ethos of materialism and commercialism owing to the United States' prosperity, capitalist economy, advertising industry, and cultural myths and icons, such as the self-made man and the rugged pioneer. Yet, at the same time, Americans display a great deal of generosity, philanthropy, and appreciation for nonmaterial values, as is seen when the country responds to natural disasters at home or abroad. Personal ethics takes into account the fact that individuals have mixed motives and both good and bad traits; the point of personal ethics is to help people accentuate their good traits and act on their better motives. Social ethics takes the same approach toward the complex ethos of a society.

In *Politics*, Aristotle moves from the descriptive statement that citizens have shared goals to the normative task of describing the best ways for citizens to organize a democracy to achieve these goals. This form of reflection is called *political philosophy* or *social ethics*. This book typically uses the latter term, which emphasizes the role of social groups more than that of political institutions in addressing ethical problems at the social level.[14] Citizens and groups engage in social ethics, in a normative fashion, when they work from their moral commitments to try to shape society's ethics. They wrestle with questions about how to arrange society, what social values they should hold and promote, what political policies they should support, and how they should act as individual citizens and in the civic groups to which they belong. Professors and students who conduct social ethics are doing the same thing, but in a formal, reasoned manner. Their work might be more descriptive or comparative ("How do one or more societies live out ethical values or respond to a certain ethical problem?") but usually it is normative and applied ("How *should* a certain society live out ethical values or respond to a certain ethical problem, given its history, ethos, and the values of its members?").

The simple meaning of social ethics is: the application of normative ethics to the problems that society faces and to the question of how society should be arranged. For a formal definition, the previous definition of normative ethics can be modified to express the social dimensions:

> Social ethics is (1) the normative deliberation of citizens, social groups, and public leaders (2) on ethical resources and on the results of social analysis (3) to decide on collective actions and express an ethos (4) so people can live together in a just and flourishing manner.

---

14. By contrast, "political philosophy" is a much broader term, encompassing such topics as theories of political authority, accounts of citizenship, the structure of constitutions, and voting rights.

When one is engaging in ethical analysis of either a personal or a social concern, one uses normative ethical theories. The proper use of such theories is what makes one's ethical analysis coherent, enlightening, and persuasive.

## Normative Ethical Theories

Ethical theories are coherent frameworks of beliefs, ideas, values, and assumptions with corresponding methods of reasoning about moral questions. Three normative ethical theories have occupied the greatest amount of attention in Western philosophy: deontology, consequentialism, and virtue ethics. These generally correspond to the three resources in the definition of ethics: rules and principles, consequences, and virtues. The three theories discussed here were developed and refined throughout centuries by philosophers who found that zeroing in on one of these three resources best accounts for people's moral intuitions and makes for the most rational and consistent approach to living. Although a person who adopts a particular theory does not necessarily exclude insights from the other theories, the adopter believes that the resource focused on by their preferred theory is the most important feature in ethical reflection.

### Deontological Ethics

The German philosopher Immanuel Kant (1724–1804) developed the most well-known version of deontology. Kant says human reason is the fundamental source of duty. For Kant, morality is based on a rational respect for people as the foundation of value. Kant boils ethical duty down to a single "categorical imperative," for which he gave two famous formulations. The first is: "Act only according to that maxim whereby you can at the same time will that it should become a universal law."[15] This means people should act only on the basis of rules and principles[16] that they rationally believe all people in similar circumstances should follow. The categorical imperative is normative, as described earlier: one cannot exempt oneself from following what his or her own reason dictates. If, for example, a teenager reasons that it is *morally* wrong to lie to his parents about how he wrecked the family car, he *knows* that he cannot exempt

---

15. Immanuel Kant, *Grounding of the Metaphysic of Morals*, trans. James W. Ellington, 3rd ed. (Indianapolis: Hackett, 1993), 30 (vol. 4, p. 421 of the Academy edition of Kant's works in German).

16. Kant used the term *maxim* to indicate a person's guiding principle for action. In less technical discussions of deontology, *rules* and *principles* can be used as rough equivalents for *maxims*. In many studies of ethics, rules and principles are associated with deontology, since deontology emphasizes that one should act under general, rational guidelines, such as "tell the truth" and "do not kill." But rules and principles can be, and are, employed in the other two theories. For instance, consequentialist philosophers have advocated "the principle of utility," and some virtue philosophers have proposed "virtue-rules."

himself from following through just because he is afraid of the consequences. Of course, people fail to follow through on such judgments all the time, but Kant's point is simply that people should know better. Deontologists use Kant's reasoning to block the path to self-serving rationalizations and relativism. Kant's second formulation of the categorical imperative is easier to grasp and easier to use in ethical argument: one "should treat himself and all others never merely as a means but always at the same time as an end in himself."[17] According to deontology, respect for human persons underlies all ethical principles and rules.

Contrary to popular opinion, the ethics of principle, even Kant's version, need not be absolutist and rigid. Kant does not say others cannot serve as a means to some ends, only that one cannot treat others *solely* as means to ends. For example, if someone buys something at a store, that person is treating the clerk as means to the end of the purchase, but one can and must treat the clerk as "an end in himself" by respecting his personal dignity—for instance, by being kind, not stealing, and so on. Kant further states that the highest level of morality is when one acts not because of a rule (what he calls "acting in accordance with duty") but because one knows and understands it to be the right thing to do ("acting from duty").[18] Another point in favor of deontology's flexibility is that it does not bar one from considering consequences, as long as doing so does not lead to the violation of fundamental moral principles. It is acceptable to consider the ends, but the ends can never justify the means.

Many ethical principles might be relevant guidelines to one's actions, depending on the context. Also, philosophers differ about whether some principles take priority over others. As mentioned, most Kantians believe respect for persons is the fundamental principle. The Western religions of Judaism, Christianity, and Islam feature moral codes and divine laws that are deontological in form. An influential textbook of medical ethics structures the field according to four basic principles: respect for patients' autonomy, nonmaleficence (do no harm), beneficence (help people), and justice (distribute medical resources equitably). These principles are often interpreted and applied in deontological fashion.[19] Medicine is just one of many social contexts in which deontological ethics has been widely used.

Deontology's appeal lies in its clarity, rationality, and fairness, yet it also has weaknesses. Principles can conflict, and while deontological theories offer various ways of addressing the conflicts, no approach has been entirely successful.

---

17. Ibid., 39. (A less-often discussed third formulation of the imperative is "every rational being must so act as if he were through his maxim always a legislating member in a universal kingdom of ends" (43; 4.438).

18. Ibid., 10–13.

19. Tom L. Beauchamp and James F. Childress, *Principles of Biomedical Ethics*, 7th ed. (New York: Oxford University Press, 2012). The authors' use of principles is neither fully deontological nor fully consequentialist. Their recommended approach is a case-by-case weighing of obligations based on a version of deontological ethics called "prima facie duties theory," developed by W. D. Ross.

The more absolutist theories—such as Kant's complete prohibition on lying[20] and the Catholic Church's rigorous pro-life principle—resolve conflicts but fail to convince many people that every other ethical value gives way to the main principle. Some may argue that all principles are initially obligatory but can give way on a case-by-case basis, but then disagreements ensue. For example, which should have priority—a dying patient's right to choose suicide to avoid massive pain or society's duty to prevent homicide and doctors' duties to preserve life? Some criticize deontology for overlooking tradition, social context, and moral development. So while deontology is less susceptible than virtue ethics to the charge of being relativistic, deontology might also be weak since it fails to draw upon the distinctive values of a cultural tradition for a vision of the best way to live.

## Consequentialist Ethics

Consequentialism is the youngest of the three theories, even though the practice of weighing consequences before deciding on an action is not new. Consequentialism turns this commonsense into a theory. It holds that acts are right or wrong based on their expected good or bad consequences. For this reason, consequentialism is categorized as a *teleological* (goal-based) theory in ethics, a description it shares with virtue ethics. "Teleological theories are ones that first identify what is good in states of affairs and then characterize right acts entirely in terms of that good."[21] Consequentialism defines the "greatest good for the greatest number" as the goal, while virtue ethics defines human flourishing as the goal. Yet both theories hold that actions are morally right when they contribute toward the defined goal of the theory. Deontology, by contrast, is a non-teleological theory, since it holds that right actions are defined by their conformity with moral duties.

The earliest consequentialist philosophers went by the name utilitarians, because they presented *the principle of utility* as the sole guideline in ethics. Utilitarianism focuses on the nature of happiness and the motivations of persons. Jeremy Bentham (1748–1832) made "the greatest happiness of the greatest number" the standard of what is right. John Stuart Mill (1806–1873), by contrast, argued that utility is a collection of many intrinsic values—the things that most or all persons want, such as health, freedom from pain, beauty, knowledge, and so on.[22] Mill agreed with Bentham that the greatest happiness

---

20. See Kant's short essay, "On a Supposed Right to Lie from Philanthropic Motives," bound with the Ellington translation of *Grounding*, 63–67.

21. "Theological Ethics," in *Encyclopedia of Philosophy*, ed. Donald M. Borchert, 2nd ed. (Farmington Hills, MI: Macmillan Reference USA, 2006), 9:382.

22. The classic sources are Bentham, *An Introduction to the Principles of Morals and Legislation* (1789) and Mill, "Essay on Bentham" (1838) and *Utilitarianism* (1863).

of the greatest number of people is the guideline, but he gave a more robust picture of happiness.

The broader term, consequentialism, focuses on the *method* of weighing good versus bad consequences. Two methods are commonly used.[23] The first, *act-consequentialism*, is straightforward: weigh all expected consequences of every action and do the action that is likely to create the greatest happiness for the greatest number. The second, *rule-consequentialism*, uses the principle of utility to support rules that, in turn, tend to produce good consequences. The philosophers who developed the rule-oriented approach were trying to overcome three problems with act-consequentialism: that charting benefits versus harms for every action is cumbersome; that the act-oriented method may give undue weight to the most obvious consequences; and that the act-oriented approach allows for unsettling instances of "the ends justify the means." For example, act-consequentialists see nothing inherently moral about keeping a promise; rather, for each opportunity one might have to keep or break a promise, act-consequentialism requires figuring out which course leads to better results overall. Rule-consequentialists assert that their approach is better, since one does not have to think through every single action and since a society that respects the adage "honesty is the best policy" will be more stable in the long run.

Consequentialist ethics initially seems disruptive to traditional morality, and it can be—in both good and bad ways. On the positive side, consequentialists are often social reformers who use this ethic to bring into focus the fact that all persons and, indeed, all beings who can experience pleasure and pain deserve consideration. Mill, for instance, was an early and strong advocate for the rights of women. Peter Singer, a contemporary philosopher, pioneered the cause of animal welfare on the utilitarian ground that since animals can suffer, they have interests that must be incorporated in a consequentialist calculation. Consequentialism has also proven beneficial in social ethics by applying the method of cost-benefit analysis to complicated decisions about public policies.

On the negative side, many remain troubled by the willingness of consequentialists to make rules provisional and, perhaps, to override longstanding values. For instance, given the demand for transplantable human organs, a consequentialist might enact a law to harvest organs from everyone who dies, regardless of the families' wishes, because, overall, the benefits would be tremendous. Further, why not allow living donors to sell their kidneys and benefit those in need of the organ as well as the seller? Based on "the greatest happiness for the greatest number," consequentialists are more supportive of these practices than other theorists. However, consequentialist arguments for organ sales often overlook values such as bodily integrity and concerns about the vulnerability of those whose desperate poverty would drive them to consider selling their organs.

---

23. See "Act and Rule Utilitarianism" in *Internet Encyclopedia of Philosophy*, *http://www.iep.utm.edu*; and "Rule Consequentialism" in *Stanford Encyclopedia of Philosophy*, *http://plato.stanford.edu*.

## Virtue Ethics

Julia Annas, a philosopher of ancient ethics, says, "In ordinary life, although we may not often use the term 'virtue,' we think and talk all the time in terms of virtues. We think (and frequently say) of others and ourselves that we are generous or stingy, kind or mean, helpful or selfish."[24] Virtue ethics is ancient theory that identifies virtues, that is, character traits, as the foundation of actions leading to human flourishing. The ancient Greek and Roman philosophers—though affiliated with various schools, such as Stoicism and Epicureanism—understand virtue to be the core of ethics. Virtue also has been central to the moralities of the world's religions.

Virtue ethics says that morality should not be as focused on *what to do* so much as on *what kind of person to be*. Virtue ethics is flexible in two ways: it is tailored to the unique features of each person's life story, and it resists giving a simple procedure for decisions, suggesting instead that people develop the habit of wise reflection. This theory considers the external purposes that people have in their roles and relationships and the internal purposes they have for moral, spiritual, and intellectual growth. As Annas puts it, the entry point for virtue ethics is the question, "How ought I to live?" or "What should my life be like?"[25] After looking at what one is trying to become, one must discern the courses of action and qualities of acting that help achieve those purposes. The Greeks described the ultimate goal of human activity—and thus of virtue—as "happiness" or "human flourishing."

*Virtues* are character traits disposing one to act, feel, perceive, or think in a way generally recognized as excellent—excellent because such actions, feelings, perceptions, or thoughts are admirable, humane, and beneficial to self and others. Examples of such character traits are justice, temperance (self-control), courage, practical wisdom, compassion, patience, forgiveness, good humor, and more. The first four items in this list emerged from the Greek tradition as the four foundational virtues, later dubbed *the cardinal virtues*. Classical authors, such as Plato, Aristotle, and Thomas Aquinas, broadly distinguish moral from intellectual virtues. Other authors recognize an even greater diversity. There are intellectual virtues, virtues for creative and artistic endeavors, and virtues for physical activity. There are virtues for specific roles, professions, and practices—such as business, parenting, sports, and so on. What is common to all virtues is that they lead one to act effectively and excellently in the field of the virtue, whatever it happens to be, and they contribute to human flourishing.

*Vices* are the character traits that lead one to perform badly. In Aristotle's system, most vices reflect a deficit or an excess of a virtue in the sense of not being on the target for rational, excellent action. For example, cowardice and rashness are opposed to courage, and impatience and being overly patient (i.e.,

---

24. Julia Annas, *Intelligent Virtue* (New York: Oxford University Press, 2011), 8.

25. These are Annas's two phrasings of the fundamental question of ancient ethics, which was classically posed by Socrates in the first book of *The Republic* (352d), in *The Morality of Happiness* (New York: Oxford University Press, 1993), 27.

so willing to wait that one would be used) are opposed to patience. For such traits of character, Aristotle says virtue consists in the proper "intermediate state," or the *mean*, between the two extremes. Virtue is the state of character in which a person acts excellently and ethically—in just the right way, at the right time, with the best motivation.[26] Vices as well as virtues are *habits*—not in the sense of rote, unthinking routines, but as a person's settled dispositions developed through a process of learning and practice called "habituation"; thus virtues can, in theory, be changed if one so chooses. However, change is not easy. Aristotle says that an everyday human action, such as "giving and spending money, is easy and everyone can do it; but doing it to the right person, in the right amount, at the right time, for the right end, and in the right way is no longer easy, nor can everyone do it. Hence doing these things well is rare, praiseworthy, and fine."[27] People know how to spend money, but not everyone knows how to spend it excellently and ethically. Almost everyone knows how to speak in a friendly manner to people they like, but not everyone knows how to relate respectfully and kindly to many sorts of people in many situations. In short, Aristotle says, it is "hard work to be excellent."[28]

*Character* is the integration of one's beliefs, perceptions, feelings, and habits, whether in a good, neutral, or bad fashion. "Having virtue" or "being a virtuous person" refers to having a predominantly good character. Aristotle says the point of ethical philosophy is to move from acting virtuously because one has been taught to do so, to acting virtuously because one sees the point of it and wants to do so.[29] In a principle-based theory, a principle, rule, or description of an action serves as the paradigm for one to follow. But in virtue ethics, real human beings are the paradigms, because only people in all their particularity and complexity can be exemplars of character. Thus, role models and moral educators are crucial resources for the theory.

As with the other ethical theories, philosophers have identified weaknesses of virtue ethics.[30] Proponents of consequentialism and deontology often say virtue is insufficient for guiding action. The exhortation, "Be virtuous," even when citing a specific virtue, doesn't tell one enough about what to do in a specific

---

26. Aristotle first describes the concept of the mean in *Nicomachean Ethics*, 2.6, and he uses it throughout.

27. Aristotle, *Nicomachean Ethics*, 2.9 (1109a27–30), trans. Terence Irwin (Indianapolis: Hackett, 1999), 29.

28. Ibid, 2.9.

29. Ibid., 1.4. Indeed, Aristotle thinks people need to have a starting point for the study of ethics: they need to have the beginnings of a good character through early education, else they will have no character with which to work. See also 2.1 and 10.9.

30. For these and some additional objections to virtue ethics, see section 3 of "Virtue Ethics," in *Stanford Encyclopedia of Philosophy*, *http://plato.stanford.edu/entries/ethics-virtue/*; and Robert B. Louden, "On Some Vices of Virtue Ethics," in *Virtue Ethics*, ed. Roger Crisp and Michael Slote (New York: Oxford University Press, 1997), 201–16.

situation. In response, virtue ethicists have employed various strategies, such as developing insights into the philosophy of action, exploring strategies for moral education and habituation, and developing a place for rules in the theory. Another concern is that virtue theory is relativistic. Virtue ethicists typically praise cultural and religious traditions for forming character, but traditions can be inflexible, even oppressive. For example, in the American South prior to the 1960s, many familial, cultural, religious, and political traditions conveyed attitudes of the racial superiority of white people. A warped understanding of virtue followed. While virtue ethics certainly does not recommend bigotry, the charge against the theory is that it does not have a vantage point from which to criticize a particular community in which members think they are teaching their children virtue instead of vice. This objection is met by acknowledging the potentially negative pull of community on character and identifying strategies for resisting it (ch. 4).

Virtue ethics is not flawless, and the other theories have important contributions to make to ethical reasoning (for a summary comparison of the theories, see table 1). One of the strengths of virtue ethics is its ability to recommend humility and prudence, so virtue ethicists themselves are inclined to learn from the limitations of their theory. Virtue ethics is a realistic ethical theory, because everyone is imperfect but capable of improvement.

## TABLE 1  Three Main Ethical Theories Compared

| | Deontological Ethics | Consequentialist Ethics | Virtue Ethics |
|---|---|---|---|
| **Focus of the Theory** | What to do | What to do | Who to be |
| **The Goal Proposed for Human Life** | Upholding the moral law | Promoting the greatest happiness for the greatest number | Achieving happiness through human flourishing |
| **What Makes Actions Right?** | Right actions are those that one has a duty to perform, regardless of the consequences | Actions are right or wrong based on their expected good or bad consequences | Right actions are those based on virtue and that promote flourishing |
| **Strengths of the Theory** | • Proposes principles that are rational, clear, and fair<br>• Resists rationalization and relativism | • Treats all persons and sentient beings with consideration<br>• Not constrained by outdated rules and traditions | • Tailored to unique features of each person's life story<br>• Resists giving an overly simple procedure for decisions |

| | Deontological Ethics | Consequentialist Ethics | Virtue Ethics |
|---|---|---|---|
| **Three Main Ethical Theories Compared** *Continued* | | | |
| Weaknesses | • Principles often conflict<br>• Overlooks tradition, social context, and moral development | • Difficult to predict all consequences of an action<br>• Makes all rules provisional<br>• Might override longstanding values | • Insufficient for guiding actions<br>• Sometimes appears egoistic<br>• Relies on tradition, which may be limiting<br>• Risk of situationism |
| Offers a Definitive Action-Guiding Procedure? | Yes: apply a categorical imperative, principle, rule, or moral law to a proposed action | Yes: weigh the consequences and do the action that will produce the best consequences overall | Partially: role models and the doctrine of the mean give guidance, but the virtuous way to act is specific to the person and the context |
| Versions | • Natural Law Theory<br>• Social Contract Theory<br>• Kantian ethics<br>• Legal codes in many religions | • Hedonist interpretation<br>• Utilitarianism<br>• Act-consequentialism<br>• Rule-consequentialism | • Platonic philosophy<br>• Aristotelian philosophy<br>• Stoicism<br>• Epicureanism<br>• Virtue traditions in many religions |
| Classical Representative Thinkers | • Immanuel Kant<br>• W. D. Ross | • Jeremy Bentham<br>• John Stuart Mill<br>• G. E. Moore | • Plato<br>• Aristotle<br>• Seneca<br>• Confucius<br>• Thomas Aquinas |
| Contemporary Representative Thinkers | • John Rawls<br>• Onora O'Neill | • Peter Singer<br>• R. B. Brandt<br>• Philip Pettit | • Phillipa Foot<br>• Rosalind Hursthouse<br>• Julia Annas<br>• Alasdair MacIntyre |

# Applying the Three Theories—A Case Study

One can see how the three normative ethical theories work and how they compare by using them to analyze a case study, such as the following from the medical profession.[31]

---

31. Hinderer and Hinderer, *A Multidisciplinary Approach to Healthcare Ethics*, 97.

Sandy R., R.N., has been a capable nurse whose generous nature and outgoing personality have made her popular with her patients and colleagues. About two months ago, however, her husband filed for divorce and custody of their two children because, he told Sandy, "we just can't compete with your job; you just don't have anything left for us when you get home; we're just your codependency, not a family." Although her colleagues try to be supportive, Sandy has become extremely depressed; and, probably because of this, she has made several medication errors.

Ann J. is doing quality assurance reviews and has discovered that Sandy incorrectly transcribed a physician's order for morphine as 15mg q4h instead of 5mg q4h [15 instead of 5 milligrams every 4 hours]. Two doses were given at the higher level, but Ann checked on the patient and assessed him as having had no ill effects from the error. Seeing Sandy in the hall, Ann went with her to the conference room and explained the problem.

When confronted, Sandy fell apart. In tears she begged Ann to conceal the error because if it became known, hospital policy would require that she be suspended or even fired for having made more than three medication errors within a six-month period. But her upcoming divorce hearing makes it crucial that she have continuing, stable employment; otherwise she will probably lose custody of her children. What should Ann do?

No one would envy being in Ann's position. Even if it were clear to her from the outset that she must report the error, she is likely to feel bad about Sandy's unfortunate situation. According to the case study, Sandy is a capable, generous, and well-liked nurse and coworker. Must Ann report the error? What do the normative theories say?

## Applying Deontology

If Ann reasons as a deontologist, she has three related tools to use. First, she should look to relevant rules, principles, and duties. Ann's job is quality control for the sake of patient protection. Her job-related duty is to report the error. As a medical professional, Ann should also follow medicine's ethical standards. The principle of nonmaleficence—"do no harm to patients"—is a paramount principle. Patients are at risk if Sandy keeps committing errors, so Ann has a duty to protect them by ensuring that Sandy's problems are addressed immediately.

Second, Ann should consider what "respect for persons" requires in this situation. Based on Kant's second formulation of the categorical imperative, Ann should treat others as ends in themselves and not (merely) as means to other ends. While Ann probably feels sympathy for Sandy, to give her a pass on the error would be treating the patients as means to the end of helping Sandy: it would mean putting their health at risk to help Sandy keep her job. This response does not pass muster with the categorical imperative. In addition, it is probably more respectful to Sandy to require her to take responsibility for her actions than to let her off the hook out of a sense of pity.

Third, respecting the universal scope of deontology, Ann should ask herself whether all people in similar situations should do the same thing. Thus she will avoid making her situation a special case and focusing too closely on her own interests or feelings. While it may be difficult to consider all people in similar situations, it does seem more reasonable to say that every quality-control person should report morphine dosing errors than to say that every quality-control person should hide those errors if the person who made them is having a personal crisis. Working from these three tools, deontological ethics supports Ann's reporting of the error.

## Applying Consequentialism

The ethics of consequences says to weigh the positive versus negative consequences of the possible courses of action. So Ann would think through the two main courses of action. The first option is reporting. If Ann reports the error and Sandy loses her job, Sandy will be unhappy: she may not be able to support herself and she may not retain custody of her kids. Moreover, the hospital will lose a capable nurse. There is much disvalue here, especially for Sandy but even for patients and coworkers. The positive results of this action would be that no other patients would be at risk from Sandy's recent tendency to errors. The risk could be significant, namely, a patient's death.

Ann's other option is to keep quiet about Sandy's error. If she chooses this course, all the negatives for Sandy will be avoided. In the long run, the world will be better off with Sandy being happy and functional: she and her patients and coworkers will flourish. However, if Sandy gets this reprieve and fails to address the stresses in her life, her patients remain at risk. If Ann chooses this course, it would make sense that she would do so only if Sandy agrees to take a leave of absence to get her life in order. Or, similarly, Ann might work with Sandy and keep careful watch on her work until Sandy overcomes her current problems.

If Ann reasons as a rule-consequentialist, she is likely to recommend reporting, because she would reason that it is too complicated and risky to try to predict the future; "honesty is the best policy," including when it comes to reporting medication errors. If Ann reasons as an act-consequentialist, her decision is not easy to predict: it depends on how Ann reads the situation, weighs the gravity of the consequences, and decides how she will monitor Sandy. Some consequentialists will be impressed by the strong negatives for Sandy and the positives that could result if she gets her life together. So there is a consequentialist case to be made for Ann not to report—*if* Sandy shows resolve to improve.

But is it wise for Ann to take on the responsibility for breaking her duty to report? And has she weighed *all* the consequences? For instance, what happens if Ann's failure to report is discovered? What if Sandy doesn't improve? Does Ann know that Sandy's kids would not be better off in the custody of their father? Is it even clear that Sandy's worst-case personal scenario will happen as she fears? These considerations suggest the complications of conducting act-consequentialist reasoning, for it is difficult to anticipate consequences, know how to measure different kinds of consequences against each other, and be sure that one is not being pulled by emotional factors. This is not to say that consequentialism has no value, but its best use might not be as the primary approach to cases such as this—cases where disparate consequences compete and, therefore, are difficult to measure and weigh, and cases where deontological obligations are already in force, as with medical and job-related obligations.

## Applying Virtue Ethics

To use virtue ethics in this case, Ann would begin by thinking about the kind of person and professional she tries to be. If Ann is virtuous, she strives to be careful and responsible in her duties, respectful and just toward patients, and compassionate and supportive toward coworkers. What would that kind of person do in response to Sandy? A seeming problem is that some of Ann's traits favor reporting the error to protect patients, but other traits favor being a compassionate coworker or friend who helps Sandy avoid dire personal consequences.

Virtue ethics has some tools to help resolve such tensions. First, the person who is fully developed in virtue has practical wisdom. If Ann possesses this skill, she will be able to reason through her obligations, the consequences of her possible actions, and the personal factors involved. Then she will be able to make the best decision and carry it out. Second, if Ann is unsure, virtue ethics recommends she consider what other virtuous people do or would do. If possible, one can seek out the wisdom of others who have faced such situations. If Ann is in the early years of her career, she should think about what the person who trained her would say or what a seasoned professional would do. The tool Ann would use in this situation has been called a virtue-rule or v-rule: for example, "Do what a wise and responsible person would do in this situation."[32]

A wise and responsible person in Ann's situation would likely report the error or ensure that Sandy reports on it herself. The virtue approach sometimes deemphasizes the importance of determining what rule to follow, since it depends on the situation. But some situations carry obligations because the person in that situation has a specific role or relationship or has made a prior

---

32. On v-rules, see Rosalind Hursthouse, *On Virtue Ethics* (New York: Oxford University Press, 1999), 36–39 and 58–61.

promise. A virtuous person in such a situation needs to acknowledge the relevant obligations. This is true of Ann: she is engaged in a professional role that carries an expectation of reporting. Where virtue ethics gives Ann more leeway is in *how* to fulfill her duties. As a virtuous professional, Ann could say to Sandy:

> I understand that you are in a bad place, and I feel really badly for you. But please understand that I cannot put patients at risk to cover up this error. I know you want to do your best for the patients and so do I, but that system of care is going to fall apart if we start taking into our own hands what to report. I know that you are a terrific nurse, and I would like to help you if I can, as long as it fits with my duties. If you've made errors more than once recently, you really need a break to get yourself back on track. What I suggest is that we both go to the supervisor and report the error, and I will strongly urge her or others involved that you should be given a short leave of absence. Or you could go self-report, and I'll hold off on turning in my report until tomorrow.

Since this speech might not please Sandy, Ann would need to listen patiently and console her but hold her ground with conviction. Virtue ethics leads Ann to the same basic conclusion as deontology and, perhaps, rule-consequentialism, but it gives her more help in reasoning out how to communicate and carry out that decision. It gives her more help in being the sort of person who communicates to Sandy with both compassion and courage.

## Comparisons and Contrasts among the Theories

In the case study involving Ann and Sandy, the application of the three normative theories illustrates broader similarities and differences among them. Each theory has several characteristics that are true:

- *It considers relevant rules and guides action.* A thoughtful use of consequentialism and virtue ethics does not ignore these features.
- *It requires critical reasoning.* Ethical situations are often complex. The users of each theory have to think carefully about the competing values and potential consequences.
- *It considers the context.* While virtue ethics and consequentialism seem more attentive to context, in deontology the situation also must be described properly so the relevant principles can be determined.
- *It involves acknowledging and responding appropriately to values and goods.* All moral theories give accounts of the values and goods that moral agents should support. In deontology, one honors the moral law and the dignity

of others; in consequentialism, one promotes the greatest happiness for the most people (or sentient beings); and in virtue ethics, one promotes flourishing by acting virtuously. In the case study, Ann is called upon to promote values and goods that are important to each theory.

- *It disdains egoism and relativism as legitimate options.* Each theory establishes that there is a right or better way for Ann to act, rationally defends the course of action, and recommends it to anyone in Ann's situation.

However, the theories differ in regard to other characteristics:

- *Primary focus.* Each theory respectively emphasizes principles, consequences, or character traits.
- *Concern for end results.* Deontology is least concerned with a good end result—not that it doesn't want to see good results, but it doesn't want to let ethical reasoning slip into the mentality of "the ends justify the means." Consequentialism is highly concerned with promoting good end-results, such that the act-version affirms that the ends do justify the means. The concern of virtue ethics for end results lies in the middle of these. It wants to promote the result of flourishing, but in a way that is consistent with moral values—good means are expected to lead to good ends.
- *Emphasis on procedure.* Deontology and consequentialism offer clear procedures for applying their norms to cases. Virtue ethics is less codifiable and provides more tentative answers to the question, "What should one do?" Instead, virtue ethics gives its most concise answers when a person acts in light of his specific virtues and relationships after reflecting on the particulars of a situation.
- *Attention paid to the particularities of the agent's life.* Consequentialism and deontology rely upon an understanding of human nature. They appreciate that people are emotional and social beings but assert that moral decisions are to be guided by reasons that transcend feelings and culture. These theories recommend how *any* person should act. Virtue ethics, on the other hand, takes a greater interest in how a *particular* person makes a *particular* decision and carries it out.

After considering the differences among the theories, the question arises: must one choose among them and adopt a preferred theory? The answer is both "no" and "yes," depending on whether one is engaging in applied ethics or normative ethics. Since all of the theories contain moral wisdom, and each highlights a feature that is part of the ethical life, there is no reason not to use all of their resources when making ethical decisions. Checking the options against all three theories is more likely to produce the best choice. Ann (indeed, anyone making significant decisions in the workplace) would benefit from using each theory as a resource. Applied ethicists recommend decision-making procedures that incorporate the insights of all three theories.[33] When responding to a specific case or real-world problem, the point of using normative theories is not to drive the person reflecting on the case to choose exclusively one of three irreconcilable options. Rather, it's to develop a strong answer that promises to build consensus among the people involved in the situation.

Yet even so, one has to make choices. In making formal, ethical arguments, one argues for a particular theoretical framework as the most defensible approach. Such a framework need not be limited to a single normative theory, but the framework must be coherent and informed by at least one normative theory. The argument must be backed with explanations as to why it is reasonable and essential to adopt this theory's beliefs, ideas, values, and assumptions about the world. The argument should also take account of potential objections from those with competing interpretations of the theory and advocates of other theories. At the normative ethics level, moral philosophers adopt single theories or develop frameworks in which one or more theories are given a larger guiding role. It is necessary to do so, for the theories have enough differences that they cannot be completely harmonized. In Ann's case, the differences among the theories suggest a comparative strength of virtue ethics: it pays more attention to the particular person making a decision and how she or he becomes a person who can act well in such situations. One could say that a virtue-ethical method of reasoning and decision making has a greater role for emotional intelligence than do the other theories.[34] When addressing the social dimension of ethics, which is the focus of this book, virtue theory overcomes some limitations of the debates between deontology and consequentialism. Even so, to perform social ethics well, the other theories must be part of the conversation and their resources drawn upon when making applied ethical arguments.

## Three Elements of the Moral Life: Norms, Purpose, and Context

Ethics involves several dimensions, as seen in this chapter: it conducts various types of inquiry, such as normative and applied; it attends to being and doing; it speaks to persons and communities; and it uses three major resources, each of which is matched with a theory that champions that resource. There is a big picture that keeps the details organized. At minimum, all ethical theories address guidelines for acting and living, goals for acting and living, and ways to think about the situations in which people act and live. In short, all ethical theories attend to three features of the moral life: norms, purpose, and context.

---

33. See, for example, Panicola et al., *Health Care Ethics*, 75–77.

34. The concept of emotional intelligence was popularized by psychologist Daniel Goleman in *Emotional Intelligence* (New York: Bantam, 1995). On virtue ethics and emotion, see Hursthouse, *On Virtue Ethics*, ch. 5.

**Norms.** Norms in ethics are guidelines for how to act and live as a person. These are explained and defended by normative ethical theories. Regardless of whether one adopts deontology, consequentialism, virtue ethics, or some other approach as a primary theory, the ethical resources of rules and principles, consequences, and virtues figure into normative analysis. When reasoning regarding an ethical decision, a person should ask these questions:

- Are there moral rules, principles, codes, or laws in force here?
- What decision is likely to promote the best overall consequences?
- Are there teachings or expectations in my culture or religion that give guidance?
- What is the best way to be or respond? What would a virtuous person, a role model, or influential teacher of mine do?
- Are there ways of acting that would be too much or too little of a good thing (that is, expressions of vice)? Am I prone to one of these extremes?
- Have I taken enough time to think through all aspects of a difficult decision? Have I reasoned creatively and courageously? Have I prayed, meditated, or deeply reflected upon it?
- Have I consulted my conscience, and is my conscience normally trustworthy? Is this a decision of which I will be proud?

**Purpose.** Purpose refers to an account of the basic goal or goals of life. Ethical theories are situated in philosophical or theological traditions that pose basic questions about the meaning of life. If an ethicist aspires for a theory to be more than simply a decision-making process, that theory must be guided by a vision of a well-lived life. To restate a major theme of this chapter, ethical visions are typically both personal and social. A key task of ethical reasoning is to clarify personal and societal purpose by reflecting upon questions such as these:

- What kind of person do I aspire to be?
- What kind of community do I aspire to help create and participate in?
- What is flourishing for me? What is flourishing for the community?
- Are others in the community flourishing or failing to flourish?
- Am I living in line with my values? Are we, as a community, living in line with our values?

**Context.** Context refers to the role of ethical theory in providing a critical understanding of situations that influence ethical living. The *general* moral context includes people's personal histories and personalities; their identities in terms of race, ethnicity, nationality, gender, religion, and worldview, and particularly, the meanings they assign to those identities; their physical, psychological, and material resources; their interpersonal relationships; and their roles and responsibilities in the institutions and social networks in which they participate. In other words, at the general level, context is everything that makes a person who he or she is, and it is all the personal and social relationships in which the person participates.

When making a particular moral decision, the *specific* context includes questions of what is happening and why, who is involved, what happened before the moment, what might happen after, what responsibilities one has to others, and so on. In short, context is everything that makes a person who he or she is at a given moment, and it is the people influencing and affected by one's potential decision. A few of the possible contextual features can be mentioned by example. First, the *practical and psychological features* of the situation can create opportunities and constraints. For example, an important choice is significantly constrained if one only has five minutes to decide, while many decisions can be improved when there is time to research and consult. Second, *institutional features* can make it easier to act in some ways and more difficult to act in others. For example, if a professor catches a student plagiarizing and the school has a policy in place about this, the policy can help the professor respond. Indeed, the professor probably warned the students about the policy. But if the school has no policy or does not reinforce its policy with meaningful consequences, this laxity might make it difficult for the professor to enforce standards of academic integrity.

Communal relationships and contexts are major features of moral living. Each ethical problem arises in a particular social context. A problem has to be understood and analyzed in that context, which requires looking, for instance, at the people and institutions that might be *causing* the problem, are *affected* by the problem, and can *help resolve* the problem. Contextual analysis, then, requires reflection on a diverse set of questions, including analysis of the total situation, consideration of the persons involved, and attention to nurturing better ethical responses throughout the long term. Contextual questions include the following:

- What is the ethical problem? Why is it a problem? Do others define the problem differently or not see it as a concern?
- What is relevant in the context surrounding an ethical problem? For instance: people and institutions affected; applicable laws, rules, and codes; practical opportunities and constraints, such as finances, available time, etc.
- What research should be done on the problem? What experts and relevant parties could be consulted?
- Who is involved? Who has expectations, rights, stakes, and vulnerabilities in this situation?
- What does it mean to respect the dignity of others in this case?
- What special relationships am I involved in that I must honor?
- How is the context helping or hindering my own and others' decision making?

- How do I, and we, learn from this problem and the decisions made? How should we teach others, based on this experience?
- What habits have to be developed so that I, and we, might act better and more reliably in the future?
- What changes should be made to rules, systems, policies, and so on, after reflecting on this situation?

## Conclusion

Personal ethics is a process for deciding how one should act and what kind of person one should be. The critical, creative thinking that informs ethical decision making helps one live a meaningful and upright life. The same style of thinking is necessary for social ethics, which enables people to live together in a just and flourishing manner and encourages them to embrace an ethos that inspires and sustains them. The three normative theories—deontology, consequentialism, and virtue ethics—are methods for conducting both personal and social reasoning in ethics. Deontology emphasizes the rules and principles that should guide actions, consequentialism emphasizes weighing the consequences of actions, and virtue ethics emphasizes developing character traits so one can deliberate and act well. While each theory can be consulted when making a decision, it makes sense to adopt one as the leading approach if it consistently has more strengths and fewer weaknesses than other approaches.

By this standard, virtue ethics is attractive as a primary approach. It pays more attention than the other theories to the particular person making a decision and how he or she becomes a person who can act well in all situations. Moreover, virtue ethics is especially well suited to exploring the connections between the personal and social dimensions of ethics and between personal and social flourishing. The next three chapters give a complete picture of how virtue ethics works as a normative theory, focusing, in turn, on the theory's norms, its understanding of life's purpose, and its analysis of the contexts in which character and community shape each other.

## Questions for Review

1. What is the meaning of *ethical* and *moral*, and what is the difference between ethics and morality?
2. How does consideration of the social dimension influence each part of the definition of ethics?
3. What is normativity?
4. What is the difference between the first and second versions of Kant's categorical imperative?

5. What is the difference between act-consequentialism and rule-consequentialism?

6. What is the entry point for virtue ethics?

7. Why are virtues and vices considered habits?

8. Describe a weakness ascribed to each of the ethical theories.

9. Describe some ways the three normative theories are similar in their approach to ethical issues.

10. Describe some ways the three normative theories differ in their approach to ethical issues.

11. What are norms, purpose, and context?

## Discussion Questions and Activities

1. Evaluate Randy Cohen's advice to L. T. Support your position using concepts from the chapter.

2. Do you agree that it makes sense to talk about the ethics of an entire society? Would you characterize the United States as a virtuous country? Why or why not?

3. Which of the three normative ethical theories most appealed to you initially, and why? Did anything in the chapter change your mind or give you stronger reasons for your initial preference? An activity that can assist you in this reflection is to take an informal self-assessment quiz that matches your responses to ethical issues to theories.[35]

4. Using the responses to the case of Ann and Sandy as models, describe an ethical issue that you or someone you know faces and use concepts from the normative ethical theories to analyze possible responses.

5. Write a reflection on your personal ethical framework, based on the three elements presented. (a) By what values, virtues, and principles do you try to live? Where did you get your values? (b) What do you see as the purpose of your life, and what is flourishing for you? (c) Which people and contexts have helped you grow as a moral person, and which have, perhaps, held you back?

## Recommendations for Further Reading

"The Ethicist." *New York Times Magazine. http://www.nytimes.com/column/the-ethicist.*

An archive of letters to the newspaper's ethical advice column and the responses from the current columnist. Good fodder for discussion.

---

35. A highly recommended quiz is in Panicola et al., *Health Care Ethics,* 31–39. Another quiz can be found at *http://selectsmart.com/philosophy/.*

Kyte, Richard. *An Ethical Life: A Practical Guide to Ethical Reasoning*. Winona, MN: Anselm Academic, 2012.

An accessible introduction to ethics. Kyte first clears away several misconceptions about ethics, such as, "ethics is just a matter of opinion," and, "ethics consists of a set of rules," and then presents four ways of ethical thinking: truth, consequences, fairness, and character.

Panicola, Michael R., et al. *Health Care Ethics: Theological Foundations, Contemporary Issues, and Controversial Cases*. 2nd ed. Winona, MN: Anselm Academic, 2011.

A medical ethics textbook that begins with an excellent overview of ethical theories and ethical decision-making. Includes many short case studies.

Marino, Gordon. *Ethics: The Essential Writings*. Modern Library Classics. New York: Random House, 2010.

A comprehensive and affordably priced anthology of primary readings from both classic and contemporary authors.

Sandel, Michael J. *Justice: What's the Right Thing to Do?* New York: Farrar, Straus and Giroux, 2009.

Based on the author's famous course, "Justice," at Harvard University. Deontology and consequentialism are presented as conflicting interpretations of the right thing to do. Videos from the course and further resources are at *http://www.justiceharvard.org*.

Weston, Anthony. *A Practical Companion to Ethics*. 4th ed. New York: Oxford University Press, 2010.

A handbook for ethical reasoning and argumentation that shows how to build strong, ethical positions through creative thinking and constructive dialogue. Each chapter concludes with several "try-it-yourself" exercises.

# Virtues
## Norms for Acting and Living

*If virtue can be taught, as I believe it can, it is not through books so much as by example.*

*—André Comte-Sponville, contemporary philosopher*[1]

---

### Chapter Overview

- gives a four-part definition of virtue
- illustrates this definition of virtue through a case study of courage
- presents a scheme of five categories of virtue
- lists and defines specific virtues that fall within each category

---

## Understanding Virtue

Norms, or normative guidelines, are one of three elements of the moral life that all adequate ethical theories address (as introduced in chapter 1—see sidebar). This chapter examines virtues as normative guidelines for action. For example, honesty is a virtue; therefore, in the perspective of virtue theory, an important moral guideline is to be honest. More specifically, the guideline is to speak and act honestly as well as to be an honest person. To engage in virtue ethics is not merely to apply virtue-rules to a situation to determine action; it is also to form one's own character. A good character then becomes a norm—a paradigm for action. Virtue ethics is learned more from life-experience than formal education. The tools for virtue ethics are developed inside persons through many years and are improved only by continual use. To be virtuous, then, one does not have to be

---

1. André Comte-Sponville, *A Small Treatise on the Great Virtues*, trans. Catherine Temerson (New York: Metropolitan Books, 2001), 1.

an intellectual genius, but one does have to work hard on oneself, with the goal of overcoming human tendencies toward selfishness and inordinate self-concern. To complete the process, a person of developed virtue works to make his or her communities as virtuous as possible and educate others in virtue.

## Three Elements of the Moral Life Addressed by Ethical Theories

- **Norms:** guidelines for acting and living
- Purpose: the goals of human life
- Context: an understanding of situations that influence ethical living

One of the easiest ways to explain what virtues are is to name some. To tell someone "a virtue is a character trait" may elicit a furrowed brow until one adds, "such as, honesty, courage, wisdom, and compassion." Virtues are recognized in how people talk, live, and evaluate themselves and others. Therefore, an effective understanding of virtue ethics begins with identifying traits that contribute to "being good" and "living well." Many of these are identified through common sense, upbringing (for example, what parents and role models deem good traits), and the group, cultures, and society in which one participates. Although such traits shouldn't be accepted unexamined, one can rely on the intuitive appeal of courage, wisdom, compassion, and so on as a scaffold for understanding virtue ethics.

The most basic definition of *virtue* is the power to accomplish an end.[2] Many things can be described as having virtue in a non-moral sense: for example, the virtue of a knife is to cut.[3] Virtue further conveys excellence in achieving that end, which is why people say things such as, "The virtue of this argument is that it makes clear. . . ." So, "virtue" in everyday use means that something does *well* what it is supposed to do. This second layer of meaning is captured in the Greek term for virtue, *aretē*, often translated as "excellence." This twofold concept of power and excellence brings the ethical definition of virtue far along: a moral virtue, such as kindness, is a power of the person who possesses it, in this

---

2. The Latin *virtus* connotes strength and power, as it derives from *vir*, meaning "man, a male," which conveys those qualities in a male-dominated culture. According to classicist Pamela Gordon, there is less of a gendered implication in the Greek term for virtue (*The Invention and Gendering of Epicurus* [Ann Arbor, MI: University of Michigan Press, 2012], 116–17).

3. The example of a knife is regularly used by commentators in explaining Aristotle's views of an item's use and virtue. Aristotle, *Nicomachean Ethics*, ed. Terrence Irwin, 2nd ed. (Indianapolis: Hackett, 1999), 332 and 352–53.

case to act and live in a kind manner. The ancient philosophers, such as Socrates, Plato, Aristotle, and Seneca, believed humans should live in an exemplary manner, so they identified virtues as the powers that help people do so.

In the Middle Ages, Thomas Aquinas, a theologian who adapted Aristotle's philosophy for Western Christianity, defined virtue as "a good habit of the mind, by which we live righteously, of which no one can make bad use."[4] The key point in Aquinas's definition is that character ("a good habit of the mind") leads to excellent, upright living. Many contemporary virtue ethicists echo Aquinas when they speak of virtue. For example, here are definitions from four modern philosophers:

- "Virtues are in general beneficial characteristics, and indeed ones that a human being needs to have, for his own sake and for that of his fellows. . . . Human beings do not get on well without [virtues]." —Phillipa Foot[5]
- A virtue is "a character trait—that is, a disposition which is well entrenched in its possessor. . . . To possess a virtue is to be a certain sort of person with a certain complex mindset." —Rosalind Hursthouse[6]
- A virtue is "a disposition of the person to be a certain way, a disposition which expresses itself in acting, reasoning, and feeling in certain ways." —Julia Annas[7]
- Virtue is "excellence in being for the good." —Robert Merrihew Adams[8]

Recurring through these definitions are claims that might be combined in a composite definition with four elements:

A virtue is (1) a complex, holistic character trait (2) developed through habituation that (3) displays human excellence and (4) contributes to, and is at least partly constitutive of, human flourishing.

## Illustrating the Four Elements of Virtue— A Case Study

The case study that follows illustrates both the four elements of virtue and the core ideas of virtue ethics.[9]

---

4. Aquinas, *Summa Theologica*, I–II, question 55, article 4, trans. Friars of the English Dominican Province, 1920; 2008 web ed., *http://www.newadvent.org/summa/*.

5. Phillipa Foot, *Virtues and Vices* (Berkeley: University of California Press, 1978), 2–3.

6. Rosalind Hursthouse, "Virtue Ethics," in *Stanford Encyclopedia of Philosophy*, Fall 2013 ed., sec. 2, *http://plato.stanford.edu/archives/fall2013/entries/ethics-virtue/*.

7. Julia Annas, *Intelligent Virtue* (New York: Oxford University Press, 2011), 8–9.

8. Robert Adams, *A Theory of Virtue: Excellence in Being for the Good*, 2nd ed. (New York: Oxford University Press, 2009), 11.

9. This summary is based on Gary Smith, "Frank Hall, American Hero," *Sports Illustrated*, June 24, 2013, *http://www.si.com/vault/2013/11/29/106399345/frank-hall-american-hero*.

On February 27, 2012, Chardon High School in Chardon, Ohio, was the scene of a shooting in which a student, armed with a handgun and a knife, shot at students in the cafeteria and hallways, killing three students and wounding three others before being chased from the school and arrested. Frank Hall, a 38-year-old assistant football coach at the high school, was monitoring a first-period study hall in the cafeteria when loud pops startled him. He saw students falling from gunshots as more than a hundred other students screamed and ran for safety. Coach Hall immediately bolted from his seat, running toward the shooter, T. J. Lane, and yelling, "Stop! Stop!" Lane turned to fire at him, but Hall avoided harm by ducking behind a soda machine. Three times in the ensuing minutes, as Lane moved out of the cafeteria and down the hallway, shooting continuously, Coach Hall ran after the boy, yelling, "Stop!" and, "Don't!" Hall was trying to distract or disrupt the shooter, and hoping to get close enough to tackle him. Lane carried a second clip of ten bullets, but did not have time to reload, probably because of Hall's pursuit. Lane eventually made it outside. When Hall followed, he could no longer see the boy, but he heard police sirens. Help was on the way. He went back to the cafeteria to tend to the bleeding victims.

Two preliminary concerns about virtue and this case study should be addressed. First, is this dramatic and exceptional story a good way to think about everyday virtue? Yes, it can be, because Hall, by his own admission, is not an exceptional person. He was simply a staff member who responded with courage to an uncommon crisis. Neither at Chardon High, nor in most similar crises, is there only one person who responds virtuously. However, to learn from such cases, one needs to look at those who responded in the best fashion, as they are the role models for virtue-based responses to moral and social challenges. Second, is it possible to discuss a person's character, instead of simply his actions, based on a news report? Hursthouse warns that it is reckless to attribute a virtue to a person on the basis of a single action or even a series of actions,[10] yet the profile in *Sports Illustrated* on which this case study is based gives enough detail that it seems safe to identify Hall as a person of great courage. As will become clear, a virtue such as courage is rarely found alone. Hall emerges in the story as a person of good overall character.

## Virtues Are Complex, Holistic Character Traits

Aristotle describes the virtue of courage in this way: "He is courageous who endures and fears the right things, for the right motive, in the right manner, and at the right time, and who displays confidence in a similar way. For a courageous

---

10. Hursthouse, "Virtue Ethics," sec. 2.

man feels and acts according to the merits of each case and as reason guides him."[11] Hall's decision to chase after the shooter did not mean that he had no fear. Rather, he was properly fearful for the other students' safety and judicious about his own, which is why he took care as he chased Lane, ducking as he proceeded and continually yelling to other students to stay down or run the other way. Because Hall had the stable disposition to care about the students and protect them, he was able to act upon his values without a great deal of thinking. He didn't have to think about whether he should act or whether he cared enough to act; thus he could put all of his mental energy into the most effective practical response. Hall already knew and valued "the right things" and had "the right motive"; what he had to determine, in the moment, was whether this was the right time to act and the right way to do so.[12]

The definitions of virtue by Hursthouse and Annas mentioned in this chapter describe the complex dispositional nature of virtue. Adams says, "The territory of virtue is larger than that of action and tendency to action. Virtue depends on appropriate emotions as well as actions."[13] These philosophers mean that the operation of virtue depends on multiple faculties working together. Virtue involves, one might say, "a desiring reason and a reasoning desire"[14]—a person whose reasoning is suffused with feeling and whose feelings are guided by intelligence. Nancy Sherman explains that, when a child is taught to discern what is morally relevant, in certain ways the learning will support the child's emotions and reactions. "By tutoring the child's vision of the world, by instructing the child to attend to these features rather than those, desires become focused and controlled in certain ways."[15] The process is one of "learning to see aright." The parent's or the educator's goal "is not to manipulate beliefs and emotions . . . but to prepare the learner for eventually arriving at competent judgments and reactions on his own."[16]

The claim that virtues express rational choices means that virtue is based on truth. There are, for the ancient Greek and Roman philosophers, truths about human nature and the world that virtuous decision must acknowledge. These truths include understandings of human nature that guide the philosophers' advice about *how* to act and understandings of personal and social flourishing that guide their advice about *what to act for*. In religious virtue traditions, there

---

11. Aristotle, *Nicomachean Ethics* 3.7 (1115b18–21), trans. Martin Ostwald (Englewood Cliffs, NJ: Prentice-Hall, 1962), 70.

12. "Right" here refers not to moral obligation (for no one would fault Hall if he just ducked under a table like the students) but to excellence in the practice of the virtue.

13. Adams, *A Theory of Virtue*, 9.

14. This is a possible translation of Aristotle's definition of choice in *Ethics* 4.2 (1139b5), one favored by Sir David Ross in *Aristotle* (orig. ed. 1923; 6th ed., London: Routledge, 1995), 139.

15. Nancy Sherman, "The Habituation of Character" in *Aristotle's Ethics: Critical Essays,* ed. Nancy Sherman (Lanham, MD: Rowman & Littlefield, 1999), 231–60, at 240.

16. Ibid., 241 and 242.

are similar truths about human nature and flourishing, as well as truths about ultimate reality, that guide moral teachings. Whatever the tradition or version of virtue theory, an ethicist stresses that the proper operation of virtue requires one to think well and to feel in a way that is responsive to the truths about the world.

## Virtue Is Developed through Habituation

Often associated with virtue is "habit," a term seen in Aquinas's definition. Some contemporary virtue ethicists avoid the term, perhaps because the English word—which conveys rote, unthinking action—is subject to being misunderstood. Annas and Hursthouse instead use "disposition." The Greek *hexis*, which became the Latin *habitus* and the English *habit*, refers to a state, capacity, or disposition in which a person is capable of actions and tends to perform appropriate actions because he or she has developed this state of readiness through repeated activity.[17] When "habit" is used, it should be understood as a complex state. Virtue ethicists still find it important to refer to *habituation*, which is a threefold process of a person becoming capable, through practice, of acting in a virtuous or vicious manner. There are three elements of the habituation process:

- *Education:* parents and teachers shape the characters of youth by rewarding and punishing, conveying expectations, and giving age-appropriate reasons for how they expect children to act.
- *Social norming:* laws, cultural ideals, and symbols; the approval and disapproval of others; and the ways others act are factors that shape one's beliefs, values, and habits.
- *Self-development:* people work on their habits by identifying their goals, examining their mental processes, making an effort to change, imitating role models, and relying on others for support. Mature people continually strive to answer the question, "How ought I to live?" through self-examination, learning, conversation, and participation in supportive communities.

If Hall has the virtue of courage, it is likely that he was educated in virtue as a youth. It is also likely that, as an adult, he further refined his character to be the kind of person who displays courageous behavior at the right times and for the right reasons. Gary Smith, the author of the *Sports Illustrated* profile, speculates that, because of Hall's experience in football, he has a more-than-ordinary capacity for physical courage that prepared him to show physical and moral courage on the day of the shooting. The article also describes the significant role that Hall's Christian faith and participation in a nondenominational church plays in his life. At various times in the story, it becomes clear that the act of praying comes naturally to Hall and that his minister and friends from the church had

---

17. On *hexis*, see Irwin's commentary in the glossary to *Nicomachean Ethics*, 349.

been instrumental in helping him overcome a depression that set in after the crisis. So all three habituation processes are evident in the case study.

Aristotle's famous "doctrine of the mean" has something to do with habituation. He says, "Virtue is about feelings and actions, and these admit of excess, deficiency, and an intermediate condition. We can be afraid, for instance, or be confident, or have appetites, or get angry, or feel pity, and in general have pleasure or pain, both too much and too little, and in both ways not well."[18] In this picture, there are two vices that correspond to each virtue, a vice of excess and a vice of deficit. In the case of courage, the excess is rashness and the deficit is cowardice. The virtue, courage, can be thought of as the intermediate condition, the mean (Greek *mesotēs*). Aristotle gives names to a dozen excess-vices and a dozen deficit-vices in books 3 and 4 of *Ethics*. So this picture of virtue was important to him and has been easy for readers throughout the ages to grasp.

Nevertheless, it is a picture that can be misunderstood through oversimplification. Even though Aristotle qualifies the doctrine in several important ways, contemporary philosophers have not been entirely satisfied with him on this point, so much so that many recent books on virtue theory do not mention the mean at all.[19] What is important to grasp is that the mean is not simply about acting in a way that is "in the middle"; it is about acting always in the reasonable way. Aristotle's approach is reflected in his definition of courage quoted in this chapter: the courageous person "feels and acts according to the merits of each case *and as reason guides him.*" As philosopher Sarah Broadie puts it,

> It is not that the right responses themselves are intermediate, although Aristotle . . . falls into this way of thinking at times; but rather that virtue itself is a disposition such that whoever has it is protected from excesses and deficiencies of feeling and impulse that *lead to* faulty particular responses.[20]

Thus, Broadie says, the idea of the mean is not helpful to a person acting in a particular moment, but it is helpful for the theoretical understanding of virtue and the theory and practice of moral education. Parents and teachers should aim to develop the habits of reasonable thinking and feeling within people.

A full and mature expression of virtue, then, is one that emerges organically and habitually from a person. Not all actions having the *form* of virtue are done *from* virtue. People act in accord with virtue but not from virtue, if they have to force themselves to go against their inclinations. People who are

---

18. Aristotle, *Ethics* 2.6 (1106b16–20) in Irwin, 24.

19. Three examples of such books are the ones, cited in this chapter, by Annas, Hursthouse, and Adams. For nuanced approaches to explaining the mean, see Rosalind Hursthouse, "A False Doctrine of the Mean," in *Aristotle's Ethics,* ed. Sherman, 105–20, and Sarah Broadie, *Ethics with Aristotle* (New York: Oxford University Press, 1991), 101.

20. Ibid.

weak-willed—or, as rendered in many translations of Aristotle, "incontinent"—need to push through their fears, temptations, laziness, or whatever is standing in the way, in order to act in accord with virtue as a first step toward developing an ingrained disposition.[21] If weak-willed people consider what virtuous people would do in a certain situation, those thoughts can help them recognize a good way to act; the weak-willed might simply imitate what fully virtuous people do by habit. Therefore, role models, mentors, and teachers are important to the practical use of virtue ethics; similarly, practical rules of the form, "When in doubt, do what a virtuous person would do," can help someone without an ingrained trait or who is unsure about that to do make a good decision.[22]

## Virtue Displays Human Excellence

The third element of the definition of virtue is that the operation of a virtue displays human excellence. Philosopher Heather Battaly's definition of virtue makes this quality decisive: "Virtues are qualities that make one an excellent person" (and so, "vices are qualities that make us worse people").[23] "Excellence" might sound as quaint as the word "virtue." Perhaps it even seems wrong to prize such a quality in a democratic society. But the concept is useful when properly understood. Consider the related term "hero," which *Sports Illustrated* applied to Hall. When people call someone a "hero," they are morally evaluating and approving of that person. In particular, the term implies that the person

- acts to help others, often with little regard for his or her own welfare (altruistically and perhaps self-sacrificially);
- acts in an extraordinary manner, demonstrating a certain trait (often, but not always, courage);
- shows consistency in helping people over time in an extraordinary manner; and
- is worthy of praise and emulation.

As befitting a person of character who acts this way, Hall rejects the title of hero; he only wishes he could have done more.

This way of describing heroic courage, however, does not mean that courage and other virtues are found only in extreme cases. Extraordinary cases disclose

21. Aristotle addresses weakness of will or incontinence (Greek *akrasia*, meaning "not in control") in *Ethics*, book 7. A good entry point into the vast philosophical literature commenting on this topic is Alfred R. Mele, "Aristotle on *Akrasia, Eudaimonia*, and the Psychology of Action," in *Aristotle's Ethics*, ed. Sherman, 183–204.

22. Role models and teachers are mentioned constantly in the literature of virtue ethics. A recent essay that philosophically analyzes role modeling is Linda Zagzebski, "Exemplarist Virtue Theory," in *Virtue and Vice, Moral and Epistemic*, ed. Heather Battaly (Malden, MA: Wiley-Blackwell, 2010), 57–71. On the use of practical "virtue-rules," see Rosalind Hursthouse, *On Virtue Ethics* (New York: Oxford University Press, 1999), 25–42.

23. Heather Battaly, 5 and 6.

the standard of excellence toward which the virtue is aiming and by which a person may be judged. In other words, to be a courageous person is to look something like Frank Hall, but few people will ever find themselves in such a dire crisis and in precisely the right place even to have the option of making a heroic choice. Still, most people have frequent opportunities to stand firm for values and the well-being of others in the face of certain fears and risks. For example, imagine two female classmates who are friends. Suppose Abby asks to look at Brianna's finished essay in such a way that Brianna knows Abby wants to cheat. It would take courage for Brianna to reject Abby's request. Other virtues likely would be called into play, such as the integrity not to be tempted to do so, the wisdom to know if the request is really about cheating, and the prudence to figure out the best way to refuse. Though not as dramatically as Hall's, Brianna's courage would be patterned the same way. If Brianna displayed consistency in such behavior over time, people would likely praise her integrity, and perhaps even say she has moral courage, even if she had not faced any truly fearsome situations. Thus, as Adams says, excellence in virtue is not "found only in an elite group."[24]

When one lives in an ethical and flourishing manner, one's virtues often reinforce each other, leading to what is sometimes called full or complete virtue. To ascribe full virtue to Hall is not possible from afar—it is only for people who know him well and, ultimately, for himself in his own conscience. Still, it can be generally observed that virtues are not isolated powers that appear at certain moments. Rather, one's virtues shape, and are shaped by, one's actions, reasons, emotions, moral values, perceptions, and social contexts, forming the psychology that makes one unique. Smith, for instance, tells of Hall's persistence in his fifteen-year effort to become the first in his family to get a college degree, "clawing it out a course or two per semester at the end as he worked in a group home for the mentally disabled." Smith notes that Hall and his wife are the parents of four adopted sons, and Hall considers himself to be "living the dream" for having a chance to coach and work with young people. Virtues tend to fit together into the story of a person's life, and there is evidence in the story that many virtues fit together in Hall's life.[25]

## Virtue Contributes to, and Is at Least Partly Constitutive of, Human Flourishing

The final element of the definition of virtue is that the operation of virtue contributes to, and is at least partly constitutive of, human flourishing.[26] "Virtues are

---

24. Adams, *A Theory of Virtue*, 25.

25. For further discussion of the complex question of whether virtues tend to fit together in a person's life, see ibid., ch. 10, and Neera K. Badhwar, "The Limited Unity of Virtue," *Noûs* 30, no. 3 (Sept. 1996): 306–29.

26. See the sidebar "Human Flourishing" in this chapter for a definition of this concept. For a more complete explanation, see ch. 3.

in general beneficial characteristics, and indeed ones that a human being needs to have, for his own sake and for that of his fellows."[27] A human being needs virtues because virtues *constitute* part of one's own flourishing just by having them. Humans also need virtues because virtues typically *contribute* to the happiness and well-being of oneself and others.

---

## Human Flourishing

*Human flourishing* is a contemporary translation of the Greek term *eudaimonia*, which is also translated as "well-being" and "happiness." Human flourishing indicates what it looks like for persons to live well as rational, emotional, desiring, and social beings. It is the ongoing activity of living well, or excellently, as a human being. The state of living well can be expected to produce happiness that is deeper than mere gladness or pleasure.

---

Virtue ethicists both ancient and contemporary hold that virtue is *necessary* for flourishing, but they have long debated the tightness of the link between the two. Chapter 3 discusses these matters, but a little reflection makes clear that there can be gaps between one's virtue and the flourishing of oneself and others. For example, acting virtuously might bring terrible consequences to oneself or to loved ones. Hall experiences this gap, in fact. He suffers because of his courage, not only by living through the trauma of the shooting, but because he doubts himself in the following months. "You should've done more," he thinks. For a while, he is an emotional wreck, unable to return to work.

Nevertheless, properly understood, Hall's courage adds much to his flourishing. He knows he did the right thing and people were deeply grateful to him. Even if he didn't stop a single shot, Hall still would be praiseworthy; but, in fact, he probably did force the shooter out of the building earlier than otherwise might have been the case, sparing some lives. Hall contributes to human flourishing—his own and others'—because his actions allow him to express great care for the students, school, and community. His social bonds are strengthened and bring benefits back to him. Support from the school staff, friends, family, and fellow church-members gradually enable Hall to overcome his depression.

Hall flourishes in the long-term because the incident forces him to revisit the basic question of virtue ethics, "How ought I to live?" Rather than coast on the laurels of being the local hero in Chardon, Hall applies to become—and

---

27. Foot, *Virtues and Vices*, 3.

is hired as—the head football coach in his hometown of Ashatabulah, Ohio. Hall's decision is guided not only by hometown ties but also by the economic struggles of the town and the needs of its student-athletes, who have been told that their football program cannot compete and should, perhaps, be terminated. For the opportunity to inspire a struggling school in a struggling town, Hall might well consider himself as flourishing, despite the pain he and the Chardon community endured. He tells *60 Minutes* about his feelings before the last game of Ashtabulah's football season, when the team played Chardon: "I was being thankful. All the blessings that I have, you know four healthy boys, a beautiful wife. I was very thankful for my players, for those kids at Chardon, for this community. Thankful."[28]

## A Brief Look at Vice: The Other Side of Virtue

When a person acts unethically—regularly and intentionally—he or she has a vice, or more than one. It is important to study vice in the context of virtue ethics. With a better understanding of how human beings develop vicious traits and act badly, people are better equipped to (1) forestall vicious tendencies in themselves and to improve their own characters, (2) educate young people more effectively, (3) anticipate the bad behavior of others and protect themselves against it, and (4) promote the development of people of good character throughout society.[29]

A vice shares two characteristics with virtue, since it, too, is a complex disposition developed by habituation. Like virtues, vices can become entrenched in one's habits through regular practice. Like virtues, vices are implicit answers to what one finds meaningful in life. But vice also has two qualities opposed to virtue: it displays badness and undermines the flourishing of oneself and others. As Adams puts it, "A vice is a trait that counts against the overall excellence of the way you are for and against goods and evils."[30] The phrase "counts against" suggests that having a vice does not necessarily mean that one has no moral character or a poor character. After all, everyone has flaws. But vice leads a person in a bad direction. Vice weakens character and makes faulty decisions more likely. Therefore, to embrace vice is to put oneself on a path toward moral decay—the opposite of flourishing.

Like displays of virtue, displays of vice can be ordinary or extraordinary. The story of Chardon High would not be a case of heroic virtue if it were not also a case of malignant vice. The shooter, T. J. Lane, showed careless disregard

---

28. CBS, *60 Minutes*, "Shooting at Chardon High," February 23, 2014, video at *http://www.cbsnews.com/videos/the-shooting-at-chardon-high/*.

29. Much of the philosophical literature on virtue gives sparse treatment to vice. Some exceptions are Adams, *A Theory of Virtue*, ch. 3, and Kevin Timpe and Craig A. Boyd, eds., *Virtues and Their Vices* (New York: Oxford University Press, 2014).

30. Adams, *A Theory of Virtue*, 36.

for human life. He displayed hate and mercilessness, not only in the attack but also a year later when he was sentenced. In court, he removed his dress shirt to reveal that he had written "Killer" on his t-shirt. Instead of apologizing to the families when given the opportunity to speak, he claimed to be happy for what he did, using vile language.[31] It is hard to fathom why people commit evil. As in the cases of other mass shooters, Lane shows evidence of being mentally ill. Sometimes, a person is so ill that he cannot be held morally or legally responsible for his actions. In Lane's case, the court found him fit to stand trial, a judgment that is related to, but not the same as, a psychological and moral judgment about Lane's responsibility. Clearly, Lane acted viciously, and he probably has deep vices; what cannot be discerned on the basis of news reports, however, is how Lane came to be the way he is.

Deeper understanding of the backgrounds of people who act viciously should be sought not for purposes of judging and shaming them, but to appreciate the social forces underlying their behavior. For instance, if a shooter is mentally ill, it would be helpful to know whether the illness had been noticed by others and whether the person had received help. Whether or not a shooter is mentally ill, cracks may be revealed in the groups who had responsibilities toward the person, such as the family, school, employer, legal system, and healthcare system. Public policy questions can be raised. Are mental health resources sufficient and easy to access for those who need them? Where did the shooter get the guns? Why have guns become so prevalent and destructive in the United States? In short, many social factors figure into the story of a person who hurts others. Understanding the social, political, economic, psychological, and medical factors can help society develop better interventions against violence and other harmful behaviors. Virtue ethics can assist in this by rigorously examining the dynamics of persona and social character and by holding up worthwhile moral ideals.

## Specific Virtues as Norms

Courage, the virtue examined in this chapter's case study, guides one in responding to situations of danger and fear. Because there are many other situations faced by human beings throughout the course of their lives, there are also many virtues. Some come to the forefront and others fade as the needs and values of communities shift throughout time. Thus there is no "official" list of virtues. However, one of the longer lists in philosophical literature is the index to Adams's *A Theory of Virtue*, in which more than fifty are named. Aristotle comments on at least a dozen moral virtues guiding how people act and seven

---

31. John Caniglia, "T. J. Lane Sentenced to Life in Prison in Chardon High School Shootings," *The Plain Dealer*, March 19, 2013, *http://www.cleveland.com/chardon-shooting/index.ssf/2013/03 /tj_lane_sentenced_in_chardon_h.html.*

intellectual virtues guiding how they think.[32] The contemporary French philosopher André Comte-Sponville wrote *A Small Treatise on the Great Virtues*, organized around eighteen virtues. While Comte-Sponville looks to Aristotle for inspiration, he does not include all the ancient virtues on his contemporary list. For instance, magnanimity, Aristotle's virtue of thinking oneself worthy of great things and actually being worthy of them, does not make sense to Comte-Sponville. By the same token, Aristotle would not highly prize Comte-Sponville's virtues of simplicity and gentleness. This difference between the ancient and modern views illustrates that understandings of virtues can change throughout time and that even virtues themselves can change.

Although there is no authoritative list, there are famous categorizations of virtues. In Western philosophy, the most influential scheme is based on four core virtues: justice, temperance, fortitude, and prudence. Plato first brought these virtues to prominence.[33] Aristotle also gives pride of place to these four, not by listing them as special, but by devoting long discussions to them. These four were later called *cardinal* virtues in the Christian tradition, because they seemed to be the hinges (Latin *cardines*) on which other virtues depended. To these four, Christianity added the three *theological* virtues of faith, hope, and love, making a core of seven that is still favored by many virtue ethicists.

So how should virtues be organized? Categorization is useful when studying and discussing the vast field of virtues—as long as it is remembered that all schemes are somewhat artificial. This book's scheme of five categories draws on two common organizing principles in virtue ethics: the subject matter of the virtues and how they are expressed in a person's activity. The first three categories gather virtues according to their moral content: whether they are directed to (1) caring for self and others, (2) respecting self and others, or (3) finding and expressing purpose in life. The last two categories collect virtues that enable excellent activity in two basic domains: (4) perceiving and reasoning and (5) acting and relating to others. This five-part categorization generally lines up with the traditional seven virtues, insofar as courage and temperance are both focused primarily on how actions are carried out, and faith and hope are both oriented to purpose (table 2.1).[34]

---

32. It is not easy to discern the exact number of virtues discussed in Aristotle, because he does not assume there is a settled official list. In the *Eudemian Ethics* (Aristotle's other book on ethics, perhaps based on lecture notes taken by his students), he provides a table of fourteen moral virtues with their excesses and deficits (2.3). In *Eudemian Ethics* 5 and *Nicomachean Ethics* 6, he describes seven intellectual virtues, but then takes two off the list because they are subject to error and, ultimately, reduces the remaining ones to the two master virtues of wisdom and prudence.

33. In the *Republic*, Plato has Socrates demonstrate that the perfectly good city is wise, courageous, moderate, and just (4.427e). Plato's extended use of these four traits gave rise to the tradition's treatment of them as cardinal. See Dorothea Frede, "Plato's Ethics: An Overview," in *Stanford Encyclopedia of Philosophy*, Fall 2013 ed., *http://plato.stanford.edu/entries/plato-ethics/*.

34. This scheme has similarities to that of psychologists Christopher Peterson and Martin E. P. Seligman, who, in *Character Strengths and Virtues: A Handbook and Classification* (New York: Oxford University Press, 2004), organize twenty-four specific virtues under six categories: strengths of wisdom and knowledge, courage, humanity, justice, temperance, and transcendence.

## TABLE 2.1 Five Categories of Virtues

| Category | Corresponding Traditional Virtue |
|---|---|
| Virtues of care | Love |
| Virtues of respect | Justice |
| Virtues of purpose | Faith and hope |
| Virtues of perceiving and reasoning | Prudence |
| Virtues of acting and relating | Courage and temperance |

In the remainder of this chapter, each of the five core virtue categories is defined with reference to representative thinkers and texts. Specific virtues in each category are listed. Each core virtue category is explained in light of this book's definition of virtue—"a complex, holistic trait developed through habituation that displays human excellence and contributes to, and is at least partly constitutive of, human flourishing"—and its normative use is described.

## Virtues of Care

Virtues of care are virtues of bonding with, valuing, and treating persons well. Specific virtues in this category include chastity, fidelity, forgiveness (mercy), friendship, generosity, hospitality, kindness, compassion, love, self-care, and solidarity (loyalty).[35] Love, the central virtue in this category, has long been recognized as extremely important for the moral quality of one's character and one's genuine happiness.

The Greek and Roman philosophers emphasize a particular type of love—friendship. So important is this activity that Aristotle devotes two of the ten books of the *Ethics* to it. Friendship is "not only necessary, but also fine," says Aristotle.[36] Among the ancient philosophical schools, the Stoics developed a broader notion of universal love as a virtue, following from their understanding of the basic connectedness of persons and nature. The Roman Stoic philosopher Seneca writes, "That line of poetry should ever be in our hearts and on our lips: 'I am human and I count nothing human as disconnected from

---

35. In this and the following sections, a list of notable virtues within the category is given alphabetically; alternative terms for a virtue are given in parentheses. The core virtue in the categories, and a few other representative virtues, are defined and illustrated. For definitions and explanations of other virtues, see the recommended readings listed at the end of this chapter, the glossary in Irwin's edition of Aristotle, Comte-Sponville, Keenan, and Peterson and Seligman.

36. Aristotle, *Ethics* 8.1 (1155a30 and 1155a1) in Irwin, 120.

me.'"[37] Later, Christian theologians were influenced by the Stoics' universalism, which fits well with their perception that human beings are children of God.

The Christian virtue of love has its roots in Hebrew Scriptures (the Old Testament), in which God speaks to the Jewish people with tender concern. Jesus drew two commandments from those scriptures and taught them as the Great Commandment: "'You shall love the Lord, your God, with all your heart, with all your soul, and with all your mind.' This is the greatest and the first commandment. The second is like it: 'You shall love your neighbor as yourself.' The whole law and the prophets depend on these two commandments" (Matt. 22:37–40, drawing from Deut. 6:5 and Lev. 19:18). Jesus' teachings and his own example of showing forgiveness led to an understanding of love as the preeminent Christian virtue. The Apostle Paul enshrined it in a famous triad—"So faith, hope, love remain, these three; but the greatest of these is love" (1 Cor. 13:13)—and the First Letter of John famously says, "God is love" (1 John 4:8). According to Christians, human love should aspire to be as universal and unconditional as God's love. In addition to Christianity, virtually all religions and moral philosophies encourage one to love family and friends and be benevolent toward others. This universal endorsement is one of the reasons love, by one name or another, should be included in any list of core virtues.

In keeping with the four-part definition of virtue, it is evident that: (1) love is a complex disposition of persons, involving their thinking, feeling, and acting; (2) habituation into the ability to be loving begins with a child's earliest experiences and depends upon parents and other adults who show the child compassion and teach the child how to act; (3) love contributes to robust happiness for oneself and others; and (4) love is excellent. There is hardly any greater compliment that can be given to a person than that he or she is genuinely kind and compassionate. Enlightenment philosopher David Hume wrote, "It seems undeniable, that nothing can bestow more merit on any human creature than the sentiment of benevolence in an eminent degree; and that a part, at least, of its merit arises from its tendency to promote the interests of our species, and bestow happiness on human society."[38] As Hume suggests, people recognize love as an excellent trait; it is a quality people want for themselves and want to see in the world, for love makes life worth living. Residents of Chardon, Ohio, praise Coach Frank Hall and continue to respect him, not merely because he has courage, but because they see his courage as flowing from love for the students.

Practicing love is an emotional, personal, and sometimes spontaneous activity. It doesn't follow a rulebook. In fact, Coach Hall did not follow the rules for a school lockdown, which were to shepherd nearby students into a classroom

---

37. Seneca, *Moral Letters to Lucilius,* Letter 95, in *The Practice of Virtue,* ed. Jennifer Welchman (Indianapolis: Hackett, 2006), 55.

38. David Hume, *An Enquiry concerning the Principles of Morals* (1777), sec. 2, part 2, in *Practice of Virtue,* ed. Welchman, 86.

and lock the door. Nevertheless, virtues of care operate as moral norms. A person with a character marked by love still must ask in many situations, "What does it mean to be loving in this context?" The guidelines for answering such a question—and this is true of every virtue—are extensive and found in areas like religious teachings, philosophical arguments, cultural traditions, the examples of role models, accumulated learning from successes and failures, and information from the sciences and other disciplines. Not all of these sources (for example, a particular religion or culture) are normative for everyone. Instead, virtue ethics draws upon universal concepts based on human reason and a normative understanding of human flourishing, as well as on particular traditions that are normative for a particular group, community, or society. In other words, all methods of ethics and even the use of principles and consequences can be employed to develop a normative account of what a loving person would do, what a loving action looks like, and what loving consequences should be promoted.

Take the hypothetical example of a person named Michael and the virtue of generosity. Generosity operates as a norm for Michael when he realizes that he should be generous and act generously. What if he is not good at that? Michael might not be aware of this flaw or care about it. But if others point out the flaw, or if he notices that a friend seems disappointed in him, Michael might come to realize that he needs to develop generosity. Then he will need to understand what generosity is. Although he probably already knows, because he has seen what generous people do, Michael might need to learn something more about this virtue—for instance, that it doesn't mean giving all his money away and that he has to give with the right attitude. Michael will need to push himself to be more generous. "Pushing himself" might mean remembering that he is working on this trait, so he should pick up the tab when he goes to lunch with someone, give to charity, and try to respond positively when someone asks for help. Eventually, these practices will become more natural to Michael, and he will develop generosity to the point where he finds it easy and enjoyable. In other words, Michael will become habituated to the virtue of generosity.

## Virtues of Respect

In partial contrast to the virtues of care, known for their emotional dimensions, the virtues of respect are generated by a rational acknowledgment of what is right and proper. Virtues of respect are traits of showing proper regard for rules and laws, rights and duties, and the dignity of oneself and others. Specific virtues in this category include citizenship, civic friendship, fairness, honesty, justice, patriotism, respect for law, responsibility, self-respect, and tolerance.

Justice is the central virtue in this category. Justice has two faces—one face involves character traits (being fair, respectful, and responsible) and the other involves social principles (an ordering of society that is fair and that respects persons' rights). Aristotle's extensive examination of justice in book 5 of *Ethics* addresses both faces. He begins with justice as state of character "that makes us do justice and wish what is just";[39] he then analyzes several forms of just relationships between persons and citizens and government. Even when the type of justice under consideration is formal and rule-based (such as legal justice and justice in financial exchanges), Aristotle assumes that a just society depends upon just citizens and rulers. Aristotle writes, "Friendship would seem to hold cities together."[40] Therefore, he says, politicians are rightly concerned to promote a rudimentary, civic form of friendship and eliminate civil conflict. This practice of civic friendship requires the same virtues that friends have—such as concern for the welfare of another and good communication skills—but scaled to the social level. Additional virtues in this area are citizenship (leading one to engage in civic duties such as voting, paying taxes, and serving in public roles) and patriotism (showing loyalty to one's country while remaining open-minded and tolerant).

Virtues of respect fit the four-part definition of virtue as complex, holistic traits developed through habituation, displaying excellence, and contributing to flourishing. These virtues are complex dispositions engaging all the faculties of the person who possesses them. They are excellent traits that contribute to the flourishing of others in society. People who show respect and practice justice are more likely to flourish than those who don't have these virtues because of the return benefits from the order, respect, and solidarity created within the community. Coach Hall offers evidence of the sense of justice that motivated his response to the shooter and that he believes should guide society's response to the ongoing spate of school shootings:

> We need to find ways to secure our schools better. We need to make a stand right now that our schools need to be the most important thing we have in this country, not Wall Street, not Capitol Hill, our schools. We need to determine that in our minds and heart, that our school and our children need to be the most important thing we have. That's the bottom line.

Finally, virtues of respect operate as norms and look similar to deontological principles. Principles of respect and virtues of respect are, generally speaking, twists on the same concept. The principle of fairness holds, for instance, "Do not cheat when you are playing a sport with others," while the virtue of fairness indicates, "Play the sport as a fair person would, which includes not cheating." Persons with virtues of respect act according to just principles and strive to promote just consequences in the world because they have the disposition to be just.

---

39. Aristotle, *Ethics* 5.1 (1129a9) in Irwin, 67.

40. Aristotle, *Ethics* 8.1 (1155a24) in Irwin, 119.

## Virtues of Purpose

Virtues of purpose help a person find and pursue meaning in life and foster enriching connections with the ultimate realities of life. Specific virtues in this category include awe (appreciation of beauty), conscience (conscientiousness, integrity), devotion, faith (spirituality), gratitude, hope, humility (simplicity, gentleness, purity),[41] and vitality.

The two leading virtues in this group were traditionally labeled, "theological virtues." Yet faith, hope, and other virtues of purpose should not be understood as limited to those who believe in God or a religious doctrine. Peterson and Seligman include a similar category that they call "transcendence" in their psychological classification of virtues: "The common theme running through these strengths of transcendence is that each allows individuals to forge connections to the larger universe and thereby provide meaning to their lives. . . . The reaching goes beyond other people per se to embrace part or all of the larger universe."[42]

When virtue theorists name a category of transcendence, purpose, or faith, they propose that an excellent life is one in which a person deeply appreciates beauty, persistently acts in the hope of contributing to a better world, and demonstrates integrity by standing for what is right regardless of the risks. In short, these theorists say that a fully flourishing person forges connections to the sacred. "The sacred" can be broadly understood as the source(s) of lasting value and meaning in one's life. While not using the term "sacred," Comte-Sponville expresses its essence when he describes the virtue of simplicity:

> Simplicity is spontaneity; it is joyous improvisation, unselfishness, detachment, a disdain for proving, winning, impressing. Hence the impression it gives of freedom, lightness, happy artlessness. . . . To be simple, then, is to forget about oneself, and that's what makes simplicity a virtue: not the opposite of egoism, which is generosity, but the opposite of narcissism, pretention, self-importance. . . . Simplicity is the virtue of wise men and the wisdom of saints.[43]

The ancient philosophers frame their ethical systems as quests for meaning. Though variously expressed, the philosophers describe the person's overriding task in life as locating true happiness in a purpose that is larger than self-interest

---

41. The three terms in parenthesis are usually considered synonymous with, or slight variations on, humility: they are all traits of acting calmly, kindly, and unselfconsciously so as to overcome the negative effects of self-interest. However, Comte-Sponville intriguingly breaks them out into four separate virtues (his chs. 11, 12, 14, and 15).

42. Peterson and Seligman, 517.

43. Comte-Sponville, *A Small Treatise on the Great Virtues*, 153, 154, and 156. In a similar vein, philosopher Iris Murdoch sees the response to beauty—i.e., awe, which is a virtue of purpose—as an occasion for "unselfing" ("The Sovereignty of Good over Other Concepts," in *Virtue Ethics*, ed. Roger Crisp and Michael Slote [New York: Oxford University Press, 1997], 104).

and more important than concerns of the body. Socrates considered it crucial to understand what piety—respect for the gods—entailed. Plato describes the goal of life as knowing what is truly just so one's soul has integrity in the afterlife. Seneca writes that the truly happy life consists in "the possession of a soul that is free and upright and undaunted and steadfast, standing beyond fear, beyond desire. . . . When a life is built on this foundation, it is accompanied by constant cheerfulness, whether wished for or not, and a deep-rooted sense of elation stemming from deep within."[44] Aristotle describes the magnanimous, or "great-souled" person, as humble, self-sufficient, "in no hurry," and "not strident."[45] His description seems to match saintly leaders such as Mother Teresa and the Dalai Lama and even political heroes such as Abraham Lincoln and Eleanor Roosevelt. These great persons as well as many "regular folks"—Coach Hall, for example—are driven by an overriding moral purpose with hope and perseverance. As such, they convey trust in the moral purpose of the universe.

Like the other categories, the virtues of purpose bear four characteristics of virtue: they involve the whole person, are developed as habits through specific practices, display excellence of character, and contribute to one's own and others' flourishing. To achieve true, deep, nonmaterial flourishing is the highest aim of these virtues. People who possess virtues of purpose, such as the historical figures recently mentioned, are widely regarded as paragons of character.

Transcendent virtues are normative and action-guiding in the same way as any other virtue. Regarding humility, for instance, people know what actions and behaviors typically display humility; this knowledge guides normative application of this virtue. To develop humility and other purposeful virtues, people should act in ways that turn their attention away from themselves—particularly from their wants, desires, frustrations, and fears. Practices that can turn one from inordinate self-focus toward transcendent focus include prayer, meditation, and attendance at religious services; sitting in beautiful settings, going for walks in nature, and observing art; abstaining from technology, media, and shopping for periods of time; identifying, each day, the things for which one is grateful; and serving others and spending time with people in need.

## Virtues of Perceiving and Reasoning

The fourth set of virtues enable people to use their mental and emotional capacities well. Specific virtues of perceiving and reasoning include creative thinking (creativity), critical thinking, curiosity (love of learning, intellectual vitality), open-mindedness, prudence (practical reason, practical wisdom), reasonableness, self-vigilance, and social-emotional intelligence.

---

44. On Socrates, see Plato's dialogue *Euthyphro*. On Plato, see *Republic*, book 10 (618d–e). Seneca is quoted from *On the Happy Life*, sec. 4, in *Practice of Virtue*, ed. Welchman, 44.

45. Aristotle, *Ethics* 4.3 (1123a35–1125a16) in Irwin, 56–59.

The leading virtue here is prudence (Greek *phronēsis*, Latin *prudentia*). Since "prudence" has a limited connotation in contemporary English, meaning being careful and cautious, some translators use "practical wisdom." Aristotle claims, "It is not possible to be good in the strict sense without practical wisdom, or practically wise without moral virtue."[46] Standing at the meeting point of mind and character, practical wisdom is the trait by which one makes good decisions and figures out how to enact them. Aristotle defines it as a characteristic "that is bound up with action, accompanied by reason, and concerned with things that are good and bad for a human being."[47] This definition indicates that *phronēsis* is intellectual (involving reason and truth), practical (deliberating about what can be done), and ethical (concerning what is good and bad for people). The virtues needed for flourishing are not limited to conceptual and critical thinking but include creative reasoning, which expands possibilities, and social-emotional intelligence, which perceives what others are feeling so that one can act appropriately and sensitively.

This category includes perception because all forms of reasoning begin with taking in information from the surrounding environment. Good reasoning requires being aware of and being able to interpret (1) facts, (2) concepts, (3) other peoples' emotions, beliefs, thoughts, and assumptions, and (4) one's own emotions, beliefs, thoughts, and assumptions. The philosopher Iris Murdoch says that compassionate, just, and perceptive reasoning is essential for virtue ethics:

> The love which brings the right answer [to everyday moral questions] is an exercise of justice and realism and really *looking*. . . . Of course virtue is good habit and dutiful action. But the background condition of such habit and action, in human beings, is a just mode of vision and a good quality of consciousness. It is a *task* to come to see the world as it is.[48]

Practical wisdom is learned from parents, teachers, and role models and is developed through daily practice. Theologian James Keenan draws an analogy between the planning parents do to steer a child's development and the planning people do for their self-development:

> If we want to transform ourselves into people of justice, fidelity, and self-esteem, we need first to know who we are as individuals and where our limits and strengths lie. . . . Using as much imagination as a parent enticing a child to try something new, we need to plan situations

---

46. Aristotle, *Ethics* 6.13 (1144b31), ed. Lesley Brown, trans. David Ross (New York: Oxford University Press, 2009), 117.

47. Aristotle, *Ethics* 6.5 (1140b5–7), in *Aristotle's Nicomachean Ethics: A New Translation*, ed. Robert C. Bartlett and Susan D. Collins (Chicago: University of Chicago Press, 2011), 120.

48. Murdoch, "Sovereignty of Good," in *Virtue Ethics*, ed. Crisp and Slote, 109.

in which the daily possibility for growth becomes real. . . . To move forward, then, we can lead ourselves as a parent leads a child: appreciating our uniqueness, anticipating the next steps, and patiently but continually guiding ourselves so that we do not tire of the nearly endless journey that lays before us in acquiring the virtues. Along the way, the imagination that helps us to plan and execute the journey will be our most prudential asset.[49]

Keenan's analogy illustrates why Aristotle said practical wisdom and character virtues cannot exist without each other: Practical wisdom is the method by which one plans to acquire and develop other virtues, while virtues such as persistence, courage, and creativity are required for practical wisdom to do its work. As norms, each form of virtuous reasoning can be spelled out in detailed traits and methods. Some of the methods of practical wisdom were just described. To take another example, critical thinking can be specified as open-mindedness, which means being open to new possibilities and responding to new information appropriately and on its own terms—not being unduly constrained by one's previous expectations.

In keeping with the first three parts of the definition of virtue, virtues of perceiving and reasoning are holistic, integrated traits of persons (as indicated by Murdoch), developed though habituation (as indicated by Keenan), and show their possessor to be excellent when practical wisdom helps that person become more virtuous overall (as indicated by Aristotle). As for the final part of the definition, virtues of perceiving and reasoning contribute to personal and social flourishing in many ways, including when they promote the moral vision that Murdoch describes. In his interview with *60 Minutes*, Hall displayed moral vision when he said it was urgent for the nation to prioritize the safety of children. His moral vision is reflected on a daily basis in his approach to coaching. At Ashtabulah, for example, when the coach learned that one player on the team had spoken disrespectfully to a teacher, he made that student, and every player on the team, apologize to the teacher. Hall was teaching the players respect, responsibility, and a new vision of themselves. One of the players explained the reason for the coach's order: "It's just based upon, like if one of us messes up, we all mess up. Like family, you know."[50]

## Virtues of Acting and Relating

While the previous category was about thinking well, the fifth and final category is about acting well. Of course, all virtues can involve action, but the ones in this category focus on *how* a person carries out the decisions that arise from his or her

---

49. James F. Keenan, *Virtues for Ordinary Christians* (Lanham, MD: Sheed & Ward, 1996), 81.

50. CBS, *60 Minutes*, "Shooting at Chardon High," February 23, 2014.

character. These virtues involve enacting decisions, achieving aims, and getting along with others. Specific virtues in this category include collaboration, communication skills, courage (bravery), friendliness, helpfulness, humor, leadership, patience, persistence, politeness, punctuality, self-control, and temperance. The category also involves skills in creative, physical, theoretical, and craft activities, because these skills involve virtues and help a person flourish. Courage is one of the two leading virtues in this category. As seen in the case study in this chapter, courage enabled Coach Hall to put aside concern for himself and act upon his deep-seated value of protecting students.

Temperance, the other leading virtue in this category, is the trait of acting with a balanced appreciation of life's pleasures. Temperance is a virtue in which the "not too much, not too little" understanding of the mean makes sense. The temperate person enjoys—in moderate, healthy, and ethical amounts—such pleasurable things as food, alcohol, material goods, and sexual activity. One might object by saying, "If these things are pleasurable, why do we need to show restraint in their use?" Anyone who has ever drank too much at a party knows the most obvious answer: overindulgence usually makes one miserable later. But *any* good thing can be used to excess, and most people have a sense of when they are enjoying something too much. For example, twenty college students taking a course on virtue ethics were asked to identify, anonymously, a pleasure in which they tend to overindulge. Five said food (portions, snacks, or eating at restaurants too much); four said phones, texting, or television; and four said buying coffee drinks. In these responses, the class might well speak for many young Americans. These items are good. Phones are useful, and food is essential. Still, the students recognized that too much of a good thing creates problems. Too much food is fattening and unhealthy; a daily trip to a coffeehouse is expensive; and phone use can be addictive, rude, and, if done while driving, dangerous. In a follow-up conversation, the students almost all recognized that it would be good for them to set limits on their enjoyment of these items but that it's not easy to do so.

In the same survey, the students were asked which pleasures they would find hardest to sacrifice for a week. Eight said using a smart phone and five said drinking or buying coffee. Again, the students know their weak spots, but what, if anything, should done about them? Philosopher Rebecca DeYoung, in a book on the Christian spiritual traditions concerning the seven capital vices, proposes, "One initial exercise in self-examination we might try is to see how hard it is to give up something for, say, a month."[51] DeYoung occasionally challenges her students to do this "fasting" exercise, each of them giving up something they enjoy too much. That some people find such fasting difficult "says something about how attached we are to certain pleasures. . . . Fasting reveals the things

---

51. Rebecca Konyndyk DeYoung, *Glittering Vices: A New Look at the Seven Deadly Sins and Their Remedies* (Grand Rapids: Brazos Press, 2009), 154–55. The popular name for the capital vices is "the seven deadly sins." The most influential listing of these is envy, vainglory, sloth, avarice, anger, gluttony, and lust—with pride as the root of all.

that control us." The practice of fasting is a strategy for resetting one's habits and reminding oneself what matters. People striving to improve their temperance do well to surround themselves with friends and acquaintances who also exhibit temperance and who offer encouragement instead of temptation.

In most activities requiring temperance, the vice of overindulgence is the more dangerous problem and an alluring temptation. Yet there is a vice in under-enjoyment as well. A person who does not have a developed appreciation for the pleasurable things in life—whether out of lack of knowledge, excessive frugality, or fear of taking chances—is missing out on opportunities for enjoyment and flourishing. If one wishes to move toward the mean of temperance from either direction, the too much or the too little side, the process is the same. Since Aristotle, virtue ethicists have recommended making oneself perform actions modeled on the virtue to start developing a new habit. In particular, there are several strategies one can employ: analyze the activities, experiences, or contexts that trigger one's bad habits and make plans to avoid them; associate new behaviors with the old habits and make a written commitment to change; tell other people of the intentions to change and ask for help; and reward oneself for following through on better behaviors. These methods, which in recent years have been confirmed by psychological experiments, can be applied to training oneself in any virtue or habit.[52]

Courage, temperance, and the other traits in this category are fittingly defined as virtues owing to their holistic nature, development via habituation, recognized excellence, and contributions to flourishing. These virtues contribute to personal flourishing by supporting one's ability to act in line with one's character.[53] They also contribute to social flourishing. In the school shooting case, Hall's courage protected students and inspired a community. A community or a nation also may show collective courage, as did the Allied nations when fighting the fascist powers in World War II. Their courage enabled them to defeat Hitler, Mussolini, and Hirohito (while their other virtues encouraged them to reconcile with the Axis powers shortly after the war). Similarly, societies benefit from acting with temperance, such as temperance in the national diet, which promotes public health, and temperance in the use of fuel and energy, which benefits both public health and the natural environment.

The normative use of these action-oriented virtues is guided by considering what's necessary for bringing an ethical decision into action. What must a person be like to act in accord with his or her virtues? One must have courage, temperance, self-control, and persistence, for starters. The normative use of

---

52. For a readable discussion of the science of habit, see Charles Duhigg, *The Power of Habit* (New York: Random House, 2012; paperback ed., 2014). His appendix (287–98) presents strategies for changing one's habits, featuring the strategies just mentioned.

53. Because these virtues help one accomplish goals, Adams labels them structural virtues, as distinguished from motivational virtues, which shape one's attitudes and actions in favor of certain goods (33).

relationship-oriented virtues is guided by considering what's necessary for inter-acting and collaborating with others. To assess whether one is doing what is necessary, one can start by asking, "Am I acting like the person I aspire to be?"

This chapter's glimpses into the rich history of commentary on the core virtues under the categories of care, respect, purpose, perceiving and reasoning, and acting and relating illustrate the general definition of virtue and show how virtues work as norms for acting and living.

## Conclusion

Virtue may be defined as (1) a complex, holistic character trait (2) developed through habituation that (3) displays human excellence and that (4) contributes to, and is at least partly constitutive of, human flourishing. The case study of Frank Hall, an assistant football coach at Chardon High School responding to a school shooter, demonstrates what virtue ethicists mean by these four elements. While Hall's most evident virtue on the day of the shooting was courage, an analysis of the case suggests he possesses a number of other virtues that support, and are supported by, his courage.

Two aspects of the case study analysis must be emphasized because they become prominent in the remainder of this book. First, virtue has a deeply social dimension. Hall is not solely responsible for his own character. Many people—his parents, the community in which he was raised, his church community, his wife and children, his friends, his colleagues—have helped form him. Just as thoughtful people should try to understand the social forces that produce vice, they should try to discern the social forces that encourage virtue, so as to protect and expand upon what works for the good.

Second, human flourishing must be pursued at the social level. The verb "must" is appropriate for two reasons: it is impossible for the authentic pursuit of personal flourishing not to have social consequences, and social flourishing is a necessary ingredient in personal flourishing. Virtues contribute to the flourish-ing of individuals and their communities, often in a simultaneous and mutually reinforcing way. The virtues of love, faith, and hope drive reformers to work for justice. Just people make society more just. Virtuous parents and teachers shape the next generation, whose character influences a society.

The fullest expression of virtue radiates outward like ripples from a stone thrown into a pond. Hall's aim in living his life as he does is not simply to satisfy his personal interests, such as his love of football, nor to connect in a satisfying way with certain individuals, such as his players and the students with whom he is friendly. While these seem to be among his purposes, and can be valuable parts of a well-lived life, Hall also wants to improve the people and communities around him. He wants his school to thrive and its members to be proud of them-selves; he wants to collaborate with fellow teachers, administrators, and parents to improve the school; he wants students to know that they are cared for and to do their best work; and he wants his struggling hometown to be revived. Such aims are shared by those who embrace virtue ethics. The rest of this book shows how virtue ethics can be employed as an analytical and motivational framework for the promotion of social flourishing.

## Questions for Review

1. What are the non-moral and moral definitions of virtue, and how do the two definitions relate?
2. What does Aristotle mean by "incontinence"?
3. Describe what a habit is, as understood by virtue ethicists.
4. What are the three elements of the process of habituation?
5. What is the meaning of "excellence" as applied to virtue?
6. What is the difference between virtue *constituting* human flourishing and virtue *contributing* to human flourishing?
7. What is the difference between moral and intellectual virtues?
8. What are the main similarities and differences between the virtues of care and respect?
9. What are the two faces of justice?
10. Why is practical wisdom (prudence) essential to all other virtues?

## Discussion Questions and Activities

1. Do an audit of your virtues, and write a reflection on what you learned about yourself from the audit. One method for the audit is to reflect on what you believe to be your most obvious virtues and the vices to which you are prone. Another way is to ask a few trusted friends and family members to name your character strengths and weaknesses. A third way is to take the "Values in Action" character strengths survey from the VIA Institute in Character (*http://www.viacharacter.org/www/*), founded by psychologist Martin E. P. Seligman. The survey is free, but there is a fee for a detailed results report (another version can be found in the appendix of Seligman, *Flourish*).[54]
2. Think of a character trait you possess. How did you develop it? Did each of the three habituation processes play a role? To maintain this trait, do you require regular practice of it? Do you require the support of others?

54. Martin E. P. Seligman, *Flourish: A Visionary New Understanding of Happiness and Well-Being* (New York: Simon and Schuster, 2011), 243–65.

3. What does courage look like for most people? What does it mean to "fear the right things," as Aristotle describes the trait? Is there an ethical argument to be made that Frank Hall did not act prudently?

4. Identify people whom you consider personal heroes and people who are widely recognized as heroes. What traits do these people have? Are there qualities that are common among them?

5. Considering the lists of virtues, are there any, in your opinion, that have been overlooked and should be included? Are there any that are questionable and might be excluded? Do some virtues deserve greater emphasis? For instance, Keenan argues that self-care deserves a place as a cardinal virtue.[55] Could you argue for such a change or for any other reprioritization?

## Recommendations for Further Reading

Annas, Julia. *Intelligent Virtue.* New York: Oxford University Press, 2011.

One of the best books by contemporary philosophers explaining virtue ethics. Annas compares virtues to practical skills and explains how virtue is part of one's flourishing.

Aristotle. *Nicomachean Ethics.* 2nd ed. Edited and translated by Terence Irwin. Indianapolis: Hackett, 1999.

This particular edition is recommended for its sound translation, effective organization, detailed glossary, and extensive notes.

Battaly, Heather. *Virtue.* Malden, MA: Polity, 2015.

Another fine introduction to virtue by a contemporary philosopher. Using brief examples from history and popular culture, Battaly clearly explains many theoretical issues in virtue theory.

Crisp, Roger, and Michael Slote, eds. *Virtue Ethics.* Oxford Readings in Philosophy. New York: Oxford University Press, 1997.

Influential essays by some of the most important twentieth-century philosophers of virtue, including Anscombe, Murdoch, MacIntyre, Foot, and Hursthouse.

Comte-Sponville, André. *A Small Treatise on the Great Virtues.* Translated by Catherine Temerson. French original, 1996. New York: Metropolitan Books, 2001.

Explores eighteen virtues, one per chapter, bringing the ideas of philosophers into vivid dialogue with the concerns of everyday life.

---

55. Keenan, *Virtues for Ordinary Christians*, 73.

Keenan, James F. *Virtues for Ordinary Christians*. Lanham, MD: Sheed & Ward, 1996.

A brief, readable, and theologically informed treatment of several virtues.

Peterson, Christopher, and Martin Seligman. *Character Strengths and Virtues: A Handbook and Classification*. New York: Oxford University Press, 2004.

Explains what psychology knows about the nature and development of the virtues, what activities tend to develop them, and what research is still needed about them.

Welchman, Jennifer, ed. *The Practice of Virtue: Classic and Contemporary Readings in Virtue Ethics*. Indianapolis: Hackett, 2006.

Selections from five classic philosophers of virtue—Aristotle, Seneca, Frances Hutcheson, David Hume, and Friedrich Nietzsche—each of which is paired with a contemporary essay applying that philosopher's ideas.

# 3

# Human Flourishing
## The Purpose of Life, the Purpose of Ethics

Call that person happy who counts nothing good or evil but a good or evil will, who reveres the honorable, is content with virtue alone, who is neither overly exhilarated nor heartbroken by chance events, who is convinced there is no greater good than the good that is self-conferred, for whom true pleasure consists in the disdain of pleasures.

—*Seneca (ca. 4 BCE–65 CE), Roman Stoic philosopher,* On the Happy Life[1]

---

## Chapter Overview

- explains human flourishing as the best way to understand happiness
- presents the debate between Aristotle and the Stoics regarding the necessity of material resources for flourishing
- offers a checklist of the elements of human flourishing, based on a contemporary interpretation of Aristotle's philosophy, and applies it to a case study of children from different socioeconomic statuses
- shows how an account of human flourishing guides ethical deliberation at the personal and social levels

---

1. Seneca, *On the Happy Life*, section 4, in Jennifer Welchman, ed., *The Practice of Virtue* (Indianapolis: Hackett, 2006), 43–44.

# The Quest for Happiness

As people make daily decisions, they usually do not stop to consider the meaning of life. But in the background of their minds, people do need a sense of what makes life meaningful, what makes them happy, and what they value. In other words, if they are going to live in a way that is likely to make them happy, they need a worldview. When people have to make big decisions—such as where to go to college, whether to marry, whether to take a job in a new city, or how to respond to an ethical dilemma—they often find it helpful to consult their sense of purpose, that is, their goals in life. If one's goal is happiness, because one sees happiness as a key ingredient in the good life—both for oneself and society—then a clear understanding of happiness is needed. Otherwise, one will pursue unrewarding and possibly immoral goals. Purpose is one of three elements of the moral life that ethical theories, to be adequate, must address (as introduced in chapter 1—see sidebar). This chapter, therefore, examines the account of the purpose of life found in virtue ethics.

## Three Elements of the Moral Life Addressed by Ethical Theories

- Norms: Guidelines for how to act and live
- **Purpose: The goals of human life**
- Context: An understanding of the situations that influence ethical living

There are several ways to talk about what makes life meaningful, but one concept has exercised a greater influence on the Western imagination than any other—happiness. Ancient Greek authors bequeathed to Western culture the idea that *eudaimonia* is the highest human good and the purpose that all people seek. *Eudaimonia* derives from the words for "good" (*eu*) and "spirit" or "divinity" (*daimōn*). So happiness was, in the origins of the term, the idea that one is blessed by the gods, or fortunate.[2] Latin authors used the words *beatitudo* and *fecilitas* for the same concept. "Happiness" has been the most common way to translate *eudaimonia*, but in the past forty years virtue ethicists and philosophers specializing in ancient Greek philosophy have adopted "human flourishing" as a better translation,[3] one that captures a sense of robust well-being. This term

---

2. Darrin M. McMahon, *Happiness: A History* (New York: Atlantic Monthly Press, 2006), 3–4.

3. It was popularized especially by John M. Cooper, *Reason and the Human Good in Aristotle* (Cambridge, MA: Harvard University Press, 1975; reprint ed., Indianapolis: Hackett, 1986).

avoids the limitations of the more common term "happiness" and connotes dynamism and vitality: people can grow, improve, and live better—that is, flourish—if they strive to live virtuously.

The notion of happiness, however, has captured the popular imagination, so the relationships among happiness, moral virtue, and flourishing should be made clear. The epigraph from Seneca sounds appealing, but it raises many questions: Does being morally good ensure happiness? If a morally right action would harm one's interests, should it still be done? What is the relationship of emotional happiness to a life of true happiness; in other words, does pleasure have any place in personal flourishing? Is individual happiness entirely in one's control, or does it depend on external factors that are subject to chance? Finally, how does a person's happiness relate to the happiness of society; for instance, does one's flourishing depend upon the actions of others, and how important is it for personal flourishing that one contribute to the flourishing of others? An investigation of these questions fleshes out the virtue-ethical approach to the purpose of life.

## Understanding Human Flourishing through the Ancient Philosophers

Darrin McMahon opens *Happiness: A History* with the words, "The search for happiness is as old as history itself," basing this claim on the first historian in Greek culture, Herodotus (ca. 484–425 BCE). Herodotus opens his own book, *The Histories*, with the story of King Croesus, who wants to identify the happiest man on earth. The king assumes it is himself, owing to his wealth and power. McMahon says that Socrates (469–399 BCE), on the other hand, has a different view: Happiness is the single-minded pursuit of knowledge and beauty through contemplation.

Higher knowledge, material success, and other sources have been contenders in the age-old quest to identify the source of true happiness. As McMahon notes, the search has not produced a widely agreed upon answer. Nonetheless, the philosophers of ancient Greece and Rome remain the best source for an answer that makes sense within virtue ethics. Greek and Roman philosophical traditions, despite the diversity of schools within them, embrace flourishing as the purpose of life and identify virtue as the key to a flourishing life. Two particular schools—the philosophy of Aristotle and Stoic philosophy as represented by Seneca and Epictetus—are of particular interest regarding the pursuit of flourishing.

Early in the *Nicomachean Ethics*, Aristotle (384–322 BCE) acknowledges both the wide appeal of happiness and the diverse opinions about it. "What is the highest of all the goods achievable in action? As far as its name goes, most people virtually agree; for both the many and the cultivated call it happiness, and they suppose that living well and going well are the same as being happy. But they disagree about what happiness is, and the many do not give the same answer as the wise."[4] Because almost everyone agrees that happiness is desirable, Aristotle believes it is the general answer. But "the many," that is, ordinary people, who do not engage in refined study, "think it is something obvious and evident—for instance, pleasure, wealth, or honor." Aristotle wants an account that takes its cues from human experience and human nature and that could, in principle, appeal to everyone, without having to accept the superficial definitions of happiness that many people create. Because people's notions of happiness can be superficial, virtue ethicists prefer to conduct their quest for the purpose of life and the purpose of ethics in terms of flourishing.

## A Thought-Experiment: What Composes Flourishing?

Take a moment to list ten things that most contribute to your personal flourishing, that bring you the greatest happiness and well-being. List them and then, difficult though it may be, narrow this list to your top five items, and finally, to your top two items.[5] Do this exercise before reading further.

The items on the list may be on it include food, shelter, good health, education, money, recreational activities, hobbies, employment, success, faith, love, friends, and family. Some of these items are typically valued only, or primarily, as means to other goods. For instance, money is nothing special in itself, but is good for the food it buys, the leisure activities it facilitates, or, for some people, the success it symbolizes. Aristotle would invite you to consider the purpose of money, food, and so on. Through such a process of questioning, you may begin to see that the top items on your list are valuable in themselves. They are not good for anything else; rather, having or experiencing them makes one happy, fulfilled, and content.

The chain of reasoning that Aristotle and other ancient ethicists pursue is clearly laid out by Raymond Devettere.[6] First, Greek virtue ethics begins with human beings' natural desires and impulses, as these are the first indications of

---

4. Aristotle, *Nicomachean Ethics* 1.4 (1095a16–20), 2nd ed., ed. and trans. Terence Irwin (Indianapolis: Hackett, 1999), 3. The next quote is from the same location.

5. This activity is based on Michael Panicola et al., *Health Care Ethics*, rev. ed. (Winona, MN: Anselm Academic, 2011), 48.

6. Raymond J. Devettere, *Introduction to Virtue Ethics: Insights of the Ancient Greeks* (Washington, DC: Georgetown University Press, 2002).

how one could answer the question, "What do I want?"[7] Aristotle begins his treatises on ethics and politics with the same idea: everyone acts in order to obtain what he or she perceives is good. The term "good" requires no technical definition; it refers to whatever humans see as desirable, helpful, or satisfying of their aims. Devettere explains, "The Greeks think that human beings, indeed all sentient beings, naturally desire what they perceive as good or valuable for themselves."[8]

The process of reflection referenced in the sidebar "A Thought Experiment" points one toward goods that are widely valued for their intrinsic worth. Michael Panicola, a medical ethicist who presents this thought-experiment to many college students and healthcare professionals, finds that people most often name *health* and *relationships* as their top two items. Health is not a surprising answer, because it is essential for being able to enjoy many other things in life. But it is not merely instrumental in value, because to be mobile, to be physically active, and to play are basic elements that produce satisfaction in human life.

The primarily intrinsic value of relationships is even clearer. A friendship enlarges one's life by providing psychological strength, social support, intimacy, and opportunities to act in good and noble ways. Naming these values of friendship is not to imply that they are a list of *mere* benefits, as if people begin and maintain friendships simply to get psychological and social support. Rather, the values experienced in being and having a friend coalesce as a total package of the goods of friendship. One might say of a close friend or a family member, "I love him just for himself," or "I value her for who she is." People think of their best relationships as involving more than instrumental value; one cares for these people for their own sake. The best way to think of friendships and other loving relationships is not that they *lead to* happiness but that the ongoing practice of these relationships is intrinsic to the ongoing activity of living well as a human being.

Aristotle stresses that flourishing is an *activity*, a claim that makes sense in the context of relationships. The flourishing person has to show virtue in action, do things that are enriching, and interact with people. People who are in medical comas or largely inactive (say, homebound people with little opportunity to connect with others or who make little effort to do so) could have wonderful characters, but others likely would not think of them as flourishing while in those states.[9] Nowhere does Aristotle give an exact breakdown of the elements

---

7. The Greek schools of thought disagreed among themselves about whether there were only rational desires (Socrates and the Stoics) or rational and nonrational desires (Plato and Aristotle). This debate need not be explored here, because these authors share a core assumption that "intelligent choices—choices mediated by practical wisdom and prudence—tend to be better choices than those made without intelligence and deliberation" (Ibid., 24).

8. Ibid., 27.

9. Aristotle, *Ethics* 1.5, 1096a1.

that compose flourishing, but the overall impression given by the *Nicomachean Ethics* is that four general types of activity are most basic for flourishing. Any flourishing, and thus truly happy, person must enjoy these four activities regularly throughout life:

- Having a good character and acting with virtue
- Engaging in study and contemplation
- Enjoying meaningful friendships
- Participating in public life—making contributions to the well-being of one's communities[10]

This specification of four activities for flourishing suggests that the specific goods people want fit within several categories of general goods. "A significant question now arises," says Devettere. "Are the individual goods that we seek in our various projects and activities the only goods we seek or is there also an overriding good in life? Are there only particular and discrete goods in our lives or is there a universal and general good?"[11] The ancient philosophers argue that humans have a highest good, reasoning from the premise that a human being is a unified entity. If something is whole, it is reasonable to think that this whole has a point or a goal; the Greeks called this a *telos* and the Latin writers a *finis*. To use an analogy, the goal of an automobile is to move effectively, and thus, the highest goal of the car is to carry its driver and passengers safely from one destination to another. The goals of the engine, the tires, and the other parts of the car come together in this overriding goal.

The goal of human beings is to flourish. This position of virtue ethics does not rule out that there are many particular things and experiences that contribute to flourishing. Virtue ethicists accept that there are various paths to happiness, but they challenge people to establish their quest for flourishing on the right foundation.

## The Security of Flourishing— Aristotle and the Stoics

To ensure the right foundation for the quest, ancient philosophy identifies three necessary qualities of the highest goal: completeness, self-sufficiency, and security. Aristotle explains the first two in the *Ethics*, book 1, chapter 7. As to completeness, "an end that is always choiceworthy in its own right, never because

---

10. Aristotle discusses the first activity throughout the *Ethics*, the second activity in *Ethics* 1.5 and 10.6–8, the third activity in *Ethics* 8 and 9, and the fourth activity in various places, including *Ethics* 1.3, 5.6, 8.10–11, 10.9, and in the *Politics*.

11. Devettere, *Introduction to Virtue Ethics*, 27–28.

of something else, is complete without qualification." As to self-sufficiency, "we regard something as self-sufficient when all by itself it makes a life choiceworthy and lacking nothing."[12] As for security, Devettere writes, "The major move of the philosophers to make happiness secure is their insistence that it depends far more on how we think and on what we choose to do than on luck and fortune. The philosophers emphasize that we, and not fate, have the primary power to make our lives happy."[13]

The word "primary" signals an important issue at stake. In the view of some philosophers, people have *all* the power to make their lives happy because, in their interpretation, flourishing consists solely of one's character. How people respond to the fortunes and misfortunes of life determines their flourishing, because they can consider themselves blessed when they act honorably in all matters. For other philosophers, notably Aristotle, flourishing is vulnerable to misfortune and bad luck. Flourishing depends *mostly* on one's character; this is the "doing well" part of the previously quoted statement from the *Ethics* (1.4): "Living well and going well are the same as being happy." The "going well" part of flourishing is influenced by resources, opportunities, and a certain amount of luck. Aristotle's view of flourishing as *having good character plus sufficient resources* is summarized in two key passages in the *Ethics*:

> Then why not say that the happy person is the one whose activities accord with complete virtue, with an adequate supply of external goods, not for just any time but for a complete life?[14]
>
> All think that the happy life is pleasant and weave pleasure into happiness, quite reasonably. For no activity is complete if it is impeded, and happiness is something complete. That is why the happy person needs to have goods of the body and external goods added [to good activities], and he needs fortune also, so that he will not be impeded.[15]

Aristotle's "external goods" refers to wide range of good things, outside of a person's mind and character, that are useful or necessary for flourishing. Though Aristotle never lists these goods, many clues in his writings suggest he means

- *material resources*, such as money, shelter, employment;
- *social resources*, such as a supportive family, teachers and mentors, education, a sound legal and political order; and
- *natural and health resources*, such as a safe environment, clean air and water, food, and other supports for one's physical and mental health.

---

12. Aristotle, *Ethics* 1.7 (1097a33 and 1097b15), in Irwin, 8.

13. Devettere, *Introduction to Virtue Ethics*, 50.

14. Aristotle, *Ethics* 1.10 (1101a15–16), in Irwin, 14.

15. Ibid., 7.13 (1153b16–18), in Irwin, 116.

External goods and decent health are at least useful and often necessary so people can engage in the four types of activity that are most significant for flourishing: acting with virtue, engaging in contemplation, enjoying relationships, and participating in public life. People need sufficiently healthy bodies and minds and enough resources to perform these activities. They need supportive families and communities to help them develop into the kind of people who know what flourishing is. This is what Aristotle apparently has in mind when he writes that people need external goods.

In contrast to Aristotle, the Stoic school of philosophy, founded by Zeno of Citium (ca. 334–ca. 262 BCE) about twenty years after Aristotle's death, adopted the position that flourishing is *completely* secure if it is considered in the right way—as located entirely within a person's reason and character—and if a person then acts appropriately based on that view. There are three differences between the Stoics and Aristotle on this score.[16]

*Invulnerability?* Can people make themselves invulnerable to sadness and anxiety? The Stoics say this is possible and desirable. It requires emotional self-control and a proper understanding of reality. Epictetus, a Greek Stoic of the early second century of the Common Era, famously claims that people should not become disturbed if their spouses or children die.[17] Epictetus does not mean people should have no feelings for their loved ones, but that they must accept the truths of life, including that people die. The Stoics believe that if a person allows external events to cause that person to lose control of his mind and thus jeopardizes his flourishing, that would be the real tragedy.[18] But Aristotelians "will not be happy" with this view, says Julia Annas, as "it seems to allow the emotions too little role in the developed moral life."[19] Aristotle agrees with the Stoics that virtuous people should be in control of their emotions, but his understanding of how deeply people should feel emotions is closer to ordinary people's "commonsense" understanding, according to Annas.

*Pleasure?* Does pleasure undermine virtue? In the second of the two previously quoted passages from Aristotle's *Ethics*, Aristotle says people are reasonable when they weave pleasure into flourishing. The Stoics think people put themselves on a slippery slope when they mix virtue (the only source of flourishing) and pleasure, for virtue then becomes less than fully honorable, and

---

16. Thanks to philosopher Jesse Bailey from Sacred Heart University for valuable feedback on this section.

17. Epictetus, *Enchiridion*, secs. 1, 3, 7, 11, 14, 15, 18, and 26, *http://classics.mit.edu/Epictetus /epicench.html*.

18. For further discussion, see Tad Brennan, *The Stoic Life: Emotions, Duties, and Fate* (New York: Oxford University Press, 2007).

19. Julia Annas in *The Morality of Happiness* (New York: Oxford University Press, 1993), 65. This section of her book (53–66) compares the Stoics and Aristotle on emotions. For a defense of the Stoics against Aristotle, see Daniel C. Russell, "Happiness and Agency in the Stoics and Aristotle," *Proceedings of the Boston Area Colloquium in Ancient Philosophy* 24 (2008): 83–112.

people following this route become increasingly dependent on fortune for pleasure.[20] As with the previous point, their view is not quite as a stark as it may seem at first. Seneca and Epictetus suggest that pleasure, in itself, is neither good nor bad. Pleasure isn't to be avoided, as long as it can be enjoyed properly, which may be difficult for people with less than full virtue, since humans are prone to follow their desires. So, while Aristotle says pleasure is a part of flourishing that should be sought and used in moderation, the Stoics say pleasure is no part of flourishing, but the virtuous person can use pleasure in moderation.

*External resources?* The previous issues flow into this one, which is the most important for the current discussion. Are resources external to a person required for flourishing? As seen in the two passages from the *Ethics*, Aristotle clearly believes such resources are part of the equation. After the second quotation, he continues to chide those of the opposing view: "Some maintain, on the contrary, that we are happy when we are broken on the wheel [e.g., being tortured in a prison], or fall into terrible misfortunes, provided that we are good. Whether they mean to or not, these people are talking nonsense."[21] Seneca, by contrast, says, "What need is there of external things if you have gathered all your assets within yourself?"[22] The life that is founded solely on virtue gives the benefit of complete security of mind and the confidence of complete inner freedom, according to the Stoics.

Once again, while there is a difference between Aristotle and the Stoics, it is not as stark as it first seems. Aristotle does not want people to become anxiously dependent on chance; rather, he wants them to be realistic about the fact that a certain amount of resources enable one's flourishing.[23] What he identifies as an ideal life is not dissimilar to what the Stoics recommend. Friendship and public activity are important to the Stoics. Indeed, Seneca was a statesman, and a wealthy one at that. Seneca does not claim that material resources are to be avoided, but he wants readers to be indifferent toward them. Speaking to a critic, he writes, "With me, wealth has a certain place; in your case, it has the highest place. In short, I own my wealth, your wealth owns you."[24] Both Aristotle and Seneca remind readers that material possessions are helpful and dangerous; they can facilitate flourishing or they can damage character.

---

20. Seneca writes, for example, "The person who allies virtue with pleasure in a partnership, inevitably an unequal partnership, blunts all the force of the one by the fragility of the other. . . . The life that follows is worried, suspicious, fearful, ever-alarmed at chance occurrences, uncertain from one moment to the next" (*On the Happy Life*, sec. 15, in Welchman, 45–46).

21. Aristotle, *Ethics* 7.13 (1153b18–21), in Irwin, 117.

22. Seneca, *On the Happy Life*, sec. 16, in Welchman, 46.

23. Aristotle is not consistent in his statements about how much external resources matter, however. He tries to do justice to both sides of the debate, because both sides appeal to common sense and both have philosophical appeal, but his account remains "unstable," according to Annas, *The Morality of Happiness*, 364–84.

24. Seneca, *On the Happy Life*, sec. 22, in Welchman, 49.

Another important similarity between Aristotelianism and Stoicism is crucial for the flourishing of individuals and communities: both traditions urge virtuous citizens and rulers to try changing social conditions in the hopes of alleviating material misfortunes. While it may seem the Stoic position on detachment from fate could lead to apathy, in fact, the Stoic philosophers were politically active and farsighted in their social concerns. They believed all humans are brothers and sisters, that people should treat each other with compassion, and that slaves should be treated well or even freed. Though Aristotle, like most people of his time, did not adopt such an egalitarian view, he too supported actions to make society just and promote civic friendship. Both of these philosophical theories of virtue, in other words, recommended ethical and political actions to help people live better. The difference between the Aristotelian and Stoic social programs lies in their understanding of human nature. The Stoics prized reason above all, which led them to respect the dignity of every rational being. Aristotle attended to the particularity of human beings and prized both reason and emotions; thus, it made sense to him that people's concern for others only extend to those with whom they are in a relationship of family, friendship, or citizenship.[25] In the contemporary world, however, it seems both possible and necessary to combine these views of humans' relationships to other humans. The challenge of pursing the common good in the global community requires linking particularity and universalism.[26]

## Summary of Human Flourishing

The ancient philosophers' understanding of flourishing yields several insights. Human flourishing is an activity; it is doing good and living well. Aristotle claims happiness amounts to virtue plus sufficient external resources for living well. Human well-being is constituted by the goods that people universally need and want. Many desirable things can be part of someone's flourishing, but a process of reflection discloses that intrinsic goods—such as virtue and the love shared with others—are the essence of a deeper, more lasting happiness for humans. But even this deeper happiness is vulnerable to chance. The Stoics urge people to see happiness as totally within their characters and thus completely secure, whereas Aristotle strives to keep happiness secure while being realistic about the limitations and misfortunes of life.

---

25. Annas, *The Morality of Happiness*, 14–15.

26. Some important works of contemporary political philosophy on this theme are Michael Walzer, *Spheres of Justice: A Defense of Pluralism and Equality* (New York: Basic Books, 1984); John Rawls, *The Law of Peoples* (Cambridge, MA: Harvard University Press, 2001); and Martha C. Nussbaum, *Political Emotions: Why Love Matters for Justice* (Cambridge, MA: Belknap, 2013).

## Specifying Resources for Flourishing— The Capabilities Approach

Attention to external resources links Aristotle's interests to those of contemporary virtue ethicists concerned about the quality of communal life. Both Aristotle and contemporary ethicists appreciate that people's access to resources such as education, income, and nutrition is not a matter of fate, but depends, in part, upon the decisions made by society. But the approach is not yet clear. What *precise* conditions make for flourishing? A reader may be disappointed to discover that Aristotle, and indeed all of the ancient philosophers, offer clues and brief examples but no extended discussions. Devettere says there are two reasons for the absence of a detailed account of the content of flourishing in ancient philosophy. The first is that ancient philosophers took it for granted that most people know what happiness generally is: having a life that goes well. The second reason is that these thinkers were "very much attuned to the particular feature of each individual moral agent and each situation where that agent makes decisions. . . . No one can give an exact definition of happiness because each person is unique and lives in a unique set of circumstances."[27]

However, there is more detail in Aristotle than first meets the eye. His insights into ethics and politics can help contemporary readers think better about their own ethics and politics. An author who ably translates the ideas of ancient philosophy into arguments for contemporary social policies is Martha C. Nussbaum, professor of philosophy and law at the University of Chicago. In 1988, she began a long-term scholarly project of systematizing Aristotle's conception of the basic goods of human life and applying it to contemporary society. This scholarly project became known as "the human development and capabilities approach," "capabilities theory," or, as it will be called in this chapter, "the capabilities approach." This theory (1) articulates a philosophical and social-scientific account of basic human capabilities and then (2) develops ethical norms and specific action-plans in such areas as human rights advocacy, economic development, women's development, civil-society improvement, domestic law and public policy, and international law and public policy.[28]

Nussbaum draws a line from Aristotle's ethical and political philosophy to the needs of contemporary societies. She says, "To answer any of the interesting, actual political questions about resources and their allocation through programs and institutions, we need to take some stand, and do all the time, on the

---

27. Devettere, *Introduction to Virtue Ethics*, 52.

28. Nussbaum explicates the approach in many writings, some of them in collaboration with Amartya Sen, a Nobel laureate economist. With Sen, she cofounded the Human Development and Capabilities Association (*http://hd-ca.org*). She has participated in development policy projects sponsored by the United Nations and nongovernmental organizations. The most accessible resource for the theory and the practice of capabilities is Martha C. Nussbaum, *Creating Capabilities: The Human Development Approach* (Cambridge, MA: Belknap, 2011).

Aristotelian question, 'What human functions are important? What does a good human life require?'"[29] Nussbaum answers the question by distilling from Aristotle's writings indications of what he finds essential for living a decent human life. Nussbaum arranges Aristotle's ideas into ten basic human functional capabilities (table 3.1). These range from basic physical functions, to operations of the mind, to forms of social interaction.

---

## TABLE 3.1 The Ten Central Human Capabilities[30]

1. *Life:* ability to live a normal lifespan

2. *Bodily Health:* ability to have health, shelter, and nutrition

3. *Bodily Integrity:* ability to enjoy freedom of movement and personal autonomy; being safe from violence

4. *Senses, Imagination, and Thought:* ability to use one's mental faculties fully; ability to attain education, engage in creative activities, enjoy freedom of thought and expression, experience pleasure, and avoid unbeneficial pain

5. *Emotions:* ability to experience and express the range of feelings, show care for others, and accept care

6. *Practical Reason:* ability to form a view of the good life and plan one's life accordingly

7. *Affiliation with People:* (1) ability to participate in a variety of interpersonal relationships, show and receive care, and participate in communal and social relationships; (2) having the social, political, and legal conditions for being treated respectfully by others

8. *Relationship with Nature and Other Species:* ability to live in relationship to and show concern for animals and nature

9. *Play:* ability to play, laugh, and enjoy recreation

10. *Control over One's Environment:* (1) *political:* ability to participate in political activities, have a voice in the creation of laws, and enjoy protection from governmental intrusion; (2) *material:* ability to own property, seek employment on a fair and equal basis, and participate in meaningful work

---

This list, which involves capabilities and limitations, is, to some degree, culturally variable and open-ended. It serves as a "starting point for reflection" about

---

29. Martha Nussbaum, "Aristotelian Social Democracy," in *Liberalism and the Good,* ed. R. Bruce Douglass, Gerald M. Mara, and Henry S. Richardson (New York: Routledge, 1990), 203–52, at 212.

30. After trying out different versions of the list through the 1990s, Nussbaum settled on this version in *Creating Capabilities,* 33–34. A few words have been added to the terms of items 7 and 8 for clarity, and the definitions of the items have been compacted.

the good life for human beings, so it is open to modification.[31] The features on the list take shape differently in the lives of different societies. Nussbaum claims, however, that people would not recognize, as human, a community that completely lacked one or more of these features. This list focuses on capabilities, rather than actual functioning, because respect for human freedom demands that individuals decide whether and how they want to act upon their own capabilities.

In keeping with Aristotle's ideas, Nussbaum supports political and economic programs that allow people to function well according to the ten central human capabilities. She says it is reasonable to take the ten capabilities "as a focus for concern, if we want to think how government can actually promote the good of human beings."[32] Political institutions should focus on providing citizens the resources for developing and acting upon their capabilities, paying attention to the many interconnections as well as the potential tensions among these functional needs.

Some national governments and international organizations have done just this; here are three examples. First, the governments of Finland and Sweden created measurements of their citizens' well-being, using a list similar to Nussbaum's, to determine how to improve conditions on healthcare and other public resources.[33] Second, the government of Bhutan in 2005 created "Gross National Happiness" indicators as a more holistic measurement of their society's well-being than Gross Domestic Product, which is merely an economic indicator. The government conducted a full survey of the nation in 2010 and is using the results to develop programs tailored to the needs of certain groups identified as less happy, such as women, farmers, and the undereducated.[34] Third, the United Nations Development Programme (UNDP) sponsors development reports employing measurements that are not narrowly economic but that see "people as the real wealth of a nation."[35]

## Capabilities, Virtues, and Flourishing

The ten capabilities relate to two major interests of virtue ethics. The first is virtue itself. Initially, one might wonder about Nussbaum's list: where are the virtues? They come into play through two capabilities—practical reason and affiliation—and from there are implicit in all capabilities. Practical reason was a

---

31. Nussbaum, "Aristotelian Social Democracy," 224.

32. Ibid., 225.

33. Ibid., 240–42.

34. Center for Bhutan Studies and GNH Research, "Gross National Happiness," *http://www .grossnationalhappiness.com*.

35. The UNDP sponsors the Human Development Reports, published annually since 1990 (*http://hdr.undp.org/en/humandev*, from which this quote was taken) and the Arab Human Development Reports (*http://www.arab-hdr.org*), which have appeared in five volumes from 2002 to 2009.

key virtue for Aristotle, because it is the power by which people effectively act on other virtues. For Nussbaum, practical reason as a central capability is the ability to form a conception of the good life for oneself and plan one's pursuit of flourishing accordingly. The centrality of affiliation makes sense because Aristotle sees humans as social and political animals; people will not flourish alone. Nussbaum identifies practical reason and affiliation as the two ordering capabilities among the ten: they are the powers by which people order their use of the other capabilities, making the whole set characteristically human.[36] If anyone is to flourish in their capabilities, he or she must express the relevant virtues. For instance, to play well, in a way that makes one flourish in body, character, and relationships, one must exercise virtues such as fairness, persistence, and teamwork.

The second major interest of virtue ethics is flourishing. Capabilities are a way of specifying areas of flourishing (similar to the list of goods discovered in the thought-experiment) and the resources needed for the pursuit of flourishing. However, because capabilities are not the same as the actual enjoyment of goods, it is worthwhile to compare the capabilities approach to the well-being theory in the field of positive psychology. The well-being theory considers both objective and subjective indicators of what it means to have a flourishing life. This theory captures a few aspects of flourishing that are not stated by Nussbaum but are compatible with her approach. Psychologist Martin Seligman describes well-being as having five measurable elements, known as PERMA:[37]

1. *Positive emotion:* feeling happiness as a general state and reporting satisfaction with one's life
2. *Engagement:* having experiences in which one feels absorbed and fully present, a state also known as "flow"
3. *Relationships:* enjoying loving and supportive relationships
4. *Meaning:* belonging to and serving something that one holds as bigger than oneself
5. *Accomplishment:* facing and meeting challenges, knowing that one achieved something because of one's effort

Seligman's list of the elements of well-being is more emotionally robust than Nussbaum's, insofar as he brings the psychological perspective into each element. He does not include anything about the body or health, but he clearly believes that these elements are connected to flourishing, for he presents ample evidence that higher levels of PERMA are correlated with being physically healthier and living longer.

---

36. Nussbaum's technical term for these two ordering capabilities is "architectonic functionings" ("Aristotelian Social Democracy," 226–27, and *Creating Capabilities*, 39).

37. Martin E. P. Seligman, *Flourish: A Visionary New Understanding of Happiness and Well-Being* (New York: Simon and Schuster, 2011; Atria Paperback, 2013), 14–26.

Seligman's and Nussbaum's frameworks are remarkably similar. The correspondence suggests a pattern of four domains of human flourishing: body, mind, character, and relationships. Aristotle's basic activities for flourishing and his mention of goods of the body also correspond well to the domains (table 3.2). As the table shows, theorists of flourishing from disparate time periods and areas of inquiry focus on much the same reality.[38] This table provides a set of four domains that reveal the similarities among these theorists.

## TABLE 3.2 The Structure of Human Flourishing according to Three Theorists

| Domains | Aristotle's Activities and External Resources | Seligman's Well-Being Theory | Nussbaum's Central Human Capabilities |
|---|---|---|---|
| Body | Goods of the body | (Assumed) | 1. Life<br>2. Health<br>3. Bodily integrity |
| Mind | Engaging in study and contemplation | Positive emotions<br>Engagement | 4. Senses, imagination, and thought<br>5. Emotions |
| Character | Having and acting with character | Meaning<br>Accomplishment | 6. Practical reason |
| Relationships | Enjoying meaningful friendships<br>Contributing to community | Relationships | 7. Affiliations:<br>(a) interpersonal<br>(b) civic<br>8. Relationship with nature<br>9. Play<br>10. Control over one's environment:<br>(a) political<br>(b) material |

---

38. In 2008, Nussbaum published a paper critical of positive psychology ("Who Is the Happy Warrior? Philosophy Poses Questions to Psychology," *Journal of Legal Studies* 37 [June 2008]: S81–S113), her main example of which was Seligman's book *Authentic Happiness* (2002). Seligman says the well-being theory in *Flourish* (2011) is an expansion of his earlier authentic happiness theory. In essence, he moved in Nussbaum's direction. In the notes to *Flourish*, he cites Nussbaum among the theorists of well-being that he finds compatible with his theory (278).

# Two Children's Flourishing—A Case Study

The list of ten central human capabilities can also be employed in social ethics to identify what resources people may be lacking and generate a virtuous response to these deficits. To illustrate this application of capabilities theory within virtue ethics, consider two American children, both age nine and in the fourth grade.

Ellie lives with her parents and younger brother in the suburb of a major city. The suburb is known for its well-kept owner-occupied houses, nice parks, library, and high-quality public schools. Ellie likes her public school, Green Hill Elementary, and does well in her studies. She is an advanced reader whose teacher provides instruction tailored to the ability levels of each student in the class. At least 80 percent of the students in the school meet or exceed the standards in reading, writing, and math that are assessed in standardized tests given by the state government. Ellie has a driven personality; when it comes to school, she never gets less than A grades and seems to put pressure on herself to stay at that level. Her parents and teacher encourage her to relax, and the teacher keeps the parents updated about Ellie's overall well-being via email. Ellie participates in Girl Scouts after school once a week; otherwise, the bus drops her off near her house at 3:45 p.m. Both parents work full-time—the father is an accountant and the mother a lawyer—but they are able to arrange their schedules so one parent or the other is home to see Ellie off the bus or to pick her up from an afterschool activity. Ellie's parents sometimes drive her to a friend's house for a play-date, but usually she plays with neighborhood kids in their homes or outside. She also plays soccer in the town's youth league. The neighborhood is safe and the parents trust one another to look out for each other's children. Like most kids, Ellie watches a little more TV than she should, spending about two to three combined hours on schooldays watching television and on the computer, but her parents also ensure that she does her homework each night and that she spends time reading. Ellie likes do crafts; when she needs more craft supplies, her parents are happy to buy her some. They make sure she sees the doctor and dentist, and she has visited an orthodontist who is planning to fit her for braces in a few years. Ellie has no health concerns presently. Her family attends church on the main holidays. Most of their weekends feature activities oriented around the kids' sports and clubs.

Robert lives less than two miles from Ellie, within the jurisdiction of the city, and with his mother, father, and older brother. Both parents work jobs that pay wages rather than salaries. Robert goes to school at King Street Elementary, a public school. He stays at an afterschool program each afternoon because of his parents' work schedules. He enjoys school at times, especially music and art classes, but performs below grade level in math and language arts, as do about 50 percent of the children in his school. Because the family does not have a car and the mother works evenings, Robert is not able to participate in organized sports leagues, but he plays with neighborhood kids outside most evenings. Robert's parents are concerned that he should stay away from youth who are involved in gangs; while this will be a greater concern when he becomes a teenager, they have heard of young children in their neighborhood being preyed on by gangs. The family does not own a computer, and Robert watches about three to four hours of television most days of the week. Thanks to state programs and federal policies, Robert and his brother have health insurance and dental coverage. Robert is being treated for asthma, but his parents will not be able to correct his overbite as they cannot afford orthodontia. The family attends church every Sunday and typically visits with other relatives on Sunday afternoons.

Ellie and Robert are fictitious characters who represent two fairly common socio-economic conditions for American children: an upper-middle-class suburban environment with robust familial, social, economic, and political resources versus a working-class urban environment with a mixture of positive resources, deficits, and challenges. Obviously, there are many variations of lifestyle, family arrangements, and so on for children living in actual suburbs and cities of the United States. These two stories are not intended to portray one child's life as wonderful and the other's as terrible. If asked, "Are you happy?" both Ellie and Robert would answer, "Yes," most of the time. *But are they flourishing?* This question is best answered using the central capabilities to assess the well-being of Ellie and Robert in specific areas of their lives.[39] One can also notice ways that resources contribute to or undermine the character-development of children, and ways that parents and others help or hinder children depending on the virtues these adults have or lack. The following sections compare Ellie and Robert in the four domains of flourishing. The comparison does not focus only on material resources, but instead on the way that relationships and character are constantly interacting with material resources in every domain.

## Body

In this domain, both Ellie's and Robert's basic health and security needs are being met. Robert has health and dental insurance thanks to government programs that make the coverage affordable for his parents. What the respective families are able to do for their children's health, nutrition, and safety is likely to be different, however, due to the differences in work schedules, transportation, and income. For instance, Ellie will get dental braces, Robert won't. Robert flourishes less than other children because of his asthma. This condition gives him discomfort and holds him back from activities that other children do readily. While a child in the suburbs could have asthma, the condition is more

---

39. Of course, a full assessment would require more knowledge about the real children involved and more research into the specific social conditions of their neighborhoods, schools, the local economy, and so on.

prevalent in low-income neighborhoods;[40] therefore, Robert's low-income status may be impinging on his health. The issues facing Robert are instances of the documented correlations between low-income status and increased health problems; there is evidence that the former causes the latter through deprivation.[41] Robert also runs a greater risk than Ellie of becoming a victim of gun violence, simply because of where he lives.[42]

Some of the children's biological "givens" could pose risks to their flourishing. For instance, if a child develops a learning disability, an emotional disability (such as clinical depression), or a mental disability, he or she will have vulnerabilities in life compared to other children and will need additional assistance. Another given is gender. As a girl, even one from the upper middle class in the contemporary United States, Ellie could face discrimination and obstacles to her flourishing.[43] Finally, neither child's race nor ethnicity is mentioned. But African-American and Hispanic children in the United States are more likely than white children to be poor. As the resources cited in this section indicate, those in low-income families are at risk of deficits in many of the capabilities related to physical well-being.

## Mind

The children's mental well-being (Nussbaum's capability 4) depends heavily on their formal education. A common pattern in the United States is that, in towns and neighborhoods where average family income is higher, public schools rate highly on many metrics: funding for the schools, level of parental involvement, student scores on standardized tests, available sports and enrichment programs,

---

40. Partners Asthma Center, "Chapter 15: Poverty and Asthma," 2010, *http://www.asthma.partners.org/NewFiles/BoFAChapter15.html.*

41. On the correlations in the United States, see Elizabeth Mendes, "In U.S., Health Disparities across Incomes Are Wide-Ranging," Gallup, October 18, 2010, *http://www.gallup.com/poll/143696/health-disparities-across-incomes-wide-ranging.aspx.* On causation, see Karien Stronks, H. Dike van de Mheen, and Johan P. Mackenbach, "A Higher Prevalence of Health Problems in Low Income Groups: Does It Reflect Relative Deprivation?," *Journal of Epidemiology and Public Health* 52 (1998): 548–57.

42. For an illustration of greater gun violence in poor, urban areas, see Richard Florida, "The Geography of U.S. Gun Violence," *CityLab at The Atlantic Monthly,* December 14, 2012, *http://www.citylab.com/crime/2012/12/geography-us-gun-violence/4171/.* For a report on research suggesting that social networks within those areas greatly predict the risk of becoming a victim of gun violence, see Allie Bidwell, "Gun Violence Significantly Increased by Social Interactions," *U.S. News and World Report,* November 14, 2013, *http://www.usnews.com/news/articles/2013/11/14/gun-violence-significantly-increased-by-social-interactions.*

43. In much of the world, women are objectively suffering in several of their capabilities because of systemic discrimination. See Nicholas D. Kristof and Cheryl WuDunn, *Half the Sky* (New York: Vintage: 2009). The situation is much better for women in developed countries, but the United States is only the twentieth best country in gender equality in 2014, according to the World Economic Forum (*https://agenda.weforum.org/topic/global-issues/gender-parity/*).

and teacher preparation, pay, and continuity.[44] In short, when towns and their residents are wealthier, their schools are better. Wealthier towns enjoy a better tax base for funding their schools and a higher proportion of well-educated households in which the adults have the interest and time to be involved in school activities. Moreover, when parents such as Ellie's decide where to buy a house, they almost always factor in the reputed quality of the public school system, as measured by test scores. Because of their higher income, Ellie's parents enjoyed more choices of where to settle down than did Robert's parents. Ellie's school is well-resourced, and her teacher is probably dealing with fewer behavior problems in the classroom, thus enjoying more time and energy for instruction. In addition to the correlations between community wealth and school quality, there are documented correlations between families' socioeconomic levels and the academic performance of their children.[45] These correlations are influenced by many factors, such as the resources families have for education, the quality of schools, the nutrition children receive, and how often children hear complex language at home.[46] For a mix of social and familial reasons, the average Ellie is likely to learn more and perform better in school than the average Robert.[47]

Concerning emotions (Nussbaum's capability 5), both children seem psychologically strong and emotionally happy, but much more needs to be considered to know for sure. In Seligman's well-being theory, children need positive emotion and engagement. Ellie and Robert seem to have healthy relationships with siblings, parents, and friends, connections that make them happy in an emotional sense and offer deeper benefits for flourishing. Both children have opportunities to play and seem to have fun in their various activities, so both children are engaged. However, Ellie enjoys a wider range of enrichment activities, such as Girl Scouts, soccer, and crafts, so she has more and varied opportunities for engagement compared to Robert.

Both children are fortunate to have two caring parents. If, however, a single parent were raising either child, the strains on some of the child's capabilities

---

44. See "America's Richest School Districts" at *24/7 Wall St.* for a sketch of the trends and an instructive comparison of the ten richest and poorest districts in the United States (*http://247wallst .com/special-report/2012/06/06/americas-richest-school-districts/*).

45. A California newspaper's analysis of data collected by the state suggests that student performance "has more to do with family income than how many students are crammed into a classroom, how much a district spends per student, how much teachers are paid, or what percentage of students are still learning English" (J. D. Velasco, "Income Level Has Strong Effect on School Test Scores, Analysis Shows," *Whittier Daily News*, November 26, 2011, *http://www.whittierdailynews .com/social-affairs/20111126/income-level-has-strong-effect-on-school-test-scores-analysis-shows*).

46. A study found that by age three, a child in a low-income family heard thirty million fewer words than a child of a middle-class family. See "Closing The 'Word Gap' between Rich and Poor," National Public Radio, December 29, 2013, *http://www.npr.org/2013/12/29/257922222 /closing-the-word-gap-between-rich-and-poor*.

47. For more analysis of all the issues in this paragraph, see ch. 6.

could be greater, because of the additional pressures on the parent's income and emotional availability.[48] In the United States or anywhere in the world, children's flourishing is greatly at risk when they live in situations of neglect, abuse, economic deprivation, or physical danger. Just as importantly, children anywhere, even those who live in financially sound households with two parents, suffer psychologically when their parents withdraw emotionally, discipline in too strict or too lax a manner, or cause physical or emotional abuse. Sometimes such parents lack genuine love for their children, but more often they need help in learning how to parent more effectively, or they need less stress in their lives and more time to spend with their children.[49]

## Character

Character-formation is one of the primary tasks of parenting and formal education. To acquire the character trait of practical reason is crucial, because it orders a person's pursuit of flourishing in every domain. In their use of practical reason, Ellie and Robert are still at an early stage of development. Being able to form a view of the good life and plan one's life accordingly is an adult capability, but it is one that adults must help children develop throughout many years. Habituation is a process of education in which parents, teachers, and mentors give children standards of good behavior, model good behaviors in their own actions, and teach children how to do the same.[50] As children grow, they take on increasing responsibility for developing their own characters. Adults plant the seeds and show children how to till their own gardens; eventually, it is up to those children to pursue flourishing. In the brief examples of Ellie and Robert, there is no reason to doubt that their parents are taking this responsibility seriously and doing well at it. Both parents are involved positively in their children's lives; they monitor how their children are doing in school and what they are doing in their free time; and they participate in activities as a family, including attending church, which exposes the children to moral education.

In Seligman's theory, it is important for children to develop meaning in their lives and have opportunities for accomplishment in the face of challenges. The case study is too short to suggest whether this is happening in each child's life. Unlike many of the other capabilities, a child's abilities to find meaning and develop character are not *heavily* dependent on his or her socioeconomic

---

48. Single Parent Wealth, a support website, mentions the range of challenges (*http://singleparent wealth.com*). A datasheet by the Population Reference Bureau notes the rapid rise of single-parent families and concludes, "Children in lower-income, single-parent families face the most significant barriers to success in school and the work force" (Mark Mather, "U.S. Children in Single-Mother Families," May 2010, *http://www.prb.org/Publications/Reports/2010/singlemotherfamilies.aspx*).

49. For more on the needs of parents and ways to meet those needs, see ch. 5.

50. For more on habituation, see ch. 2, in the second part of the definition of virtue.

status; indeed, some argue that people who are wealthier have a harder time finding happiness.[51]

## Relationships

The final four of Nussbaum's ten capabilities concern relationships to others— persons, animals, nature, and society—as a domain for flourishing. Affiliation (capability 7) is one of these capabilities because connections to other people are crucial to achieving flourishing and developing character. Since relationships run the gamut, this category can be subdivided into *interpersonal affiliations* (family and friends) and *civic affiliations* (relating to others in social clubs, civic organizations, the workplace, and the political community).[52] Parents constitute the major interpersonal relationships in Ellie's and Robert's lives. Other family members, including other involved adults, are also important. It is notable that Robert is closely connected to a church community and extended family, possibly more so than Ellie. Such affiliations bring many psychological and sociological benefits.[53] Ellie enjoys opportunities for affiliation by participating in organized soccer and the Girl Scouts. Both Ellie and Robert have friends, a great boon to emotional flourishing, although peers can also be a source of risk, especially since young people are impressionable. Based on what they see in their neighborhood, Robert's parents seem worried about peer influences on Robert.

Ellie, Robert, and all children live in larger networks of economic and political affiliations. Hardly aware of these affiliations, they nevertheless are affected by them daily. Economic networks have shaped their parents' financial prospects and thus partly dictated where Ellie and Robert live and the financial resources available for their needs. The families' socioeconomic statuses influence many aspects of the children's well-being, as has been seen throughout this analysis. Moreover, socioeconomic status in the United States is not as amenable to change across generations as people like to think.[54] As for political networks, city, state, and federal governments establish rules and provide resources that facilitate (or hamper) citizens' pursuit of flourishing. The quality of public education, the safety of neighborhoods, pollution levels, availability of public transportation, promotion

---

51. See Tal Ben-Shahar, *Happier: Learn the Secrets to Daily Joy and Lasting Fulfillment* (New York: McGraw Hill, 2007), 55–58. For a research note on the U.S. trends, complicating the sometimes overly simple picture, see Claude S. Fischer, "What Wealth-Happiness Paradox? A Short Note on the American Case," *Journal of Happiness Studies* 9, no. 2 (June 2008): 219–26.

52. This delineation of two types of affiliation is not quite the same as Nussbaum's original delineation in capability 7, but the interpersonal and civic types still cover the range of affiliations that she identifies.

53. The dual benefits of civic participation—that it promotes well-being in the people who participate and builds networks of social trust that promote social flourishing—have been documented in Robert D. Putnam's study of "social capital" in *Bowling Alone: The Collapse and Revival of American Community* (New York: Simon & Schuster, 2000), which is discussed in ch. 4.

54. See reporter Timothy Noah, *The Great Divergence* (New York: Bloomsbury, 2012) and Nobel laureate economist Joseph E. Stiglitz, *The Price of Inequality* (New York: W. W. Norton, 2012).

of public health, affordability of health insurance, and many other dimensions of well-being are significantly shaped by political policies. Ellie and Robert live in the same country and state, so some resources are equally available to them and their families. But because they live in different localities with different tax bases, tax rates, and problems to address, they experience governmental resources in very different ways, beginning with the quality of their schools.

Concerning the ability to relate to nature and other species (capability 8), the former is more salient in these two children's lives. Both play outdoors. In an urban environment, Robert's opportunities to enjoy nature and a clean environment are more limited, though sometimes people living in the suburbs, like Ellie, face the same challenges. Generally, lower-income families experience more pollution.[55] Air pollution and housing quality could contribute to Robert's asthma. The quality of the natural environment depends significantly on state and local governments, local businesses, and local civic organizations.

Children highly value the chance to play (capability 9). Ellie and Robert enjoy recreation, some of it outdoors, and participate in activities they enjoy. Play is sometimes solitary but most often social; both children enjoy playing with others. However, there is a difference between Ellie's and Robert's structured play: Ellie participates in the Girl Scouts and organized soccer, while Robert has only informal play and sports. In his recent study of "opportunity gap" between American children of different social classes, political scientist Robert Putnam reports, "Involvement in extracurricular activities has been shown repeatedly to have measurably favorable consequences." [56] The benefits for children include developing social skills and leadership skills, and such participation is strongly correlated with later college attendance and higher salaries. The benefits for the community are that young people involved in extracurriculars tend to be better students and less involved in crime. Given these benefits, Putnam comments,

> It is thus distressing to learn that every study confirms a substantial class gap in extracurricular participation, especially when it comes to sustained involved across different types of activity. Poor kids are three times as likely as their nonpoor classmates to participate in *neither* sports *nor* clubs (30 percent to 10 percent), and half as likely to participate in *both* sports *and* clubs (22 percent to 44 percent).[57]

Another potential threat to play—one that affects children of all social classes—is technology. Like most contemporary American children, "screen

---

55. See Cheryl Katz and Environmental Health News, "People in Poor Neighborhoods Breathe More Hazardous Particles," *Scientific American*, November 1, 2012, *http://www.scientificamerican.com/article/people-poor-neighborhoods-breate-more-hazardous-particles/*.

56. Robert D. Putnam, *Our Kids: The American Dream in Crisis* (New York: Simon & Schuster, 2015), 174.

57. Ibid., 176.

time" is a significant factor in their lives. Robert watches the amount of television that the average American child does, while Ellie watches somewhat less.[58] Ellie spends some of her daily screen time on a computer with Internet, while Robert has no computer at home. Ellie thus has comparatively more access to educational and enrichment opportunities online, though much of how these children will be shaped by technology and empowered to use it to their benefit depends on parental guidance.[59]

The last capability concerning relationships is control over one's environment (capability 10). Like other items on the list, this capability is only fully realized by adults, but children are greatly affected by it. One's ability to participate in politics (capability 10a) is significant for flourishing. Without a voice and a vote, people live at the whim of those in power. In the United States, government is accountable to the people, but, in practice, individuals can have a hard time making their voices heard. Suppose, for instance, that both Ellie's and Robert's parents vote. But because of demographic and political developments in recent decades, American suburbs hold greater clout than urban centers.[60] At the state level, which is often decisive for education policy, suburban voters and their representatives can steer resources in a direction that favors themselves.[61] The ability to navigate bureaucracies is also important in influencing one's environment. Robert's family lacks a computer, a potential roadblock to accessing certain resources. Signing up for healthcare, connecting to the children's schools, applying for college, and many other activities are most easily done on the Internet. The roadblock is not insurmountable, as there are computers at school, work, and the public library, but the lack still hampers the family.[62] In their employment and financial situation (material control, capability 10b), Robert's parents are more vulnerable to loss of autonomy than Ellie's parents. The loss of a job or an unexpected major medical crisis is challenging for all families, but Robert's family is more at risk because of the parents' small bank account (so they have a weaker safety net during unemployment) and lower levels of education (so they are less competitive for higher-paying jobs).

---

58. The average American child age two to eleven watches three-and-a-half hours of television per day. The hours dip a bit for young adults and then rise steadily for older Americans. David Hinckley, "Average American Watches 5 Hours of TV Per Day, Report Shows," *New York Daily News*, March 5, 2014, *http://www.nydailynews.com/life-style/average-american-watches-5-hours-tv-day-article-1.1711954.*

59. See Danah Boyd, *It's Complicated: The Social Lives of Networked Teens* (New Haven: Yale University Press, 2014) and the discussion of cultural influences on families in ch. 5.

60. Richard Florida, "The Suburbs are the New Swing States," CityLab at *The Atlantic Monthly*, November 29, 2013, *http://www.citylab.com/politics/2013/11/suburbs-are-new-swing-states/7706/.*

61. See Eduardo Porter, "In Public Education, Edge Still Goes to Rich," *New York Times*, November 5, 2013, *http://www.nytimes.com/2013/11/06/business/a-rich-childs-edge-in-public-education.html?_r=0.*

62. See Alfred Lubrano, "Lack of Computer Access a Major Hurdle for the Poor," *Philadelphia Inquirer*, June 12, 2012, *http://articles.philly.com/2012-06-12/news/32175613_1_internet-access-computer-food-stamps.*

## Summary Assessment of Ellie's and Robert's Flourishing

In table 3.3, readers may attempt to assess the children's flourishing by rating Ellie's and Robert's well-being in each capability as high, moderate-high, moderate, moderate-low, or low. Admittedly, this is difficult given the limited and hypothetical details of the children's lives, but it is still possible to get a rough sense and to compare the children's situations.

### TABLE 3.3 Assessment of the Flourishing of Two Children: The Reader's Answers

|  | Ellie | Robert |
|---|---|---|
| 1. Life |  |  |
| 2. Bodily health |  |  |
| 3. Bodily integrity |  |  |
| 4. Senses, imagination, and thought |  |  |
| 5. Emotions |  |  |
| 6. Practical reason |  |  |
| 7a. Affiliations: interpersonal |  |  |
| 7b. Affiliations: civic |  |  |
| 8. Relationship with nature |  |  |
| 9. Play |  |  |
| 10. Control over one's environment |  |  |

One would be justified in thinking that Ellie is highly flourishing overall, especially when compared to children in many parts of the world and even to other American children. Ellie enjoys health and security, a good education, and the ability to participate in activities that help her develop holistically. Ellie has parents who love her and support her both materially and emotionally. Benefitting from a wide array of social networks, she and her family can make meaningful choices about how to live their lives. The risks to Ellie's well-being are twofold. The first is the stress that can accompany the attempt to be a successful child in a success-oriented family and community. Virtue ethics calls into question status quo notions of success. As some books and documentary films have illustrated, American children across the spectrum—especially those from families of the middle and upper class—are often put under strong pressure by parents, peers, and cultural norms to be the best in everything they do.[63] Some students, therefore, work hard at school and sports, with sacrifices to their sleep and happiness.

The second risk to Ellie's well-being lies in her experience of a nuclear family and a typical American suburb. Her relationships with extended family are thinner and less frequent than Robert's. While close, primary family relationships are crucial for a child's well-being, so are extended kin relationship; a paucity of these in a child's life might leave her with fewer psychological and social supports.[64] Families throughout the United States, and especially in the suburbs, have tended, in recent years, to know fewer of their neighbors.[65] Also, Americans tend to live in areas where everyone else is much like them—ethnically, socioeconomically, and politically. This trend, which has been dubbed "the Big Sort," arguably is having negative effects on the fabric of civil society.[66] Ellie's flourishing will be, to some extent, reduced if she grows up not knowing many children like Robert.

Robert has many of the same familial and emotional positives in his life as Ellie: caring parents, friends, and family relationships. He is being raised with an eye to his moral and spiritual development. His health is good except for his asthma, but this is being treated (his orthodontic needs, however, are not), just as Ellie's slight emotional vulnerability is being watched by caring adults. Robert's well-being is lower than Ellie's insofar as his capabilities are constrained by family income and resources, social resources, and civic affiliations. Robert does not have the same opportunities that Ellie does for structured extracurricular activities. His public school does an acceptable job, but is not of the same quality as Ellie's, just as schools in poorer communities, urban and rural, are weaker compared to suburban schools in the United States. The Big Sort influences Robert and his family as well, and they are left in a community with weaker civic and political affiliations. These weak affiliations constitute one of the greatest risks to Robert's flourishing. The government, the economy, and social networks are not working optimally for families like Robert's. Robert's parents have less experience and less clout in securing benefits from these organizations and networks. Therefore, they have less control over their well-being. An important benefit

---

63. See for example the film *Race to Nowhere* (Reel Link Films, 2009, *http://www.racetonowhere.com*) and William Deresciewicz, *Excellent Sheep: The Miseducation of the American Elite and the Way to a Meaningful Life* (New York: Free Press, 2014).

64. For scientific studies that find evidence of the benefits of extended family, see Mads Meier Jæger, "The Extended Family and Children's Educational Success," *American Sociological Review*, 77, no. 6 (Dec. 2012): 903–22; and Judith A. Crowell et al., "Partnership and Extended Family Relationship Quality Moderate Associations between Lifetime Psychiatric Diagnoses and Current Depressive Symptoms in Midlife," *Journal of Social and Clinical Psychology* 33, no. 7 (Sep. 2014): 612–29.

65. "A 2005 Georgetown University study, for example, found that 47 percent of Americans knew 'none, almost none or a few' of their neighbors by name," writes Marc J. Dunkelman (*The Vanishing Neighbor: The Transformation of American Community* [New York: W. W. Norton, 2014], 118).

66. Bill Bishop, *The Big Sort: Why the Clustering of Like-Minded America Is Tearing Us Apart* (Boston: Mariner Books, 2009).

to Robert's flourishing is his family's participation in a church. Religiousness is associated with greater psychological well-being and the development of virtues.[67] Active participation in a religious community contributes to the development of social skills and tends to build social capital among people across lines of social difference. In other words, religious participation could be a partial antidote to the Big Sort phenomenon.[68]

A possible summary assessment (table 3.4) might be considered from four angles: personal flourishing, social flourishing, character, and community.

## TABLE 3.4 Assessing the Flourishing of Two Children: A Possible Set of Answers

|  | Ellie | Robert |
|---|---|---|
| 1. Life | High | High |
| 2. Bodily health | High | Moderate |
| 3. Bodily integrity | High | High |
| 4. Senses, imagination, and thought | High | Moderate |
| 5. Emotions | Moderate-high | Moderate-high |
| 6. Practical reason | High | High |
| 7a. Affiliations: interpersonal | Moderate-high | High |
| 7b. Affiliations: civic | Moderate-high | Low |
| 8. Relationship with nature | High | Moderate |
| 9. Play | High | Moderate-low |
| 10. Control over one's environment | High | Low |

---

67. See the summary of the scientific evidence in Christopher Peterson and Martin E. P. Seligman, *Character Strengths and Virtues: A Handbook and Classification* (New York: Oxford University Press, 2004), 609–11.

68. See Bishop, *The Big Sort*, ch. 7 on the shift to socially divided and privatized religion. See Putnam, *Bowling Alone*, ch. 4 and *passim* (see index), also Sidney Verba, Kay Lehman Schlozman, and Henry Brady in *Voice and Equality: Civic Voluntarism in American Politics* (Cambridge, MA: Harvard University Press, 1995), *passim* (see index) for evidence on the benefits of religion for social bridging and the development of civic skills. However, a more recent study by the latter authors finds persistent inequality between social classes in political participation and influence, which religious activity has not been powerful enough to overcome (*The Unheavenly Chorus: Unequal Political Voice and the Broken Promise of American Democracy* [Princeton: Princeton University Press, 2012]).

*Personal Flourishing.* Both Ellie and Robert *deserve* to flourish because they are human and members of the same political society. The moral bottom line is: where and how one happens to be born shouldn't determine one's basic well-being. This case study is entirely realistic in setting up the families as living only two miles apart. Just a little distance separated by a line of political jurisdiction can represent a world of difference for a family's flourishing. In some societies, including the United States, the socioeconomic class into which one is born can largely cast the die for one's flourishing. The assessment of Ellie's and Robert's flourishing draws attention to the fact that children like Robert need assistance in specific areas. The individuals and institutions involved in Robert's life can, and should, collaborate to give that assistance.

*Social Flourishing.* An individual's flourishing seems to go hand-in-hand with the strength of civic networks. The benefits flow in both directions. First, *when society is healthy, people are healthy.* The analysis directs attention to systems and programs that promote flourishing. Almost all analyses of the well-being of American children identify quality of education as a major concern. Other resources of recent public concern are children's health insurance and access to doctors, the capacity for getting good nutrition and avoiding obesity, and the development of skills for emotional self-regulation and constructive resolution of conflicts. Second, *when people are healthy, society is healthy.* To the extent that children grow up without acquiring a decent education, developing practical reason, seeing the value of political participation, trusting in neighbors and institutions, and so on, as adults they will be less likely to contribute to their communities. Individuals and families whose flourishing has been stunted, in part from social constraints, are less likely to make their local communities and society flourish.

*Character.* Virtues are the norms that carry people toward the goal of flourishing. The analysis of Ellie's and Robert's flourishing spoke only generally of their characters, because of the limits of the case study and the fact that they are still children. It is the responsibility of parents and communities to help children develop character. Children need to develop virtues in all five of the main categories (care, respect, purpose, perceiving and reasoning, and acting and relating). They need to develop self-control, patience, and practical wisdom so they can take on more responsibility for themselves as they mature. Each and every virtue has something to do with developing one's capacity to flourish and help others flourish.

*Community.* From the perspective of community, the goal is the same: to support the flourishing of persons, which promotes the flourishing of society, and to support the flourishing of society, which promotes the flourishing of persons. The goal is *integrated flourishing* or, in other words, *the common good.* A definition of the common good that highlights its connection to flourishing is "the sum of those conditions of social life which allow social groups and their individual members relatively thorough and ready access to their own fulfillment."[69] To create, protect, and promote such conditions is an enormous task, since the conditions are varied. It is the responsibility of every group in society. A group working for integrated flourishing is practicing social ethics, as defined in chapter 1.

Social ethics is

- the normative deliberation of citizens, social groups, and public leaders
- on ethical resources and the results of social analysis
- to decide on collective actions and express an ethos
- so people can live together in a just and flourishing manner.

When social groups and their members work together to promote flourishing, they make life better—not just for those in need but for everyone. In the act of promoting flourishing, they contribute to developing the ethos of their society.

## Conclusion

Flourishing is a complex phenomenon. It is about being happy, doing good, and living well. Flourishing holds intuitive appeal, since everyone wants to be happy, but the meaning of "happiness" needs careful specification: human flourishing includes positive emotions, but it is about much more than emotions.

The specific conception of human flourishing advanced in this chapter comes from Aristotle and has been interpreted and applied to the contemporary world by Nussbaum. The Aristotelian view is that *human flourishing consists in having a good character plus sufficient material resources for exercising central human capabilities in domains of body, mind, character, and relationships.* The structure of human flourishing, which can encompass several theoretical approaches (table 3.2) is a gauge for measuring, even if only roughly, the areas in which specific people in specific contexts experience high, moderate, or low levels of well-being—as illustrated in the case study of Ellie and Robert.

People who see how the flourishing of their fellow citizens varies greatly based on factors largely outside those citizens' control might take action to

---

69. Vatican Council II, *Gaudium et spes* (1965), no. 26, *http://www.vatican.va/archive/hist_councils /ii_vatican_council/documents/vat-ii_const_19651207_gaudium-et-spes_en.html. Gaudium et spes (Pastoral Constitution on the Church in the Modern World)* is part of the Catholic Church's social teaching.

improve the flourishing of those less fortunate. Action is warranted by the virtues of justice, solidarity, and compassion: citizens and communities who claim to be virtuous cannot fail to act in some way, lest they violate the tenets of virtue ethics. However, virtue ethics does not prescribe one clear and precise way of responding. It is up to virtuous people to deliberate and decide, based on the specifics of the situation. Social responses are more effective when people ethically deliberate and act in virtuous groups. Hence the chapters of part 2 examine in more detail how certain groups can promote social flourishing. Before turning to groups' application of virtue ethics in society, the moral dynamics of groups as such must be examined, which is the focus of the next chapter.

## Questions for Review

1. Why do virtue ethicists prefer to conduct their quest for the purpose of life and the purpose of ethics in terms of "human flourishing" instead of "happiness"?
2. What does Aristotle mean by saying that flourishing is an activity? What are his four key activities for flourishing?
3. What are the differences between Aristotle and the Stoics on the matter of how flourishing is made secure?
4. In what ways do Aristotle and the Stoics agree about how flourishing is made secure?
5. What does Aristotle mean by "external resources" that are necessary for flourishing? What are some examples of these resources?
6. What does Martha Nussbaum mean by central human capabilities?
7. How has the list of central capabilities been used by policymakers?
8. Give examples of ways that lower socioeconomic status can hamper the flourishing of a person in body, mind, character, and relationships to others.
9. How does an individual's flourishing go hand-in-hand with a community's flourishing? Use details from the case study to illustrate.

## Discussion Questions and Activities

1. Discuss, with others, your answers to the thought-experiment on the elements of human flourishing.
2. Defend a position on the debate between Aristotle and the Stoics concerning whether one's happiness, in the sense of flourishing, is completely under one's control.
3. What external resources are essential for flourishing, and why?

4. Develop, defend, and discuss your answers regarding the relative levels of Ellie's and Robert's flourishing in the case study.

5. Find a story in Nicolas Kristof and Sheryl WuDunn's *Half the Sky* (see "Recommendations for Further Reading") or a similar news story of a person or family struggling with a lack of resources. Analyze the case using the methods of this chapter.

6. Examine the *World Happiness Report 2015* (see "Recommendations for Further Reading"). Discuss whether the standards for "happiness" in the report are compatible with the approaches in this chapter. What economic and political initiatives does the report recommend? Are these initiatives ethically warranted?

## Recommendations for Further Reading

Devettere, Raymond J. *Introduction to Virtue Ethics: Insights of the Ancient Greeks* Washington, DC: Georgetown University Press, 2002.

A clear introduction to the themes of ancient Greek virtue ethics for the beginning student.

Kristof, Nicholas D. and Cheryl WuDunn, *Half the Sky: Turning Oppression into Opportunity for Women Worldwide.* New York: Vintage: 2009.

Powerfully illustrates the multiple forms of oppression that women worldwide experience and shows how women can improve their flourishing markedly with support from education, healthcare, and small business loans.

MacIntyre, Alasdair. *Dependent Rational Animals: Why Human Beings Need the Virtues.* Peru, IL: Carus Publishing, 1999.

Argues that virtues are indispensible to human flourishing, because virtues enable humans to adequately protect themselves in the face of their biological needs, vulnerability to deprivations, and dependence on others.

McMahon, Darrin M. *Happiness: A History.* New York: Atlantic Monthly Press, 2006.

A study of the quest for happiness ranges from ancient Greek drama and philosophy through various Western philosophers to the contemporary science of happiness.

Nussbaum, Martha C. *Creating Capabilities: The Human Development Approach.* Cambridge, MA: Belknap, 2011.

Nussbaum's accessible explanation of the capabilities approach covers economic, legal, and philosophical angles, and discusses the relevance of the approach to contemporary issues, such as poverty, education, and the environment.

Seligman, Martin E. P. *Flourish: A Visionary New Understanding of Happiness and Well-Being*. New York: Simon and Schuster, 2011; Atria Paperback, 2013.

A co-founder of positive psychology updates his earlier "authentic happiness theory" to become "well-being theory": an account of human flourishing and the character traits and relationships needed to enhance it.

Seneca. *On the Happy Life. Moral Letters. On the Shortness of Life.* Multiple editions.

Seneca was not only a philosopher, but lived a dramatic life as a statesman, eventually being forced by the emperor Nero to commit suicide in 65 CE. These texts are the main resources for his virtue ethics.

Sustainable Development Solutions Network (SDSN), *World Happiness Report 2015. http://worldhappiness.report/*.

Commissioned by the United Nations, this report, now in its third edition, summarizes how citizens in all countries rate their happiness and satisfaction with life, as well as how they fare in various objective measurements of physical, mental, and economic well-being.

# Communities

## The Contexts for Becoming Good and Living Well

It is easy, from a safe distance, to overlook the fact that in under-cities governed by corruption, where exhausted people vie on scant terrain for very little, it is blisteringly hard to be good. The astonishment is that people are good, and that many people try to be.

—*Katherine Boo*[1]

## Chapter Overview

- explains the importance of groups as mediating institutions
- charts the mutual relationships among persons, groups, and society
- details six hindering influences of community on character and flourishing
- examines four helping influences of community on character and flourishing
- presents the sociological concept of social capital and the ethical concept of the common good as frameworks for social ethics

## Community Matters

Katherine Boo is a journalist who spent several years getting to know the residents of an undercity—in other words, a slum—called Annawadi. The undercity is home to thousands of poor people living in crudely constructed shacks

---

1. Katherine Boo, *Behind the Beautiful Forevers: Life, Death, and Hope in a Mumbai Undercity* (New York: Random House, 2012), 284. The book has won several prestigious awards, including the National Book Award and the PEN Literary Award.

close to the airport of Mumbai, India. The residents contend with few jobs, little schooling, inadequate sanitation, police corruption, and a political system that is concerned with them only at election time. Boo profiles the lives of several Annawadians in *Behind the Beautiful Forevers*. Unfortunately, it is a story more tragic than hopeful.

Fatima, a one-legged prostitute, sets herself on fire and then blames Abdul—quite literally, the boy next "door" (the two residences are separated only by a hanging bedsheet). Since Fatima resents the neighboring family, which is more successful than hers owing to Abdul's hard work as a trash scavenger, she injures herself out of jealousy, blaming Abdul. Fatima is sad and angry at the world. Driven to prostitution by her disability, she is routinely degraded by her customers and scorned in the community. Although Abdul does nothing to harm Fatima, he serves as a convenient scapegoat.

For Abdul, the situation turns dire when the burns worsen and Fatima dies in the hospital, largely because of inadequate care. Abdul and his father are jailed. The police and public defense lawyer pressure Abdul's mother for bribes. She does not want to pay—indeed, cannot afford to—especially since there is no guarantee that paying will bring her husband or son home. The family has little confidence they will get justice within a corrupt legal and political system. Can Abdul's family maintain its belief that working hard and doing the right thing pays off? After what Fatima did, would they be foolish to trust their neighbors again? Considering their treatment at the hands of the police, courts, and politicians, why would they try to be good if their virtue might be a disadvantage?

*Behind the Beautiful Forevers* raises these and other ethical questions. In the book, the dilemma facing Abdul's family is one of the many stories concerning vicious people, virtuous people, and people with mixed characters. What unites their struggles is expressed when Boo says that, in a context in which people are disrespected and given no social support, it is "blisteringly hard" for them to be good. Yet character shines through: Abdul is diligent and hopeful before his arrest and maintains his hope and composure as the case continues. The education he received from his mother and father is among the reasons he is a conscientious and hard-working young man, and their love and dedication support him throughout the ordeal. Thus, as the tragedies and occasional successes of the Annwadians illustrate, communal contexts are crucial for character and flourishing.

Proponents of normative ethical theories recognize that the theories' guidance for living cannot remain abstract but must be applied by real people in real-world contexts. Therefore, *context* is the third major element of the moral life addressed by ethical theories (see chapter 1). Although community matters in all ethical theories, virtue ethics pays it particular attention. This chapter presents a virtue-based analysis of community in four parts. First, the chart "Community Connections" introduces the mutual relationships among groups, persons, and society. Second, the negative influences of community on individual character and flourishing are detailed. Third, the positive influences of community are detailed. Fourth, the sociological concept of social capital and the ethical concept of the common good are presented as frameworks that help social ethicists move from normative values to applied recommendations.

---

## Three Elements of the Moral Life Addressed by Ethical Theories

- Norms: Guidelines for how to act and live
- Purpose: The goals of human life
- **Context: An understanding of the situations that influence ethical living**

---

# The Art of Association: Groups as Mediating Institutions

Alexis de Tocqueville, a nineteenth-century French author and civil servant, was commissioned by his government to visit the United States and report back on the function of its prisons. In 1831 and 1832, he visited and gathered impressions, not only of the prison system, but also of the politics of the young nation. His keen interest in American politics led him to write a masterwork of political thought, *Democracy in America*, published in 1835. In this book, Tocqueville describes American civic culture, which he finds crucial for making democracy thrive. Tocqueville writes, "Americans of all ages, all conditions, and all dispositions, constantly form associations" to address their social needs.[2] These civic organizations include philanthropic charities, schools, political parties, civic clubs, museums, business associations, churches and religious communities.

According to Tocqueville, civic organizations are tremendously important for instilling and enacting the virtues that make possible an orderly and free society.

He observes that, by participating in groups, Americans learn skills and develop values that they carry into other sectors of life, including politics. What people learn is "the art of association."[3] This art produces positive synergy: the pro-social influences of the virtues instilled in people in one communal context transfer to other contexts as the individuals participate in many associations. As

---

2. Alexis de Tocqueville, *Democracy in America*, 2.2.2.5, ed. Richard Heffner (New York: Signet Classic, 2001), 198.

3. Ibid., ch. 5 and 7, in Heffner, 198–209.

more of the small- and medium-size associations experience the positive influence of character, society's larger institutions—such as the national government, the economy, and culture—do so as well.

Associating in groups and communities helps persons develop character, pursue flourishing, and collaborate with others in the pursuit of social flourishing. This claim will be demonstrated, but first, a few terms must be defined and their relationships explained.

*Person* refers to individual members of groups, communities, and society. *Community* is a catch-all term referring to any of the many ways people share life. *Groups* are small- and medium-sized communities. Groups are also called "voluntary associations" because, typically, people choose to join or be active in them—examples include schools, clubs, churches, philanthropic organizations, and so on. Some groups are not voluntary, like one's biological family, yet people still make choices about how to associate with their families and whether to start their own families through parenting. Whether fully voluntary or not, all groups have the possibility of serving as "mediating institutions," because they stand "between the individual in his private life and the large institutions of public life . . . giving private life a measure of stability . . . [and] transferring meaning and value to the megastructures."[4]

*Society* is a large system of persons and communities bound by cultural, economic, geographic, legal, and political ties. In many cases, a society is roughly equivalent to a country; for example, the United States of America is a country (or nation) and a society. Despite the great diversity within it, U.S. society coheres through its history, language, political system, and public culture.

## The Community Connections Chart

The network among persons, groups, and society is illustrated in a diagram of mutual relationships (fig. 4.1).

### Community Connections

**Figure 4.1.** A Chart of Community Connections

Each part of the network has a state of flourishing:

- Individual flourishing begins with the development of, and ability to act from, the capabilities (ch. 3) that persons develop in their families and

---

4. Peter Berger and Richard Neuhaus, *To Empower People: The Role of Mediating Structures in Public Policy* (Washington, DC: American Enterprise Institute, 1977), 2–3.

intimate communities. Flourishing depends on the quality of affiliations with others and the communal groups and societies to which one belongs.

- A group's flourishing depends on its ability to fulfill its functions, work toward its mission, and nurture and sustain its members.
- A society's flourishing depends on its ability to fulfill its functions, work toward its mission, and nurture and sustain its citizens and the communities that compose it. The flourishing of a society is also called *the common good*: the sum of social relationships and availability of conditions that enable the individual members and immediate communities of society to progress toward flourishing.

Each part of the network has moral character:

- Individuals have characters—the integrated sum of their virtues and vices, as expressed in their decisions and actions.
- A group has a character based on the virtues, vices, and actions of its members. For instance, a family whose members show consistent love to each other has a loving character; it exhibits the virtue of love.
- A society has an ethos, which is composed of the values for which the society is established; how it incorporates and validates the ethics of its subcommunities; the values, virtues, and principles that guide its daily activities; and whether or not it shows relative consistency in how it conducts itself.[5]

The three parts of the network—persons, groups, and society—with their constituent types of flourishing and character, stand in relationships of mutual influence. The double-headed arrows signify that the entities contribute to each other's flourishing and character. To see these mutual influences at work, consider the example of a youth sports league (fig. 4.2).

## Sports League

**Figure 4.2.** Community Connections: A Youth Sports League

---

5. On ethos, see ch. 1, in the section "The Personal and Social Dimensions of Ethics." The terms "character" or "ethos" can be applied to both groups and society, but, when it comes to society, the most commonly used term is "ethos."

The relationship between the youth sports league and its participants, teams, parents, and volunteer adults (relationship no. 1) helps the children and adults. Volunteers make the playing of games possible by organizing the league. Children in the community are thus able to thrive in some basic human capabilities: play, physical health, and affiliation. Coaches teach the players how to play well, stay safe, develop physical stamina, practice teamwork, and be good sports.[6] Coaches teach virtues, in other words, and they rely on parents or guardians to have already taught virtues and to reinforce them at home. Benefits flow in the other direction, too: if most of the league participants communicate well, support the league, and show good character, the league will flourish in carrying out its mission of promoting healthy play, enjoyment of the sport, and children's development.

The sports league also contributes to the common good of the local neighborhood, town, city, or county (relationship no. 2). Local sports give residents something fun to do, as participants and spectators. A town with good youth leagues is a place where families are willing to settle down and invest their energies in improving the community. In the other direction, benefits flow from the local community to the league, making its operations possible. The league needs assistance from the government and other civic groups. The league benefits from well-maintained parks where children play the sport, exemptions from taxes as a nonprofit entity, financial sponsorship from local businesses, and partnerships with schools and sports leagues.

The relationship between the league and the community mediates a relationship between citizens and society. For example, the league supports the health and character of children who, therefore, are more likely to be happy, healthy, and productive in the community. Adults who volunteer in the league are more likely to engage in other productive behaviors for the benefit of society. The prevalence of youth sports likely enriches the ethos of the society and the civic sensibilities of citizens.[7] As one can see, the entire scheme is synergistic, as the flows of support are mutually reinforcing, and the benefits in one part of the network transfer to other parts of the network.

The synergy, however, can be negative in two major ways. First, limitations of resources in any part of the network can undermine flourishing. The absence of youth leagues in a community, or an insufficient number of them, removes opportunities for people to participate, reducing the benefits just described. When it is expensive for players to participate in the sport, some

---

6. For virtue-oriented discussions of the benefit of sports on persons, see Patrick Kelly, "Experiencing Life's Flow," *America*, October 20, 2008, 19-21; James F. Keenan, *Virtues for Ordinary Christians* (Lanham, MD: Sheed and Ward, 1996), 134–39; and Michael McNamee, "Sporting Virtue and Its Development," in *The Handbook of Virtue Ethics*, ed. Stan van Hooft (Durham, UK: Acumen, 2014), 375–85.

7. For an argument along these lines, see Scott Ganz and Ken Hassett, "Little League, Huge Effect," *The American* (May/June 2008): 64–67, EBSCOhost (AN 32109976).

families and children are potentially excluded. If a town does not have adequate parks and the budget to maintain them, the league and its members might miss out on a higher-quality experience or have to pass on upkeep costs to the member families.

Second, weakness of character in any part of the network can harm one or more of the parts. For instance, if the participating parents make little effort to support the league (by volunteering, participating in fundraisers, etc.) or if some parents are overly competitive and yell at the children during games, such character flaws can harm the children and the league. Officials who are overly competitive or who communicate poorly with parents could ruin a league. The officials and coaches might schedule too many practices and games, such that they crowd out the families' other activities. Slowly but surely, the culture around a given sport in a community can become self-centered and morally cramped.[8] Most parents and youth who have been involved in sports know of examples when a sport has become too demanding on people's time and when a focus on winning distorts the purpose of amateur athletics. When such imbalance occurs, some participants might wish for change but be unsure how to effect it. A parent who feels, for instance, that his or her child's league is too focused on winning may find the culture of the league too powerful to combat. Often such a parent won't try to change the culture but will opt out and find another activity for his or her child.

Any group, even a well-meaning volunteer group such as a youth sports league, can develop a corrupt ethos. Groups are too important to society to ignore issues of corruption. Thus people need to know how to effect change. Social ethics analyzes how, in general, positive person-group-society synergies can be promoted and negative synergies prevented. Virtue ethics is a helpful resource for such social analysis.

## Community as a Hindrance to Character and Flourishing

As is evident in *Behind the Beautiful Forevers*, a local community and a large society can threaten character and flourishing. Reinhold Niebuhr, arguably the most influential American theologian of the twentieth century, diagnosed community's threats to character in *Moral Man and Immoral Society* (1932). Niebuhr describes a dichotomy: although individuals might be morally decent, the egoism and diffusion of responsibility that occurs in large groups and society causes these communities to act less virtuously than would their individual members. Niebuhr contends that groups are almost always a bad influence on people: "In

---

8. An expression of concern about these trends is Fred Engh, *Why Johnny Hates Sports*, rev. ed. (Garden City Park, NY: Square One, 2002).

every human group there is less reason to guide and check impulse . . . less ability to comprehend the needs of others and therefore more unrestrained egoism" than in the individuals who compose the group.[9] These bad dynamics even can happen in the family, Niebuhr says, but they are more prominent in larger groups.

From the writings of virtue ethicists, it is possible to distill six ways communities can hinder the character and flourishing of individuals. These six are patterns of *potential* negative influences of a group, institution, or society on individuals. The actual influence of a specific community on a specific individual throughout time is complex and difficult to summarize. There are some qualifications on communal influence: a community does not dictate how the people within it develop; there are multiple influences on people inside a community and additional outside influences; people have freedom to make up their own minds; and people influence the community, sometimes ending or alleviating the negative influence. Virtue ethics aims to stop or ameliorate the following communal influences.

## 1. Communities Can Control and Corrupt People

Some groups (and individuals) are so powerful that they can negatively shape the character of people under their control. A child raised by an abusive parent can turn out in a number of ways, one of which is to be self-abusive. Parents might also fail to instill character in their children. Parents are not the only influence on children, of course. Peers are a powerful influence, often for good yet sometimes for ill. An example of negative influence is when a youth associates with a gang that encourages him to commit crimes. Society can also negatively impact people. For example, a dictatorial government uses fear, punishment, and propaganda to brutalize citizens; sometimes these consequences are so dire that citizens act in ways that go against their nature, such as betraying a friend to the police. Interestingly, some people rise above even the most brutal and corrupting contexts. A child raised by a racist parent may accept racist ideas when she is too young to know better but later find a way out of that bigotry. People and their characters are resilient, in the sense that people can act with character in the face of tremendous threats. Even deprived children can grow up well if they receive a little help.[10]

---

9. Reinhold Niebuhr, *Moral Man and Immoral Society* (New York: Scribners, 1932; reprint ed., 1960), xxix.

10. A dramatic narrative example is Ishmael Beah, *A Long Way Gone: Memoirs of a Boy Soldier* (New York: Farrar, Straus and Giroux, 2007). As a twelve-year-old boy in Sierra Leone, Beah was kidnapped by rebel forces and indoctrinated as a soldier who then committed atrocities. Through a long process of recovery in a United Nations' camp, he became a well-adjusted adult. For a discussion of the psychology and science of children's resilience, see Paul Tough, *How Children Succeed: Grit, Curiosity, and the Hidden Power of Character* (Boston: Houghton Mifflin, 2012).

## 2. Communities Can Constrain Individuals' Moral Responsiveness

The very existence of a group can constrain a person's moral responsiveness through peer pressure, groupthink, and the like. For this reason, to exercise virtue, people need to develop habits of critical thinking and courage. But can people really resist a group's constraining influences? Some philosophers and psychologists, known as "situationists," posit that because people act differently in different situations, there is strong reason to doubt that enduring character traits exist. Situationists point to experiments in social psychology suggesting that character is highly variable. One experiment often cited involves seminary students who had just heard a sermon about the Good Samaritan. The students were then told they were late for an appointment. On their way to the appointment, given the opportunity, the students failed to stop and help a person in need. The infamous Milgram experiments, in which people were willing to administer shocks to an innocent person when goaded by a scientist, provide another example.

Virtue ethicists have answered the situationist challenge most effectively by showing that the experiments do not show what the situationists claim; rather, more character is revealed in the subjects' actions than has been realized or reported. The hurrying students felt conflicted about stopping, because they felt they needed to help the person who was waiting for them at their appointment. With Milgram, many of the subjects openly or shrewdly defied the scientists and some tried forcibly to aid the apparent victim of the shocks. The judicious response to situationism, then, is to agree that situations and groups influence people's behavior, sometimes significantly, but to affirm that virtue traits exist and that good and bad Samaritan behaviors can be better interpreted by asking how the people involved understood the situation.[11]

## 3. Communities Can Constrain Individual Flourishing

A group, community, or society may possess limited material or social resources. These deficits likely undercut each member's ability to flourish. In chapter 3, a case study comparing two schoolchildren illustrates how social context might constrain one's ability to achieve well-being in body, mind, character, and relationships to others. Compared to an upper-middle-class child of the suburbs, a child living in a low-income household and neighborhood has a higher risk of health problems such as asthma, becoming a victim of crime, and doing poorly in school, among other threats to his flourishing.

---

11. This paragraph summarizes complex issues. An excellent resource is Nancy Snow, *Virtue as Social Intelligence: An Empirically Grounded Theory* (New York: Routledge, 2010). In ch. 5, Snow recaps the famous experiments and makes the counterarguments summarized here. Her bibliography lists the important books and articles in the situationism debate.

Since communities are composed of persons who are moral beings, some people bear moral responsibility in a case of constrained flourishing. For example, when Hurricane Katrina struck the Gulf coast of the United States in 2005, the natural disaster harmed the flourishing of individuals and communities. The effects lasted for years. But the damage to flourishing was not just caused by a natural disaster; there were moral failures.[12] Local, state, and federal governments were underprepared. Mismanagement of preparation and response made the suffering worse and disproportionately burdened poor minorities. The role that racism may have played in the decisions of some officials remains a point of controversy. Global warming and environmental degradation of wetlands likely contributed to the severity and destructiveness of the hurricane. Human activity and human choices are at least partly responsible for these environmental trends, which in turn exacerbate suffering. To say people bear responsibility is not to say that anyone wanted the hurricane to strike or anyone to be hurt. Niebuhr suggests that large groups are limited in their ability to reason well, consider long-term consequences, overcome egoism, and notice the needs of others. If he is correct, then the problem is not so much that people with privilege and security are bad, but that they fail to notice.

## 4. Communities Can Encourage an Unbalanced Pursuit of Goals

Similar to the way groups can constrain flourishing, groups can also encourage unbalanced pursuit of goals. This occurs when a group is so intent on its own goals that it damages the common good. Business ethicist Kenneth E. Goodpaster named this constraint "teleopathy," meaning a "sickness of goals."[13] For example, businesses are geared toward the goals of selling a product or service, realizing a profit, and returning value to stockholders. Yet when a business thinks only of those financial goals, it is prone to behave unethically. Many in the organization may not even realize the ethical risks involved, owing to bureaucracy, groupthink, and diffusion of responsibility. For Goodpaster, a classic example of teleopathy was the decision of NASA leaders and managers at Morton Thiokol to approve the launch of the Space Shuttle Challenger on January 28, 1986. The managers approved the launch despite the warnings of two Thiokol engineers that the temperature that day was so cold that the O-rings on the rockets might fail. Indeed, the O-rings failed, and Challenger exploded 73 seconds after lift-off, causing the deaths of seven astronauts. NASA had pushed for the launch

---

12. For an argument supporting several of the following points, see Michael Eric Dyson, *Come Hell or High Water: Hurricane Katrina and the Color of Disaster* (New York: Basic Civitas Books, 2007).

13. Goodpaster first coined the term in 1986 and gives it book-length treatment in *Conscience and Corporate Culture* (Malden, MA: Blackwell, 2007).

because it had been embarrassed by previous delays, and Thiokol leaders wanted to please their customer. Post-disaster investigations uncovered poor communication and decision-making on launch day and a long history of failure, by NASA and Thiokol, to fix problems with the O-rings.[14]

## 5. Communities Can Sow Discouragement

When people see one or more of the prior hindering influences at work in their community or group, they may become discouraged about making an effort to improve a situation, which becomes a fifth hindrance caused by community. This discouragement is understandable due to the many ways communities can hinder character and flourishing: *controlling and corrupting*, when a powerful group punishes those who would challenge authority; *constraining moral responsiveness*, in which it may be difficult to know if one is being subtly influenced by the group; *constraining flourishing*, where it is overwhelming for a person or small group to locate resources not provided by society; and *promoting unbalanced pursuit of goals*, in which dissenting voices are often ignored or punished. Because of these obstacles, people may find it risky or overwhelming to resist and change a powerful institution or group.

## 6. Communities Can Hinder Marginalized Persons and Groups

Philosopher Lisa Tessman says, "Moral trouble spawned by oppressive conditions can stand in the way of the good life."[15] This trouble takes two forms. First, oppressive conditions can hamper the characters of vulnerable people so they act out of the opposite of virtue, that is, vice. For example, Fatima, whose poverty and disability force her into prostitution in Annawadi, sets herself on fire and blames the neighbors. The second form of trouble is "burdened virtues, virtues that have the unusual trait of being disjoined from the bearer's own flourishing."[16] Tessman means that when people are resisting conditions of oppression, the virtues that are most admirable in them—such as solidarity, justice, courage—often also bring suffering until those conditions change, something that may not happen in their lifetimes. For example, during the 1950s and 1960s, at least forty people, mostly African-Americans and some whites, were martyred for their work in the Civil Rights Movement. Many more African-Americans were killed, hundreds

---

14. The Challenger disaster has been extensively discussed in the context of engineering ethics and business ethics. Ibid., 15–31 and 42–46.

15. Lisa Tessman, *Burdened Virtues: Virtue Ethics for Liberatory Struggles* (New York: Oxford University Press, 2005), 4.

16. Ibid. (italics removed).

brutalized, and thousands suffered deprivations and humiliations before legal segregation was ended—and, unfortunately, even afterward.[17] Tessman's goal is to recognize another way community can hinder character and flourishing, so virtue ethicists and others will be more motivated to undo systems of oppression. Among the six communal hindrances on character and flourishing, several often operate simultaneously. The general dynamic is this: an elite group or society, given its privilege, power, and size, is likely to focus on its own goals and make other, less-powerful people go along with its wishes. Therefore, ethical failures happen and the less-powerful people are harmed—forced to act against their virtues and constrained from flourishing. If the harmed people or groups try to change the situation, they can be ignored, ridiculed, isolated, and/or punished. Some may give up the struggle in the face of those consequences, others push on but may suffer for their resistance. That is the ugly face of community.

## Community as a Help to Character and Flourishing

Fortunately, community also promotes the character and flourishing of persons. Virtue ethicists note four ways this occurs. As with the list of six hindrances, these are patterns of *potential* influences. Caveats similar to those mentioned earlier should be considered, for community is not destiny. The point of the following four descriptions is to identify beneficial communal forces that should be promoted.

### 1. Communities Can Form People in Character

Virtues are learned in communities—not only in the more obvious early-educational settings of home, primary school, friends, and church, but in the civic, cultural, economic, and political settings in which one participates throughout a lifetime. Take the example of Le Chambon, a small Christian village in occupied France during World War II, whose residents, at great risk to themselves, sheltered more than 3,000 Jewish refugees throughout the war. Lawrence Blum, a philosopher specializing in ethics, moral psychology, and moral education, presents Le Chambon as a detailed case study in an important article on the relationship of community and virtue. Blum studied books and documentary films about the incident to understand "the communal nature of the rescue enterprise—the way that the community as whole had an impact on the decisions of its individual members to help with the rescue activities."[18] The rescue

---

17. The Southern Poverty Law Center created the Civil Rights Memorial in Montgomery, Alabama, to remember forty people murdered for their civil rights work (*www.splcenter.org /civil-rights-memorial/civil-rights-martyrs*).

18. Lawrence Blum, "Community and Virtue," in *How Should One Live? Essays on the Virtues*, ed. Roger Crisp (New York: Clarendon, 1996), 231–50, at 236.

effort was a heroically virtuous activity. Yet, interestingly, the villagers of Le Chambon did *not* consider themselves heroic. "In fact, after the war there was little to distinguish Le Chambon from many other villages of similar size and composition."[19] So what made the difference?

One key factor, one that always matters in the acquisition of virtue, is education. Blum sees the community itself as the educator of its adult members' characters. "It is impossible to explain the widespread collective participation without attributing to most of the villagers motives of compassion, a concern for human life, a sense of Christian (or non-Christian) duty, a concern not to co-operate with evil, an eschewing of violence."[20] These motives had developed in the villagers because of the way they were raised at home and in church, as well as from their history as an oppressed religious minority in Catholic France. "The Chambonnais were particularly well-equipped to resist these state-sponsored moral obfuscations [of the Nazi-aligned French government]. Their tradition of resistance made them generally skeptical of the state itself."[21] Thus families, church, religious identity, and historical experience shaped the Chambonnais to be the sort of people who showed compassion and justice toward those in need.

## 2. Communities Can Shape Members' Moral Agency

One's moral reality, sense of moral agency, and ability to act upon virtue can be sustained or undermined by communal forces. These capacities are learned at home, but they can be deepened and maintained by ongoing participation in a virtuous community. Blum describes how, in Le Chambon, awareness of what others were doing as well as moral leadership from the village's pastor, André Trocmé, and his wife, Magda, made it seem expected that villagers assist in the sheltering of Jews. Interestingly, the rescue effort was rarely mentioned publicly except in Trocmé's sermons—and then only obliquely. But these indirect messages were sufficient. "In his sermons [Trocmé] called people to the true teachings of Christianity as he understood them—to love one's neighbour [sic], to cherish human life, not to consort with evil, to be non-violent. Though only indirectly, he made it clear that he took the providing of refuge as instantiating these teachings."[22]

The attitude, "This is just what we do here," became the operative thinking in Le Chambon. This communal aid to moral agency is the flip side of a community's power to hinder moral responsiveness. If, as situationism holds, the presence of other people is a factor that can nudge people to act below the level

19. Ibid., 238.
20. Ibid., 237.
21. Ibid., 241.
22. Ibid., 237.

of their virtues and motivations, then the presence of other people acting in a certain way can also *embolden* people to live up to their virtues and best motivations. As Blum says, "Indeed, one thing that moral leadership (in contrast to demagoguery, manipulation, mere charisma) does is precisely to help people to find their better motives, to impress upon them moral truths," from which fear and concern for the safety of their families could cause them to turn away.[23] In a group, the forces of discouragement can be blunted. In a group, people can find the courage to endure the burdening of their virtues.

## 3. Communities Can Habituate the Virtues that Sustain Them

As a community forms character and shapes agency, its members develop into the sorts of people who are capable and motivated to help the community thrive. Healthy communities expand the traits of compassion, generosity, solidarity, and so on in their members. Members of a virtuous community tend to resonate with Seneca's words:

> That line of poetry should ever be in our hearts and on our lips: 'I am human and I count nothing human as disconnected from me.' Let us possess what we possess as members of a community. Into it we were born. Our society is like an arch of stones that will collapse unless each stone lends its weight to the next, allowing the whole structure to support itself.[24]

Among the virtues instilled by a community are those suited to making the community operate well and achieve its distinctive goals. These traits can be called "social virtues," following a coinage by eighteenth-century virtue philosophers and authors from the Catholic tradition.[25] Social virtues, traits that help the community flourish, develop in members through their participation in the community. For example, as a child learns to resolve conflicts with a sibling under the guidance of a parent ("Use your words!" "Why don't you take turns?" "See how nice it is when you two find something you can play together?"), the

---

23. Ibid.

24. Seneca, *Moral Letters to Lucilius*, Letter 95, in *The Practice of Virtue* (Indianapolis: Hackett, 2006), 55. Seneca's thought is discussed in ch. 2, ed. Jennifer Welchman (under "Virtues of Purpose") and ch. 3.

25. The identification of benevolence and justice as the main "social virtues" is found in Frances Hutcheson, *An Inquiry into the Original of Our Ideas of Beauty and Virtue* (1726) and David Hume, *An Enquiry Concerning the Principles of Morals* (1751), both of which are excerpted in Welchman (see esp. 85–87, 92–95). The Catholic Church uses the term in a similar way, denoting virtues of justice, solidarity, and civic responsibility; see Pontifical Council for Justice and Peace, *Compendium of the Social Doctrine of the Church*, 2004, no. 19, 193, 238, 343, and 546, *http://www.vatican.va/roman_curia /pontifical_councils/justpeace/documents/rc_pc_justpeace_doc_20060526_compendio-dott-soc_en.html*.

child develops the skills of communication, negotiation, and cooperation. These traits help the child and sibling flourish—by not fighting and by learning to cooperate. In turn, the family flourishes, as the parents take pleasure in their children's smoother relations. A child who has been well guided in sibling relations throughout many years will take his or her habits of association into the world, and be more likely to relate well to others in different social settings. In the example of Le Chambon, the virtues of faith, justice, and courage instilled in the villagers by the community made it possible for villagers to demonstrate a remarkably other-centered attitude. These virtues made it possible for them to hold strong as a community despite the risk that they could be discovered and punished by the Vichy regime.

## 4. Communities Can Make Flourishing More Achievable

The three positive influences already mentioned—that communities help members develop character, moral agency, and social virtues—contribute to the flourishing of a community's members, which is the fourth contribution. To flourish, people also require a variety of resources, many of which are best provided by society (ch. 3). No human being is entirely self-made and self-reliant. To say that humans are interdependent is not to denigrate the importance of hard work and personal diligence but to recognize a practical and moral truth.

The practical truth is that no one is self-made. Someone who builds a multimillion-dollar company from the ground up by sheer creativity and hard work shows impressive perseverance, industry, and autonomy. But he or she never does it alone, getting assistance from employees, the legal system, the banking system, and other infrastructure.[26] Americans value hard work, but there is also good reason for them to acknowledge "the self-made man" as "America's most pliable, pernicious, irrepressible myth."[27] The moral truth of interdependence is expressed in Seneca's metaphor of the arch and in John Donne's famous line, "No man is an island."[28] People cannot, in fact, do without others. For that reason, they ought to show concern for the health of their groups, communities, and society; to do so is both right and pragmatic. Experiencing community also can make one care about it, which certainly seems to be the case among the Chambonnais.

26. This claim was a point of controversy in the 2012 U.S. presidential campaign, when President Barack Obama made remarks along these lines, which challenger Mitt Romney and his supporters criticized. See "'You Didn't Build That,' Uncut and Unedited," Annenberg Public Policy Center, July 24, 2012, *http://www.factcheck.org/2012/07/you-didnt-build-that-uncut-and-unedited/*.

27. John Swansburg, "The Self-Made Man," *Slate*, September 29, 2014. This article delves into the stories of six Americans who shaped this myth. Ironically, such iconic figures as Benjamin Franklin and Andrew Carnegie do not valorize self-reliance as greatly as the lore about them suggests.

28. John Donne, *Devotions upon Emergent Occasions*, Meditation 17, *http://www.luminarium.org/sevenlit/donne/meditation17.php*.

Niebuhr's challenge, nonetheless, remains: in societies and large institutions, it is easy for people to lose touch with the human dimension. One might care about family, friends, and neighborhood but not give much thought to distant people. One might not appreciate distant people's life experiences in more than stereotypical ways. Therefore, a moral task for virtuous communities is intentionally to develop social virtues.

## The Character of Our Communities

Former Florida Congresswoman Carrie P. Meek is reported to have said, "Until we all start to take responsibility, until we do all we can to improve the character of our communities, we'll never break the cycle of violence and indifference."[29] This statement, with a central phrase resonant of the speeches of Martin Luther King, captures connections between personal and social flourishing and between personal and social character. The ethical idea behind "the character of our communities" is the claim that people *ought* to take responsibility and *ought* to care for each other. Later in the chapter, this "ought" will be expressed by the principle of the common good. The practical need behind "the character of our communities" is to understand why some people's sense of civic responsibility is weak and what could make it stronger. For that analysis, the concept of social capital proves useful.

## Social Capital Is Important

Social capital describes and quantifies the contributions of social participation to the flourishing of society, its groups, and their members. This chapter emphasizes that people belong to many groups and associations—families, neighborhoods, schools, sports leagues, clubs, and churches. According to British psychologist David Halpern, "These everyday networks, including many of the social customs that define them and keep them together, are what we mean when we talk about social capital."[30] The term, which had been used by some sociologists and economists earlier in the twentieth century, gained popularity among academics and policymakers beginning in the 1980s. In the United States, political scientist Robert Putnam brought social capital into the mainstream with his 2000 book *Bowling Alone*. Because Putnam clearly explains the connections between social capital, civic virtue, and flourishing, his books are the primary resource in the following section. Yet it should be noted that his work is just the tip of an

---

29. As listed at *www.brainyquote.com* and other famous-quotation sites on the Internet; however, the legitimacy and source of the quote could not be confirmed. There is no other famous use of the phrase "the character of our communities," except as the title of a 1995 book by theologian Gloria Albrecht.

30. David Halpern, *Social Capital* (Malden, MA: Polity, 2005), 2.

iceberg of studies in sociology, development economics, education, and public health that suggests that social trust and cohesion are positively correlated with various benefits for communities and their members.[31]

Putnam defines social capital as the "connections among individuals—social networks and the norms of reciprocity and trustworthiness that arise from them."[32] John Field says, "Social capital must be understood as a relational concept. It can only provide access to resources where individuals have not only formed ties with others but have internalized the shared values of the group."[33] Thus there are character-based and relational dimensions to social capital. The character dimension is that social capital takes root in persons and groups in the form of social virtues, such as justice and citizenship. The relational dimension is that virtuous persons and groups create a social ethos characterized by trust and civility. Both dimensions are essential, says Putnam: "Civic virtue is most powerful when embedded in a dense network of reciprocal social relations."[34] So, while social capital allows a society to work well no matter what its goals are, it also fosters moral character. When citizens see that their fates are linked, they are more likely to develop compassion and a sense of solidarity. When citizens and groups must work together to resolve common problems, their virtues of fairness, prudence, and cooperation are likely to be reinforced.

Modeled on the concepts of physical and financial capital, social capital increases productivity and gets things done in the social sectors of life, just as the other forms of capital get things built, created, and traded. Social capital helps people achieve goals, especially the goals they share with others in society. Putnam sees three general features of social capital that make it effective for social flourishing: it "helps citizens resolve collective problems more easily"; it "greases the wheels that allow communities to advance smoothly"; and it "widen[s] our awareness of the many ways in which our fates are linked."[35] Putnam further identifies three types of groups based on how their social capital operates: groups that *bond* (communities united over shared interests and demographics, such as ethnic fraternal societies and country clubs); groups that *bridge* (helping people work across differences to accomplish goals, such as philanthropic groups, ecumenical religious organizations, and some political and advocacy groups); and groups that combine bonding and bridging.[36]

---

31. For accessible overviews of the concept and the research, see Halpern, *Social Capital*, and John Field, *Social Capital*, 2nd ed. (New York: Routledge, 2008). For a strong argument against the use of the concept, see Ben Fine, *Theories of Social Capital: Researchers Behaving Badly* (London: Pluto, 2010).

32. Robert D. Putnam, *Bowling Alone: The Collapse and Revival of American Community* (New York: Simon & Schuster, 2000), 19.

33. Field, 161.

34. Putnam, 19.

35. Ibid., 288.

36. Ibid., 20–23. This distinction has been widely adopted by social capital researchers.

People and families enjoy greater well-being in places with more social capital. To measure these connections in the United States, Putnam and his research team created an index of social capital, drawing on data from social surveys and government archives. Data points include, for example: voter turnout in presidential elections, the number of nonprofit organizations in a state per thousand residents, and people's answers to survey questions about the average number of club meetings they attended in the past year and whether they believe most people can be trusted.[37] Geographical variations were discovered: the states with the highest social capital are the New England states, upper Midwest states, and Utah. Social capital is low in Nevada and the Southern states.[38] The findings are not intended to disparage any state or region. Rather, if citizens understand the forces that erode social capital they may be able to forestall or reverse the decline.

Putnam then compares the level of social capital in each state with various indicators of personal and social flourishing. He continually finds positive correlations.[39] As for personal flourishing, the states that score highest on the social capital index have better rates for children's health and educational performance, overall public health and life-expectancy, and self-reports of happiness. The situation is exactly the opposite for low social capital states. As for social flourishing, there are likewise impressive correlations: states high in social capital have lower crime rates, less tax evasion, higher tolerance, more equality, and certain economic benefits, while states low in social capital tend toward the opposite.

Social capital researchers have sought—and found—similar correlations in many areas of social life around the globe:

- Social capital has a profound impact on developing countries. "It affects the provision of services, in both urban and rural areas; transforms the prospects for agricultural development; influences the expansion of private enterprises; improves the management of common resources; helps improve education; can contribute to recovery from conflict; and can help compensate for a deficient state. More generally, it helps alleviate poverty for individuals and for countries as a whole."[40]

---

37. Ibid., 291, table 4.

38. Why do these patterns exist? The most plausible factors are historical and cultural (Ibid., 292–95). New England states, for instance, have histories of strong participation in local governance dating back to the colonial era. Utah has a large Mormon population, whose religious solidarity has promoted social capital. Finally, the states lowest in social capital practiced slavery for generations, which suggests that enduring patterns of social inequality eat at the foundations of social capital.

39. The rest of this paragraph gives a brief summary of Putnam's discussion in chs. 17–22.

40. Christiaan Grootaert and Thierry Van Bastelaer, eds., *The Role of Social Capital in Development: An Empirical Assessment* (New York: Cambridge University Press, 2002), 344.

- There is "fairly consistent evidence of association between social capital and physical health"—although more for self-rated health and less for objective health measures and mental health.[41]
- Education researchers have examined how social capital can be developed in schools to increase children's sense of inclusion and educational outcomes.[42]
- Attendance at religious services is a strong predictor of altruism and empathy. Britain's Chief Rabbi says, "Religion creates community, community creates altruism and altruism turns us away from self and towards the common good."[43]

Also valuable are narrative studies of social capital in action. In *Better Together*, Putnam and Lewis Feldstein write profiles of organizations—such as the branch libraries of Chicago, a workers union at Harvard University, the delivery business UPS, and a large California church—that improved the flourishing of themselves and their communities using the tools of social capital to address problems of common concern.[44]

## Is Social Capital in Trouble?

While these studies are encouraging for countries, states, cities, neighborhoods, and groups with strong social networks, the national trends in the United States are troubling. Overall, American society has been on a path of decline in social capital for more than fifty years. The title *Bowling Alone* symbolizes Putnam's concern. What happened, he asks, to bowling leagues, which were a major social institution in the United States in the 1950s? It is not that bowling declined in popularity, because, in the 1990s, more Americans than ever were bowling—but not in leagues.[45] Putnam demonstrates that the decline of bowling leagues is emblematic of a widespread decline in civic association memberships in America in the second half of the twentieth century. Chart after chart in *Bowling Alone* documents that membership and active participation in a host of associations peaked around 1960 and then declined steadily.

---

41. Ichiro Kawachi, S. V. Subramanian, and Daniel Kim, eds., *Social Capital and Health* (New York: Springer, 2008), 22.

42. See, for example, Julie Allan and Ralph Catts, eds., *Social Capital, Children and Young People: Implications for Practice, Policy and Research* (Bristol, UK: Policy, 2012).

43. Jonathan Sacks, "If You're Searching for the Big Society, Here's Where You May Find It," *New Statesman*, June 15, 2011, 21.

44. Robert D. Putnam and Lewis Feldstein, *Better Together: Restoring the American Community* (New York: Simon & Schuster, 2004).

45. Putnam, *Bowling Alone*, 111–13. Since the 1990s, even casual, non-league bowling has declined, but the bowling industry has enjoyed success by adding amenities, such as food, drink, and arcades to alleys.

Like a modern-day Tocqueville, Putnam warns that this trend could negatively affect the quality of American political life and the ability of citizens to flourish fully. As the years pass, Americans report decreasing satisfaction with personal health and happiness, with the young and middle-aged reporting more dissatisfaction. "Roughly half the decline in contentment is associated with financial worries, and half is associated with declines in social capital: lower marriage rates and decreasing connectedness to friends and community."[46] Putnam concludes: "In our personal lives as well as in our collective life, . . . we are paying a significant price for a quarter century's disengagement from one another."[47]

What *caused* the erosion of social capital in the United States in the second half of the twentieth century? It is difficult to prove causation and separate out the factors, but there are four likely culprits, says Putnam:[48]

- *Work.* Trends such as women entering the workforce in large numbers starting in the 1960s and the decline in middle-class wages starting in the 1970s, have meant that parents can experience a time crunch reducing their time for civic activities and family life.[49]
- *Sprawl.* Through the later twentieth century, the suburbs grew massively and commuting times lengthened, cutting down on time for civic activities.
- *Electronic entertainment.* The popularity of television exploded during this time period. Rather than going to theaters, plays, club meetings, and church-based events, Americans increasingly got their entertainment at home, missing out on the bonding and bridging opportunities that develop from socializing.
- *Generational change.* Older Americans (the WWII generation) are more active in civic clubs, more likely to vote, and so on, than younger age cohorts. The historical, cultural, economic, and political experiences of the generations that follow are significantly different, leading members of these generations to varied interests.

Putnam acknowledges that, while contemporary views on civic participation are *different* from those in the past, current views are not necessarily bad. There are countertrends and hopeful signs. In social attitudes, Americans since the 1950s have grown more tolerant of individual differences.[50] Women and African-Americans have reached high levels of accomplishment in almost every profession. Some of the trends that are problematic for civic engagement, such as

---

46. Ibid., 334.

47. Ibid., 335.

48. Ibid., chs. 10–15. Putnam also considers—but gives reasons for rejecting—the following as major contributors: departures from traditional family structures, racism, and the growth of government.

49. Sociologist Arlie Russell Hochschild has written several significant books examining these trends, including *The Second Shift* (1989), *The Time Bind* (2001), and *The Outsourced Self* (2013). See also chs. 5 and 7.

50. Putnam, *Bowling Alone*, ch. 21.

families having two working parents and the spread of television, may have also contributed to increased tolerance. As for participation, Americans remain active in sports leagues and local schools when their children are enrolled. Most high schools and colleges provide a wider range of organized volunteer activities than in prior generations. Volunteerism has grown in popularity among young people. One research report indicates that youth volunteer more than adults and that the number of high school and college students who have volunteered occasionally or at least once in the previous year has risen every year since 1990.[51] The Internet and social media have provided new ways for people with similar interests to connect, both virtually and in person. Studies indicate that use of the Internet (not using it to watch television) is positively associated with indicators of social capital, suggesting that digital participation can benefit social participation and cohesion.[52]

These counterexamples are promising, but they are not enough to remove worries about the overall decline of social capital. There are three limitations to the counterexamples. First, new forms of connection through the Internet and social media emphasize the like-mindedness of members. Putnam is concerned that such connections *bond* like-minded people but don't *bridge* people across socioeconomic divides, as unions, churches, and political clubs once did. People need both kinds of social capital, as this example illustrates: "Strong ties with intimate friends may ensure chicken soup when you're sick, but weak ties with distant acquaintances are more likely to produce leads for a new job."[53] Likewise, on the issues that matter for social flourishing, both types of capital are needed, for different reasons. For instance, for the healthy development and effective education of children, bonding social capital is essential in the children's families, neighborhoods, and schools. And for political decision making that shapes education and economic policies for families, "surely it is social capital of the most broad and bridging kind that will most improve the quality of public debate. In short, for our biggest collective problems we need precisely the sort of bridging social capital that is toughest to create."[54]

---

51. Occasional volunteerism among high school seniors has gone from 65 percent in 1990 to more than 75 percent in 2004 and, among college freshman in the same time period, from 65 to almost 85 percent, according to Mark Hugo Lopez, "Volunteering among Young People," Center for Information & Research on Civic Learning & Engagement (CIRCLE), February 2004, *www.civicyouth.org/PopUps/FactSheets/FS_Volunteering2.pdf*.

52. Marc Hooghe and Jennifer Oser, "Internet, Television and Social Capital: The Effect of 'Screen Time' on Social Capital," *Information, Communication & Society* 18, no. 10 (October 2015): 1175–99.

53. Putnam, *Bowling Alone*, 363.

54. Ibid., 363. Ongoing research complicates Putnam's hunch. One study, based on an Australian election survey, finds that online participation of the bonding, not the bridging, type is a good predictor of political engagement (Rachel Gibson and Ian McAllister, "Online Social Ties and Political Engagement," *Journal of Information Technology & Politics* 10, no. 1 [2013]: 21–34). Two articles in the *Journal of Ethnic & Migration Studies* find bonding capital is equally or more efficacious for group members' political participation as bridging capital (Marco Giugni, et al., "Associational Involvement, Social Capital and the Political Participation of Ethno-Religious Minorities," 40, no. 10 [2014]: 1593–1613; and Wahideh Achbari, "Bridging and Bonding Ethnic Ties in Voluntary Organisations," 41, no. 14 [2015]: 2291–2313).

The second limitation of the appeal to new forms of connection is that the commitment needed to sustain civic organizations remains soft. Consider that the growth in volunteerism has been in *occasional* service.[55] Volunteers of all ages can plug into an activity now and then, such as serving at a soup kitchen or working for a day on a Habitat for Humanity house-building project. But for the soup kitchen and the Habitat chapter to exist in the first place, volunteers with a deeper level of commitment are needed. The hope of those who lead volunteer organizations is that the occasional participants will become enthused by what they are doing and get more involved. Capturing the hearts of new volunteers happens enough to allow such organizations to survive, but in contemporary society, the task of maintaining organizations is a continual effort.

The final limitation is that new forms of connection are not sufficient to overcome economic inequality. In his recent study, *Our Kids*, Putnam addresses the dire problem of the growing inequality between rich and poor children. There are many factors contributing to the opportunity gap between social classes in the United States, differences in social capital being one of them. Americans' disengagement and growing social isolation "constitute a trend that, even if common to individuals of all classes, affects members of lower classes disproportionately, ultimately reinforcing differences between social classes."[56] The fact that poor and minority Americans have mostly caught up to others in their Internet access does not mean they have gained equal benefit. "Affluent Americans use the Internet in ways that are mobility-enhancing," such as following the news, pursuing education, looking for jobs, and engaging in politics, "whereas poorer, less educated Americans typically use it in ways that are not."[57]

So is social capital in trouble? There is plenty of evidence for concluding, yes, it is, especially in neighborhoods, cities, and states with histories of lower engagement and/or with lower socioeconomic status. In addition, social capital is at a historically weak point throughout the United States owing to such factors as two-parent working families, sprawl and commuting, electronic entertainment, and generational change. Other countries are not exempt from these trends. In fact, the United States rates well, but not among the highest nations in social capital—and not as high as its prosperity and long tradition of democracy would indicate. A vast number of studies throughout the past three decades show that social capital is not a mysterious entity. It can be described, measured,

---

55. According to Lopez, *regular* volunteerism by youth has remained steady throughout many years, at a rate of 10 to 15 percent of survey respondents.

56. Robert D. Putnam, *Our Kids: The American Dream in Crisis* (New York: Simon & Schuster, 2015), 211 (citing Ivaylo D. Petev, "The Association of Social Class and Lifestyles: Persistence in American Sociability, 1974 to 2010," *American Sociological Review* 78 [Aug. 2013]: 633-61).

57. Ibid., 212.

tracked, and assessed. Social capital is an expression of people and their social choices, so it can be improved, given the will to do so.

## Seeking the Common Good

Virtue ethicists agree that the well-being of a society and its citizens is better when groups are healthy. Thus there are practical and ethical reasons for promoting the flourishing of mediating institutions. The common good is the ethical rationale that matches well with the practical concerns about social capital. It is also the name for an ethical goal in which the well-being of individuals and that of society fit together and support each other.

The common good is related to all three normative theories (ch. 1), which suggests its strength in creating consensus in ethical debates. In terms of virtues, commitment to the common good goes by various names: justice, solidarity, responsibility, citizenship, civic friendship, or some combination of these. As a teleological principle, the common good is oriented to promoting personal and social flourishing. Flourishing is obviously the goal in virtue ethics, as it is in consequentialism, often with the emphasis placed on *social* flourishing ("the greatest good for the greatest number"). The potential risk in a consequentialist account of the common good is that the wants of the majority always overwhelm the needs of some individuals. To avoid that risk, the common good also requires deontological norms: protections for people's rights (such as their rights to life, liberty, education, and the ability to work) and the provision of resources (such as education and health care) on a fair and equal basis.

To secure citizens' rights and promote their flourishing, government has a significant responsibility. Among its duties to the common good are ensuring law and order, providing for a common defense, directing tax monies to programs of social benefit, and assisting the civically beneficial activities of other groups in society. All levels of government, citizens, and institutions in society have responsibilities for ensuring that the common good is morally good (by meeting basic human needs and respecting freedom) and truly common (by ensuring that all members of society have meaningful and equal opportunities to participate in it). Theologian and ethicist David Hollenbach expresses three principles of justice reflecting these social responsibilities:[58]

1. The needs of the poor take priority over the wants of the rich.
2. The freedom of the dominated takes priority over the liberty of the powerful.

---

58. David Hollenbach, *Claims in Conflict: Retrieving and Renewing the Catholic Human Rights Tradition* (Mahwah, NJ: Paulist Press, 1979), 204.

3. The participation of marginalized groups takes priority over the preservation of an order that excludes them.

How these principles could and should be put into practice is a highly contextual matter. Hollenbach's goal in stating them so starkly is to establish a sense of moral urgency around key priorities for social institutions. An example of the rhetorical use of these principles is when Putnam argues that Americans "don't have to believe in perfect equality of opportunity to agree that our religious ideals and our basic moral code demand more equality of opportunity than we now have."[59]

Yet the common good is about more than social programs and governmental activities. As this chapter illustrates with the example of Le Chambon and Putnam's research, groups are tremendously important for promoting the common good. Families, churches, schools, civic organizations, volunteer groups, and even businesses promote the common good by instilling social virtues in their members, enacting virtues as they carry out their day-to-day activities, and fostering the conditions for social harmony by the way they cooperate with other groups. The principle of the common good holds that with civic rights come civic responsibilities. Everyone in society should contribute to the common good, and every person is understood as having dignity, unique gifts, and something valuable to contribute. The common good is a moral reality: its full flourishing is when people in society respect one another, help one another, and see each other as civic friends.[60]

## Conclusion

Putnam's analysis suggests an ethical agenda for promoting social flourishing. It is not a matter of considering oneself lucky to live in a geographical place with high social capital or a matter of moving to such a place. Social capital is not magic; it depends on whether and how people participate in groups. The good news, then, is that social capital can be promoted anywhere. Wherever one lives and in any sort of community or group, one can connect with other people. Any civic participation makes a small but real contribution to one's social virtues—one's willingness and ability to promote the common good. A few people working together in a group can find ways to collaborate with others on a matter of common concern. People working together can address, directly or indirectly, one or more of the standard causes of social erosion that are manifested in their community. They can advocate for the needs of working parents. They can press the government to

---

59. Putnam, *Our Kids*, 242.

60. Catholic philosopher Jacques Maritain said that the common good is morally good because, in it, persons interact with each other in reason, freedom, and love (see *The Person and the Common Good* [Notre Dame, IN: University of Notre Dame Press, orig. 1947, reprint, 1966], 52). Aristotle speaks of friendship among citizens in *Nicomachean Ethics* 8.1 (1155a24–30).

create better public transportation to reduce traffic and commute times. They can create public activities such as concerts and farmers' markets.

Such pro-social activities are instances of people motivated by their virtues and working together to promote social well-being in their community, prudently aware of the challenges and opportunities provided by that context. In short, virtues, flourishing, and community are mutually reinforcing. The method for combatting the erosion of social capital is to build social capital by practicing Tocqueville's "art of association." Through group participation and civic action, people grow in social virtues and develop the habits by which they can work with others for the common good. In part 2 of this book, the "art of association" is further explained and illustrated in the communal contexts of families, schools, workplaces, and service organizations.

## Questions for Review

1. Why, according to Tocqueville, did Americans form so many associations? What were the benefits of associations to the fledgling democracy of the United States?
2. What is meant by referring to groups as "voluntary associations" and as "mediating institutions"?
3. Why did Niebuhr title his book *Moral Man and Immoral Society*?
4. How can the mere presence of others constrain one's moral responsiveness?
5. What is situationism, and how do virtue ethicists respond to the challenge posed by situationists?
6. What is teleopathy, and what factors seem to encourage it?
7. What are burdened virtues? Why are such virtues a problem for virtue ethics, given what the theory claims about flourishing?
8. Why did Putnam title his book *Bowling Alone*?
9. What is social capital? What are its bonding and bridging styles?
10. What is the definition of "the common good"?

## Discussion Questions and Activities

1. What conditions, according to Boo, can make it "blisteringly hard to be good"? Do you agree with her observation? What are other examples of social conditions that impinge negatively on character and flourishing? What makes it possible for some people to overcome these obstacles?
2. Give other examples of the negative impact of groups on individuals that fit Niebuhr's description. Do you agree with his argument that groups are almost always a bad influence on individuals?

3. Using the chart in figures 4.1 and 4.2, take your own example of a group and describe the mutual positive influences among the group, its members, and society. Describe the possible negative mutual influences as well.

4. Some people act as Good Samaritans and others fail to do so. What might be the reasons for these differences in behavior? Are there strategies that can be employed to encourage people to act altruistically more often?

5. Discuss your own examples of groups that display one or more of the helping influences on character and flourishing.

6. Assess Putnam's argument about the decline of social capital. How deep is the trouble? Do you think social media and newer forms of social networking have more positive benefits than Putnam and the author state? Is social capital weak in the United States or your local community? If yes, what strategies could rehabilitate it?

## Recommendations for Further Reading

Bellah, Robert J., Richard Madsen, William M. Sullivan, Ann Swidler, and Steven M. Tipton. *Habits of the Heart: Individualism and Commitment in American Life.* Berkeley: University of California Press, 1985; rev. ed., 1996.

This modern classic of sociology takes inspiration from Tocqueville's original observations.

Dunkelman, Marc. J. *The Vanishing Neighbor: The Transformation of American Community.* New York: Norton, 2014.

This book is in the tradition of Tocqueville's, Bellah's, and Putnam's projects. Dunkelman says there is little to be gained by arguing about whether the changes in American communities are good or bad. The need is to adjust the institutions of politics, education, and communications to meet the new realities.

Moore, Wes. *The Other Wes Moore: One Name, Two Fates.* New York: Spiegel & Grau Trade Paperbacks, 2011.

Wes Moore, the author, discovers a man with his same name serving a life sentence in prison. This gripping memoir suggests how social circumstances and luck can lead to completely different outcomes for personal flourishing.

Niebuhr, Reinhold. *Major Works on Religion and Politics.* Edited by Elisabeth Sifton. New York: Library of America, 2015.

This anthology contains the famous book discussed here, *Moral Man and Immoral Society,* and related works, such as *The Children of Light and the Children of Darkness* and *The Irony of American History.*

Putnam, Robert D. *Bowling Alone: The Collapse and Revival of American Community*. New York: Simon & Schuster, 2000.

A must-read study of social capital.

Putnam, Robert D. *Our Kids: The American Dream in Crisis*. New York: Simon & Schuster, 2015.

Putnam was so shocked by the changes in his boyhood hometown in Ohio that he took on the project of documenting and explaining the widening opportunity gap between rich and poor children. Parents' levels of education and children's educational opportunities are crucial factors in this narrative that relies on stories as well as data.

Snow, Nancy. *Virtue as Social Intelligence: An Empirically Grounded Theory*. New York: Routledge, 2010.

Snow argues that virtues, psychologically speaking, are forms of social intelligence. Against the situationist critics, she defends the existence of stable character traits with support from both philosophy and psychology.

Stiltner, Brian. *Religion and the Common Good: Catholic Contributions to Building Community in a Liberal Society*. Lanham, MD: Rowman and Littlefield, 1997.

Defines and defends the principle of the common good, drawing upon classic and modern political philosophy and Catholic philosophy, particularly the work of Jacques Maritain.

# PART

# The Pursuit of Flourishing in Social Contexts

Part 1 of *Toward Thriving Communities* provides an in-depth summary of virtue and flourishing and shows how virtue ethics offer a compass toward a happier, healthier, and more just society. Part 2 addresses, from the perspective of virtue ethics, some challenges of contemporary social life that people experience on a daily basis. The goal is to recommend ethical principles and concrete practices that will help persons, groups, and society flourish. Chapter 5, "Families: First Teachers and Promoters of the Common Good," focuses on the crucial role families have in forming character and providing children with the capabilities to become ethical and productive members of society. Schools continue developing young people so they flourish in mind, body, character, and relationships, as seen in chapter 6, "Schools: Education for the Good Society." People's careers and workplaces are the focus in chapter 7, "Work: Meaning on the Job, Responsibility in the Economy." These are places where people can be empowered to pursue flourishing and contribute to the common good. Finally, chapter 8, "Service: Groups That Promote Charity, Justice, and Purpose," explains how nonprofit volunteer groups enrich the well-being of the people they serve, which in turn makes society more compassionate and just.

Each chapter in this section highlights the positive contributions of groups to the development of character and the pursuit of personal and social flourishing. Yet, since chapter 3 has shown that people's well-being can deteriorate when they do not have access to necessary resources and chapter 4 has shown that groups and society can undermine character and flourishing, part 2 also examines the challenges associated with groups. Some challenges occur within groups, while others are generated by outside cultural, economic, and political forces. In each context discussed in part 2, a virtue-ethical analysis recommends practices that enable these groups to rise to each challenge and, hopefully, overcome them. Society will never arrive at perfect flourishing, but people and groups making use of the resources of virtue ethics can make meaningful progress in their pursuit of flourishing.

# Families
## First Teachers and Promoters of the Common Good

What goes on in the home becomes a model for society.
                                    —*Julie Hanlon Rubio, theological ethicist*[1]

---

## Chapter Overview

- describes how various aspects of family life develop family members' characters and promote their flourishing
- illustrates how the family as a whole flourishes from engaging in intentional practices, such as eating meals together
- describes the material and ethical benefits of families to society and the assistance that society provides families
- examines the challenges of communication and commitment facing families from within and the virtuous responses families can make to these challenges
- assesses challenges to families from outside forces and possible responses by government, businesses, and families themselves

---

## Family Matters

The positive and negative influences among families, their members, and society are critical to the well-being of all. Family is one of the most important communities people experience, and it is universal. Family nurtures and protects children in their crucial, formative years. It is the first teacher, not just of virtue, but

---

1. Julie Hanlon Rubio, *Family Ethics: Practices for Christians* (Washington, DC: Georgetown University Press, 2010), 142.

of everything fundamental in human life. Additionally, family is where children and adults most often experience deep bonds of caring. For many people, relationships to family members are the most important affiliations throughout life. Thus family is an essential focus for virtue ethics.

But family life can be difficult for children and parents alike. Certainly being a parent is tough. Parents need sufficient character for the task, as it often takes "an act of courage and consciousness to break the negative and destructive patterns that may unconsciously control our interactions with our children."[2] Parents also need help handling cultural and economic stresses. Likewise, childhood is no easy task. In every developmental stage of a child's life, there are psychological and social challenges. In contemporary society, children are under great pressure. People often say, "Children grow up too fast these days," referring to insistent stressors, such as media, technology, peer pressure, the anxiety to perform well in school, and more. To have the greatest chance at a flourishing life, children need many things, including loving caregivers, stable homes, good education, financial resources, and opportunities to strive for their dreams. But many children lack some or all of these supports. Rightly or wrongly, families are expected to ensure that children get what they need to succeed in life, but families can't do it alone. Thus the flourishing of children depends not only on the character of their parents but on the resources and obstacles encountered within their social context.

## Families Are Universal and Varied

Families are varied and people's feelings about what constitutes family run the gamut. Accounting for all these experiences would be cumbersome, so a wide diversity of definitions and experiences will be assumed from the outset. A working *sociological* definition of *family* is any group of persons related by blood, adoption, or the decision to marry or partner and who share an emotional life and household responsibilities.[3] Since most ethical issues in this chapter concern children, it also is assumed that a child's family begins with at least one parent or guardian with whom the child lives in a household and might include other members of the household as well as extended kin in other households.[4]

A *virtue-ethical* perspective on family considers it a foundational social group, a key mediating institution, and a fundamental teacher of character. To

---

2. Jack Canfield, foreword by Dorothy Law Nolte and Rachel Harris, *Children Learn What They Live* (New York: Workman, 1988), ix.

3. This definition is similar to one used by the U.S. Census Bureau. See David M. Newman, *Families: A Sociological Perspective* (New York: McGraw-Hill Higher Education, 2009), 4–26.

4. For simplicity's sake, in this chapter and book, the term *parent(s)* is intended to include guardian(s).

invoke a phrase used in secular and religious contexts, families are the fundamental building blocks of society.[5] As mediating institutions, they are the group best able to give members the social skills for navigating society. Families develop the characters of their members. Parents teach children about virtue and vice. They provide rules and order to encourage their children to act well and develop good habits. All expressions of care and respect among family members build, in them, confidence and the ability to show love and respect to others. Strong family relationships help family members live healthy, happy, connected, and virtuous lives. This is not to say that all family experiences are positive; this chapter's point is not to defend a certain experience of family as correct, but to help the reader understand how families can live well. Healthy families contribute to society's ethos and flourishing. Indeed, families are indispensable promoters of social and cultural change for the common good.

## Families and Family Members

The community connections chart from chapter 4 indicates two basic social relationships: persons to groups and groups to society. As applied to families (fig. 5.1), the goal in examining relationship number 1 is to understand the contributions of families to character and flourishing. Four main benefits derive from the relationship between families and their members. In sum, family life (1) creates capabilities in children and promotes their flourishing throughout life, (2) enriches the well-being of members, (3) develops virtues in members, and (4) develops the character of the family itself.

### Family and Members

**Figure 5.1.** Community Connections: A Family and Its Members

## Family Life Creates Capabilities in Children

Families provide shelter, safety, nutrition, and other basic needs. Children rely on parents and guardians to watch out for their health and safety, provide meals and a roof over their heads, ensure they are educated, and so on. Although families

---

5. The 1949 *Universal Declaration of Human Rights* claims in article 16, "The family is the natural and fundamental group unit of society and is entitled to protection by society and the State" (*http://www.un.org/en/documents/udhr/*). Religious leaders, including, for example, Pope Francis, also often use the phrase ("Message of Pope Francis to Cardinal Kurt Koch," October 4, 2013, *http://www.news.va/en/news/pope-francis-to-wcc-show-solidarity-to-the-most-vu*).

are supposed to meet these needs, not all families can accomplish this or accomplish it well, as illustrated in the chapter 3 case study about Robert's family. In other families, parents are not sufficiently responsible or competent to meet basic needs. If children are to flourish, they need families that are sufficiently resourced and in which the adults are caring and responsible.

The process starts with the first days of life. Infants benefit from the love they receive by being held, played with, talked to, and caressed. The inherent value of such everyday practices seems like common sense, and it is supported by a plethora of research that specifies the long-term practical impact of such nurturing on the capacities and character of children. Those nurtured well are not only less stressed and more likely to thrive in school and work, but are also more likely to develop characters conducive to flourishing. Paul Tough, a journalist and author of *How Children Succeed*, explains what the most recent studies in neuroscience show about the relationship between nurturance and character: there is a "powerful connection between infant brain chemistry and adult psychology"; therefore, an important factor for children becoming "brave and curious and kind and prudent" is to ensure that they are protected, loved, and cuddled as infants.[6] The research validates what already seems beyond debate—that infants need loving attention.

The importance of loving attention does not mean children can or should be shielded from the stresses and difficulties of life. Quite the opposite is true, in fact. Tough reports that the second major ingredient for the initial development of character is facing difficult situations and having opportunities to fail. Psychologists have developed a short survey, the Grit Scale, to measure people's persistence, courage, hope, and self-care.[7] One's grit is indicated by how strongly one agrees with statements such as, "I am a hard worker" and, "Setbacks don't discourage me." Grit is a character strength that helps one face life's challenges, whether intellectual, physical, or emotional. For instance, psychologists found that children at the National Spelling Bee who scored higher on the Grit Scale were more likely to survive to the later rounds and that West Point cadets with higher grit were more likely to complete a grueling summer training course. What this research suggests is that parents and similarly situated adults, such as teachers and coaches, should not shelter children from the risk of failure, but allow them to face real, age-appropriate challenges so they can learn how to manage failure.[8]

---

6. Paul Tough, *How Children Succeed: Grit, Curiosity, and the Hidden Power of Character* (Boston: Houghton Mifflin, 2012), 182. Tough's notes provide references to some of the scientific literature, including the pioneering work of Dr. Michael Meaney on maternal care and stress response in rats, work he later applied to humans.

7. Ibid., 74–75. "Grit" is not a classic name for a virtue, but it seems to include the four virtues listed here, especially persistence.

8. Ibid., 183.

## Family Life Enriches All Members

Children receive enrichment within their families, especially when those families are virtuous and flourishing. According to psychologist Martin Seligman's well-being theory, people flourish most when they experience Positive emotions, Engagement, Relationships, Meaning, and Achievement (PERMA).[9] Opportunities to experience PERMA are readily available within family life. Consider children first. Central to children's experience of flourishing are positive *relationships* with their parents, siblings, and extended kin. Children experience *positive emotions* when their parents show them love and build their self-esteem, such as through encouragement. Children experience *engagement* in their play and hobbies (even children with few resources find ways to play). As parents teach children about purpose and morality and involve them in activities such as volunteerism and religious life, children are encouraged to develop a sense of *meaning*. Finally, parents can provide children with opportunities to *achieve* through participation in school, sports, music, and other activities that promote persistence, commitment, and the habit of winning and losing gracefully.

Adults can also thrive in relationships with their family of origin and the families they may create through marriage and procreation. These *relationships* are potentially great sources of *positive emotions*. Parents experience *engagement*—a sense of being fully present—when they join their children in play and leisure, share conversation and laughter with them, and involve children in household chores and responsibilities. Parents also experience engagement through serious conversations that help a child handle problems, such as dealing with a difficult friend or a challenging course in school. Parents experience *meaning* by addressing these situations and shaping the development of their children throughout time. Adults who are not parents also experience positive emotions, engagement, and meaning by participating in relationships with spouses and other family members. Adults encounter opportunities for *achievement* in the quest to be better parents, partners, and family members. Looking at family relationships from both a child's and an adult's vantage, it seems clear that family life offers opportunities—though, of course, not guarantees—for flourishing.

## Family Life Develops Virtues in Its Members

Family life teaches virtue. Few people would deny the power of early moral education; it seems self-evident that character development begins at home. Inculcating habits (habituation) is a process of guiding, modeling, forbidding, and rewarding. It involves shaping a child's understanding and desires. It is a process

---

9. Martin E. P. Seligman, *Flourish: A Visionary New Understanding of Happiness and Well-Being* (New York: Simon and Schuster, 2011; Atria Paperback, 2013), 14–26. See the discussion in ch. 3.

of socialization—drawing the child into the social dynamics of the family and then, through the family, into wider social networks. By habituating the child into virtues, such as politeness, kindness, self-respect, and collaboration, parents help the child live well among others.[10]

Parents are also educated in virtue as they manage their children's moral development. James Keenan's example of developing prudence through parenting,[11] illustrates how parents' imaginative and compassionate planning to help their children flourish develops the parents' prudence, which is a skill the parents can apply to themselves to manage their own moral growth.[12] It is not uncommon to hear adults—whether teachers, nurses, managers, etc.—say that being a parent helped them learn how to do their job better. When people say this, they typically mean the parenting experience gave them a deeper understanding of other people and helped them develop character traits that carried over into their work. This benefit of family life is not limited to those who are parents. Through working with young people in jobs, volunteerism, and in relationship with nieces, nephews, and cousins of various ages, adults can develop this sort of prudence.

## Family Practices Develop a Family's Character

In addition to family members having individual character, families possess and act from a collective character. Through their actions, family members and communities form their characters throughout time. For this reason, virtue ethicists pay particular attention to what are known as "practices."

The concept of a *practice* was given currency in contemporary virtue ethics by the philosopher Alasdair MacIntyre, who describes it as any cooperative social activity that involves the pursuit of intrinsic goods, in addition to whatever extrinsic goods are pursued. His examples include "arts, sciences, games, politics in the Aristotelian sense, [and] the making and sustaining of family life."[13] These activities have both extrinsic and intrinsic value, but people only find the activities deeply meaningful when the intrinsic dimension is honored.[14] Playing basketball is a practice in this sense. There is an extrinsic good in basketball: to win the game by putting the ball through the hoop more times than

---

10. For a more detailed explanation of the habituation process, see M. F. Burnyeat, "Aristotle on Learning to Be Good," and Nancy Sherman, "The Habituation of Character," both in *Aristotle's Ethics: Critical Essays,* ed. Nancy Sherman (Lanham, MD: Rowman and Littlefield, 1999), 205–30 and 231–60 respectively.

11. See the section "Virtues of Perceiving and Reasoning" in ch. 2.

12. James F. Keenan, *Virtues for Ordinary Christians* (Lanham, MD: Sheed & Ward, 1996), 76–81.

13. Alasdair MacIntyre, *After Virtue,* 3rd ed. (Notre Dame, IN: University of Notre Dame Press, 2007), 187–88.

14. On extrinsic and intrinsic, see ch. 7, the section "Meanings of Work."

the opposing team does. There are also intrinsic goods in basketball: playing the game well and gracefully, making one's best effort, practicing teamwork, and enjoying the flow of the game. Only by embracing these intrinsic goods does a basketball player experience flourishing through the game. This flourishing is inevitably social: "It is characteristic of [intrinsic goods] that their achievement is a good for the whole community who participate in the practice."[15] MacIntyre defines virtue in relationship to practices: "A virtue is an acquired human quality the possession and exercise of which tends to enable us to achieve those goods which are internal to practices and the lack of which effectively prevents us from achieving any such goods."[16]

Notice that one of MacIntyre's examples of a practice is the making and sustaining of family life. All members of a family can develop virtues and achieve greater flourishing if they understand the daily activities of family life as practices and conduct themselves accordingly. Such an understanding of family life has been thoroughly developed by theological ethicist Julie Hanlon Rubio. In her book *Family Ethics*, she defines a practice as "an intentional, shared action, situated in the context of a tradition, ordinary in outward appearance but transcendent in its association with fundamental human goods."[17] Practices are everyday activities that convey deeper meaning for those who do them thoughtfully. There are many such activities in family life, including talking, reading, consuming media, using technology, teaching and learning, traveling, playing, communicating sexually, eating meals, spending money, serving, and, for religious families, praying.[18] Most families engage in most of these activities to some extent. Rubio's goal is to help families think about how they can perform these everyday activities as intentional practices so they can develop their characters and experience greater happiness and flourishing.

Consider eating. At a practical level, eating meals together benefits each family member. Studies show that the more often a family eats together, the less likely the children are to have physical or emotional problems or to engage in problematic behaviors, such as using drugs. At the table, family members have regular opportunities to talk, which contributes to the health of their relationships. Parents seem to have heeded the advice recounted by doctors and popular media, since the percentage of teenagers who eat most dinners with their families increased 23 percent between 1998 and 2005.[19] Of course, the busyness of

---

15. MacIntyre, *After Virtue*, 190.

16. Ibid., 191.

17. Rubio, *Family Ethics*, 99. She relies for this definition on Craig Dykstra and Dorothy C. Bass, "A Theological Understanding of Christian Practices," in *Practicing Theology*, ed. Miroslav Volf and Dorothy C. Bass (Grand Rapids: Eerdmans, 2002), 13–32.

18. The first seven items in this list are the author's. The final five—from sex through prayer—are Rubio's and the topics of her chs. 4–8.

19. Ibid., 129.

many families impinges upon their ability to share regular meals. But if parents capitalize on mealtimes and other family gatherings, the flourishing that results can motivate parents to prioritize this practice. Dining as a family requires parents and children to act with virtues, such as self-control and responsibility. Regarding character, Rubio explains,

> While individuals in families can and do eat in a variety of ways, when families gather over meals, those meals are formative. In coming together to eat, a family recognizes bonds they share, shapes its members' characters, and sends them forth to be certain kinds of people. This is true whether families intend it or not. Around a table, a family becomes more of who it is—faithful or jaded, contentious or loving, open or closed, or something in between.[20]

Eating is, therefore, an important practice for developing a family's virtues. Rubio discusses several virtues that are developed by eating meals together as an intentional practice: respect, politeness, hospitality, and mercy.[21]

Practices are situated in traditions, and Rubio draws from her religious faith tradition to show that these virtues are deeply embedded in the Christian understanding of eating. Almost any family can locate itself in a tradition that adds depth to the practice of eating, that is, if members make the effort to become intentional about it. For some, such a tradition might be Christianity, with its practices of saying grace before meals and participating in the Eucharist at church, which is seen as a spiritual meal conveying God's blessings to those who partake in it. For others, it might be Judaism, with its rich practices of the weekly Shabbat meal and the Passover Seder. For others, it is a cultural or family tradition such as a holiday meal or occasional meals with extended family. If a family doesn't have a meal practice, it can start one by committing to have at least one weekly meal together at some leisure and without the distraction of electronic devices.

Intentional participation in practices is an effective method for implementing virtue ethics. This chapter and each chapter in part 2 describe practices groups can pursue as virtuous responses to the challenges they face.

## Families and Society

Families and society have a mutually beneficial relationship (fig. 5.2). Families help create a society in which they and all groups and persons can flourish by making material and ethical contributions to the common good. Society's

---

20. Ibid., 128–29.
21. Ibid., 142–55.

political, economic, cultural, and philanthropic institutions help families in the material and ethical dimensions of their lives.

## A Family and Society

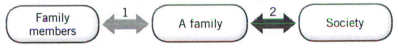

**Figure 5.2.** Community Connections: Family and Society

## Families Make Material and Ethical Contributions to a Better Society

The material contributions families make to society are varied. Families pay taxes. They maintain homes. They take responsibility for the care and education of children. They participate in civic activities. Simply by carrying on with everyday life, families contribute to social capital (ch. 4). For instance, almost no one relishes paying taxes, but the taxes paid by families make the operations of government possible. Schools, libraries, roads, police, courts, and other resources necessary for social well-being would not exist without taxes. So tax-paying families and individuals—which is almost everyone in society, at some point[22]— make possible the resources for social flourishing.[23] Families can go a further step by appreciating the importance of these activities and participating in them from the virtuous motives of justice, solidarity, and citizenship.

By acting ethically and teaching ethics to its children, families become agents for social flourishing. Families can be more or less aware of and committed to their important role in society. At the lowest level of motivation, a family is focused heavily on the flourishing of its members. At the middle level, a family sees its flourishing and societal flourishing as compatible. At the highest level, the family is motivated by its *and* society's flourishing; it sees both as inherently valuable. This level is the familial parallel to Aristotle's person of full character, who does the right things for the right reasons and finds satisfaction in so doing.[24] Families at the highest level act from a sense of social mission.

---

22. At any one time, the percent of households paying federal income taxes and/or payroll taxes is 72 percent. Even when low-income, retired, or unemployed people are not paying these taxes, they are paying other taxes and fees. See William G. Gale and Donald Marron, "Five Myths about the 47 Percent," *The Washington Post*, September 21, 2012, *https://www.washingtonpost.com/opinions /five-myths-about-the-47-percent/2012/09/21/57dc7bbe-0341-11e2-8102-ebee9c66e190_story.html.*

23. In this light, the political and ethical questions to be raised about a nation's tax system are not whether it should exist but how it should be arranged so it is fair to all and also how taxes should be allocated. These issues are addressed later in this chapter.

24. See Aristotle, *Nicomachean Ethics* 2.4 (1105a30–35) and 2.6 (1106a21–23) on the right things for the right reasons and 1.8 (1099a7) and 10.5 (1174b33) on the inherent pleasure in being virtuous.

They ask, "What should be the shape of our life?" and answer the question by working on their character and performing virtuous actions. They become families with a mission. A family's mission can take many forms, but a few of its basic elements are shared love among its members, service to those in need, educating its children in justice, acting in society from motives of love and justice, and adopting a values-oriented lifestyle.[25] By living from a sense of mission or purpose, the family can be an agent for the transformation of culture. As Rubio says, "What goes on in the home becomes a model for society."[26]

The earlier example of families eating together illustrates the social implications found in everyday practices.[27]

- Dinner conversation can be an important time in the day or week when parents educate their children about ethical values and when the family talks about social concerns. "Discussions about social issues and how family members approach money, time, charity, politics, and so on can broaden the concerns of both parents and children."[28]

- Families can make just choices about what foods to buy and eat. While acknowledging the financial and practical difficulties for some families, Rubio recommends that families consider buying more organic, local, and seasonable foods and cutting down on meat consumption, because these actions will benefit the family members' health, support local farmers, contribute to environmental sustainability, educate the family's friends and relatives, and develop virtues in the family members.

- Families can invite others to their table—not only relatives and friends but, perhaps, the lonely or disenfranchised.

- Meals provide opportunities for families to remember the hungry. This act of awareness is encouraged when a family says a mealtime grace that includes the needs of others. Families may then resolve to do something charitable to help those in need.

## Society Assists Families Materially and Ethically

In the other direction, society supports families in basic ways. "Society" refers to a number of medium and large institutions, such as government, businesses, schools, churches, and nonprofit organizations. Since federal, state, and local governments control major resources that impact families—such as public schools and universities, health insurance programs, and tax benefits—these levels of

---

25. These elements are loosely modeled on Pope John Paul II's tasks for the social mission of the family, as affirmed by Rubio (54–56).

26. Ibid., 142.

27. The bullet points summarize Rubio, ibid., 143–54.

28. Ibid., 145.

government figure prominently in the following discussion and later arguments about resources society should provide to families. Yet the ethical principle of subsidiarity, which holds that government is not the only social institution that matters, applies. *Subsidiarity* means that government (a) must cooperate with other institutions and refrain from usurping the role of other groups and (b) should implement its solutions to social needs at the most local level possible.[29] With this principle in mind, it appears that a number of social institutions should—and, in fact, do—give material and ethical assistance to families.

## Material Assistance

Three categories of social institutions figure prominently in giving material support to families. Families may not be explicitly aware of relying upon these institutions, but they form, together, the daily background of family life, offering a safe and stable context in which families and citizens can pursue flourishing.

- *Government and law.* Government ensures protection, social order, and legal justice. Legislation, courts, police, and fire departments are among the methods for doing so. Taxes are ethically important because they (a) provide for a wide range of services and (b) redistribute some income in society, helping those in need and potentially reducing economic inequality. Government, sometimes in collaboration with nonprofit organizations, provides safety nets for needy people and families. States create community hospitals, public health programs, worker disability insurance programs, job training programs, anti-drug programs, anti-violence programs, and the like to help people across the socioeconomic gamut.
- *Schools and nonprofit organizations.* Society provides education. Federal, state, and local government, as well as the nonprofit and business sectors, provide educational programming and services that are critical for the flourishing of children, families, and society. Schools are part of the wider nonprofit philanthropic sector, which helps all families at various points. Museums and cultural institutions, afterschool programs, summer camps, youth sports leagues, and the like are resources that enrich the lives of children and families. Social institutions continually cooperate to help families survive and thrive.
- *Businesses and the economy.* Businesses create jobs at which adults can earn income to support their families. Financially sound companies may also provide benefits, such as retirement accounts, health insurance, flexible

---

29. "Subsidiarity" was coined in Catholic social ethics (see the Pontifical Council for Justice and Peace, *Compendium of the Social Doctrine of the Church*, 2004, no. 185–88, *http://www.vatican.va/roman_curia/pontifical_councils/justpeace/documents/rc_pc_justpeace_doc_20060526_compendio-dott-soc_en.html*), but it is similar to the principle of federalism in American political theory and to Alexis de Tocqueville's robust civil society composed of mediating institutions (see ch. 4).

working arrangements, and tuition assistance. Many smaller businesses are unable to provide some or all of these benefits; government, then, might fill in the gaps. However, many contemporary families still have a tough time "making ends meet."

## Ethical Assistance

The types of aid mentioned are mostly material, but social institutions also contribute to the ethical development of children and families. Society, as well as government, is invested in the moral education of children and the character development of families. Society's and government's roles can be limit-setting, and indirectly and directly supportive.

- *Limit-setting.* The legal system sets boundaries on what parents can do and holds them accountable for failures. For instance, government cannot make parents love their children, but government can step in when parents neglect their duties.

- *Indirectly supportive.* Most of the time, society's and government's assistance indirectly supports the ethical development of families. For instance, educational, charitable, and governmental organizations and programs help many parents find more time and energy to focus on their children's moral and intellectual development. The tax system encourages certain ethical behaviors in families through tax incentives—for everything from charitable contributions to adoption.

- *Directly supportive.* Government and other social institutions also directly promote character development in children, families, and citizens. Public schools teach virtues such as patriotism, citizenship, tolerance, cooperation, and fairness. Governmental and charitable anti-poverty programs discourage irresponsible behavior, such as drug use, and encourage positive behaviors, such as healthy parent-children interaction, nonviolent discipline, and compassion.

## Increased Social Capital for All

All citizens, even those with no family members in their household, benefit from family-oriented policies and activities. The social capital created when families thrive is beneficial for everyone in society. For example, extensive data shows that the quality of schooling in a nation correlates directly to citizens' income levels, the nation's economic strength, and the overall well-being of citizens and society.[30] Further, as political scientist Robert Putnam's research shows, social capital within families powerfully affects youth development, which in turn benefits society. Social capital research suggests that parents' involvement in their

---

30. See ch. 6, the section "Schools Contribute to Society, Increasing Social Capital for All."

children's lives and schools helps children become more engaged in a school. Engaged children are more likely to exhibit good behavior at school. Students' better behavior makes the school more effective, benefitting every student. A neighborhood with a reputation for a good school is a draw for families who are involved in their children's lives and schools. It's a virtuous cycle and one from which communities of any socioeconomic level can benefit.[31]

## Challenges within Families and Virtuous Responses

It is true that family life benefits persons and society, but how might families better flourish and play a more complete role in social flourishing? The following case study of the Jenkins family features some challenges that families and their members encounter internally in daily life. Bear in mind that this is an example of only one U.S. family. The case illustrates challenges any family could face, with an emphasis on the way middle- to lower-income families might experience them. These challenges are internal, since families and their members can do something about them through virtuous practices.

### Striving for the American Dream—A Case Study

The Jenkins are a middle class family living in Niles, Illinois, a village that borders Chicago and has a population of 30,000 and a median family income of $64,000.[32] The father, Dave, is a plumber who earns $53,000 annually, and the mother, Robin, is a nursery school teacher who earns $21,000. The couple has three children. Olivia is a senior in high school, Trevor a high school freshman, and Kyle a sixth grader. Kyle has learning disabilities that affect his performance in math and language arts. The parents are happy with the public schools their children attend, although they see room for improvement. Only 60 to 70 percent of the students in those schools meet or exceed state standards in reading and math. Olivia and Trevor meet the standards, but Kyle, even with special education services, does not.

Until recently, the Jenkins had insurance coverage for their children through an Illinois program since neither Dave's nor Robin's employer provided it. But starting in 2014, the entirely family secured health insurance under the Affordable Care Act. Dave and Robin are concerned about paying for their children's college and saving for retirement; the little money they put away monthly for

---

31. The virtuous circle is suggested by Putnam's finding in *Bowling Alone* (New York: Simon & Schuster, 2000), 303–6. See ch. 4.

32. Data for this case study is drawn from U.S. Census Bureau data (*http://factfinder.census.gov*), Illinois's 2013–2014 "report card" on school performance (*http://www.illinoisreportcard.com*), average salaries for the parents' jobs (*http://www.payscale.com*), the Wikipedia entry for Niles, and Niles's official website (*https://www.vniles.com*).

these purposes seems inadequate. Their retirement savings are meager, because they believe saving for their children's college is more urgent.

The Jenkinses communicate well with each other most of the time, though the two teenagers are often in their own worlds of friends and activities. The family eats dinner together several nights a week, and the parents attend most of the kids' sporting events and school-related activities. The family contributes ten dollars a week to their church and donates modestly to various charities. Because the parents feel they don't have a lot of money to give, they also volunteer as a way to help others. Dave coaches Trevor's soccer team, Robin teaches Sunday school, and the whole family occasionally volunteers at a soup kitchen.

## Internal Challenges

The quality of family life begins at home and requires parents to be people of character, showing love, courage, persistence, self-control, and so on. Dave and Robin Jenkins are presented as parents who have character. They work hard at their jobs to pay their bills, provide for their children, and save for their children's college funds. In fact, to provide for their children, the parents neglect some of their own wants, such as an upgraded cell phone, for example, and even some of their needs, such as retirement savings. Importantly, Dave and Robin make an ongoing effort to be involved in their children's lives. Whatever tensions might arise, at times, between the parents and the children, Olivia, Trevor, and Kyle are likely to notice that their parents are "there for them."

However, when parents lack character or are overly strained by difficult circumstances, harm can result. Although the following major harms are not evident in the case study, people should be aware of these risks to families.

- *Abuse and neglect.* Children can be deeply, even permanently harmed when one or more parents or close adults are unloving, abusive, irresponsible, or absent owing to irresponsibility, tragedy, or other circumstances.[33]
- *Absent fathers.* The absence of a father—which characterizes the lives of one in three American children[34]—is a risk. Evidence shows that "children who live with their fathers are more likely to have good physical and emotional health, achieve academically, and avoid drugs, violence, and delinquent behavior."[35]

---

33. See specific data from the Congressional Coalition on Adoption Institute, *http://www.cca institute.org* (see "Facts and Figures," in the section "Why We Do It"), which draws upon studies from the U.S. Department of Health and Human Services, UNICEF, and other agencies.

34. U.S. Census Bureau, "Census Bureau Reports 64 Percent Increase in Number of Children Living with a Grandparent over Last Two Decades," June 29, 2011, *https://www.census.gov/news room/releases/archives/children/cb11-117.html.*

35. Jeffrey Rosenberg and W. Bradford Wilcox, "The Importance of Fathers in the Healthy Development of Children," U.S. Department of Health and Human Services, Child Welfare Information Gateway, 2006, sec. 2.3, *https://www.childwelfare.gov/pubs/usermanuals/fatherhood/.*

- *Poor parenting.* When parents or guardians do not have the necessary character or maturity, flourishing for family members is harmed. Obvious examples are parents who abuse drugs or inadequately supervise their children. Similarly, families are challenged when a parent is well-intentioned but desperate. A modest flaw in a parent's character or a poor decision can be greatly magnified when a family is vulnerable.[36]

- *Emotional neglect.* There are many children who enjoy the financial, educational, and social opportunities of an upper-middle-class or upper-class lifestyle, yet are stunted in their flourishing by emotional damage from a parent who is never satisfied with their "success," is too busy working to spend much time with them, and so on. Emotional neglect is a significant problem in many children's development.[37]

- *Single parent/divorced families.* Single parents and divorced families face additional challenges in scheduling, finances, and caregiving.[38]

- *Character-based challenges.* Children may have their own character-based challenges despite the intentions and oversight of their parents. A child may get involved in drinking or drug use, engage in early or risky sexual activity, or become involved in criminal activity. Although these behaviors may be attributed to character flaws, it is important to remember that children are impressionable and not in full command of their reason and will.

In the Jenkins family, as in any family, some of these challenges could arise. The parents could have marital difficulties and separate. One of the parents could lose a job and struggle with extended unemployment leading to depression. One of the children might hang out with friends who encourage him or her to drink or use other drugs. One of the children could impulsively make a bad decision, such as getting into a car with a drunk driver or passing along a "sext" picture on his or her cell phone. While Dave and Robin want to provide as safe and stable an environment as they can, they must also realize they cannot shield their children from every harm or take away their freedom to make bad decisions.

---

36. A recent example was when an Arizona woman, desperate for employment, went on a job interview, leaving her two-year-old and six-month-old sons in the car with the fan running and the windows cracked. See Rheana Murray, "Mom Who Left Kids in Car for Job Interview Glad for '2nd Chance,'" ABC News, July 25, 2014. *http://abcnews.go.com/US /arizona-mom-left-kids-car-job-interview-glad/story?id=24712432.*

37. Jonice Webb with Christian Musello, *Running on Empty: Overcome Your Childhood Emotional Neglect* (New York: Morgan James Publishing, 2013).

38. More controversially, some contend that divorce carries the risk of hampering children's emotional flourishing. For a summary of this debate, see Hal Arkowitz and Scott O. Lilienfeld, "Is Divorce Bad for Children?" *Scientific American*, February 14, 2013, *http://www.scientificamerican .com/article/is-divorce-bad-for-children/.*

Still, Dave and Robin must do what they can. As they attempt their best, they have questions about how they should work toward their children's flourishing.

- *Responsibility.* Will the responsibility they taught keep the children safe in their high school years? Will their kids be able to resist harmful peer pressure? How do the parents stay involved in their teenager's lives now that the teens want more independence and privacy?

- *Education.* Should Olivia go to a community college instead of a private institution, so the family will be able to better afford tuition for the children, or should she take out large student loans? Is Kyle getting the best special education services at his school, and how can the parents know? Is private tutoring needed?

- *Finances and charity.* Should the children be expected to get jobs when they are in high school? How should the family spend its money when the family budget is tight—on activities for the children, vacations, cell phones, or other things everyone in the family would like to have? Is the family doing enough to give back to the community?

The Jenkinses represent a middle-class family trying to live "the American dream." A major part of this dream is for parents to ensure that their children have the opportunities and resources to do well in life—to do better than the parents themselves did. The American dream can be problematic if reduced to material success, however. Taking a lead from Aristotle and Tocqueville, a virtuous understanding of this powerful cultural ideal is one in which parents do their best to ensure that their children have the character, material resources, and fortitude to flourish holistically, pursue a meaningful life, and contribute to the common good. Dave and Robin seem to be on the right path in this regard. Along the way, they will encounter obstacles. What can they do when they face these challenges?

## Responses to Internal Challenges

In responding to challenges, the Jenkinses, like all families, can rely on character. Dave and Robin have reason to trust that they have given their children the skills to make good decisions. However, they will have to be attuned to new developments in their children's lives as they become teenagers. Practicing prudence, parents will need to be creative and courageous in trying new avenues when challenges arise or when their current way of dealing with a challenge is not working well. The following practices are ways the Jenkinses and other families can meet their challenges virtuously.

## Nurturing Care, Respect, and Purpose within the Family

Parents can show tangible, practical love for their children. If Dave and Robin communicate well with their children, they, as parents, have the best chance of guiding them well in life. Capitalizing on family meals and opportunities for conversation (with teens, for example, this is often when driving together in the car)[39] goes a long way in guiding children toward flourishing. Parents start by teaching their children politeness and respect. It is important for parents to show the same politeness and respect to each other as to their children. Monitoring their stress levels helps parents avoid situations in which they snipe or yell at the children because of parental problems.

Parents can be thoughtful about the use of family time for play, leisure, exercise, media consumption, and socialization. They also can be deliberate about how they socialize with those outside the family. The parents' choice of friends and associates makes a major statement to the children about the parents' values; these friendships also shape the parents' characters, slowly but surely. Associating with other families who share the parents' values exposes the children to good role models, and everyone benefits from the camaraderie and assistance that good friends provide.

Family members can be cruel to each other simply because of familiarity,[40] which is why it is important to apologize and forgive when warranted. This is true for parents and children. Also, parents, couples, and families can build in mechanisms for renewal and reconnection. Examples are date nights, low-stress vacations, game nights, and activities that promote conversation.

Families can nurture the virtues of purpose by attending religious services together, praying, meditating, going for walks in nature, or practicing yoga together. Families could consider writing a family mission statement.[41] A mission statement expresses the family's core values and major goals, and the main roles and responsibilities of each member. Families could make regular opportunities to "fast" from media, cell phones, or other pleasures and activities that can distract from family life or that get taken for granted because they are experienced often.[42]

---

39. Ann Meier and Kelly Musisk, "Variation in Associations between Family Dinners and Adolescent Well-Being," *Journal of Marriage and Family* 76, no. 1 (2014): 13–23.

40. Emily Esfahani Smith, "Why Your Family Drives You Crazy," *Vox*, November 26, 2014, *http://www.vox.com/2014/11/26/7254589/family-crazy*.

41. Stephen R. Covey, *The Seven Habits of Highly Effective People*, 25th Anniversary ed. (New York: Simon and Schuster, 2013), 146–47. See resources in the websites listed in "Recommendations for Further Reading" at the end of this chapter.

42. Rebecca Konyndyk DeYoung suggests various sorts of fasting as a strategy for countering vices in one's character in *Glittering Vices: A New Look at the Seven Deadly Sins and the Remedies* (Grand Rapids: Brazos Press, 2009), 76, 114, and 151–57.

## Educating Children at Home

Education starts from day one in a child's life. Before children have any words for the concept, they know if they are loved. As noted earlier, when parents touch, cuddle, and speak compassionately to their children, the children's brains are stimulated such that the children are more likely to develop resilience, confidence, and self-control.

Parents can teach their children to name their emotions and address their problems through communication. Learning to monitor and name emotions teaches children to enjoy their full range of emotions without acting inappropriately on them. Everyone in the family can work on the skills of active listening and nonjudgmental speaking.[43]

As they grow, children can be taught to think critically, a skill and virtue that applies to all areas of one's life. For example, parents can teach children to think critically about the media the children consume. Parents can engage children in conversations about the values and assumptions about the world reflected in television programs and movies. To do this, parents can discover what their children are watching. There is no sure guideline on the amount of time children should be allowed to watch television, play on computers, use social media, and so on; those decisions vary with the context. The important thing is for parents to show awareness of the children's media use and identify their expectations about age-appropriate content that is consistent with the family's values. Parents might consult websites that review movies and television programs from a parenting perspective.[44]

## Guiding Children's Formal Education

Parents benefit their children's education by being involved in schools as much as their schedules allow—volunteering, attending school events with the children, and communicating with teachers. Parents can promote their children's education outside of school by encouraging reading and using family leisure time for educational purposes (e.g., going to the library, visiting a museum, etc.).

Parents have an important choice in where to send a child to school. The Jenkinses want to ensure that Kyle has the best services possible and that all their children go to schools that challenge them and help them develop important life skills. Families may try to locate in a city or neighborhood with a reputation for a

---

43. Recommended for parents with children of all ages is Adele Faber and Elaine Mazlish, *How to Talk So Kids Will Listen and Listen So Kids Will Talk*, updated ed. (New York: Scribner, 2012) and, for parents of teenagers, Anthony E. Wolf, *I'd Listen to My Parents If They'd Just Shut Up: What to Say and Not Say When Parenting Teens* (New York: William Morrow Paperbacks, 2011). See also Laura Markham, "5 Steps to Help Kids Learn to Control Their Emotions," *Psychology Today*, July 13, 2013, *https://www.psychologytoday.com/blog/peaceful-parents-happy-kids/201307/5-steps-help-kids-learn-control-their-emotions*.

44. A useful resource, grounded in both media theory and a virtuous-parenting theology, is Jay Dunlap, *Raising Kids in the Media Age* (Hamden, CT: Circle Press, 2007).

good school system. Some, due to social inequities, may be unable to do so, while others will have the income and opportunity to make such a choice. Regardless of individual circumstance, parents can make the best choices possible in the interests of their children, as well as look to social institutions to address the broader dimensions of fairness. Parents, like all citizens, can advocate for political leaders to institute policies that improve education for all students in society.

Parents considering schooling options can keep a few social factors in mind. First, a good education is about more than sending children to the "best" schools. Schools can be homogeneous, depriving children of opportunities to learn from diversity. Second, private education can be expensive; parents have to be responsible with their family budget and thoughtful about how their spending influences the options for other families. For the Jenkinses, when it comes to Olivia's college choices, some universities have excellent reputations but are expensive. Robin and Dave must help Olivia think through a sensible plan for her future, remembering that her own virtues—persistence, courage, and prudence—are going to serve her well no matter where she goes to college.

There are several other practices that help family members develop character so they grow closer and happier as a family. Such practices—volunteering, being civically active, and resisting consumerism—are discussed after the section on external challenges, because these practices also concern how families can make a difference in the world.

## Challenges outside Families and Virtuous Responses

Contemporary American families face many external challenges—economic, cultural, and political. These challenges pressure family members who might rise to the challenges or struggle to do so—usually some of both throughout time. Before surveying these challenges, a stark reality, with which any discussion of the state of American families must reckon, should be mentioned: "United States children increasingly live in a diverse array of family structures."[45] So begins a study by a team of public health and social science researchers responding to the following trends:[46]

1. Between 1960 and 1996, the proportion of children younger than 18 and living with married parents decreased from 85 to 68 percent. By 2012, it had decreased to 64 percent.

---

45. Patrick M. Krueger et al., "Family Structure and Multiple Domains of Child Well-Being in the United States: A Cross-Sectional Study," *Population Health Metrics* 13, no. 1 (2015): 1.

46. The authors refer to the Child Trends Data Bank. The following points are quoted with slight adaptation from its most recent report, *Family Structure: Indicators on Children and Youth*, updated March 2015, p. 3, *http://www.childtrends.org/?indicators=family-structure*.

2. In 1960, the proportion of children living in mother-only families was 8 percent but, by 1996, that proportion tripled, to 24 percent. Since 1996, it has fluctuated between 22 and 24 percent, and was at 24 percent in 2014.

3. Between 1990 and 2013, the share of children living in father-only families fluctuated between 3 and 5 percent and was at 4 percent in 2014. The proportion living without either parent remained steady, at approximately 4 percent.

4. In 2014, 7 percent of all children lived in a grandparent's home. In two-thirds of these families, one or both parents were also present.

The changes are of concern because, as this study finds, "*all non-married* couple family structures are associated with *some adverse outcomes* among children."[47] Of particular note is that children of single mothers and cohabiting couples fare the worst among family types in children's education, health, access to health care, and other measures of well-being, even controlling for socioeconomic status. In other words, at each class level, children in non-marital families do worse on most of the well-being indicators, but the disparities are reduced, showing that financial resources alone make a difference. However, there are limitations to this and similar studies; for instance, correlation does not prove causation; these are general trends with many exceptions to the rule; there are other indicators of well-being that cannot be discerned in survey data; and there is no indication in this study of how gay and lesbian families compare to other types of families.[48]

As indicated at the start of the chapter, the point is not to be morally judgmental about any particular form of family life. These data do not necessarily show that married-couple families are better off, and they certainly do not show that married-couple families are more virtuous as a rule. Rather, ethical and sociological analyses based on such data suggest that (a) family structures insofar as they impact parental involvement do matter for family flourishing, and (b) families lacking two parents united in a stable marital commitment tend to encounter the challenges of life more intensely than others. The challenges are especially severe for poor families, who have much higher rates of non-marital family formats, with associated resource deficits, than rich families. Putnam's study, *Our Kids*, portrays the effects of changing family trends statistically and in the stories of young people from his hometown of Port Clinton, Ohio.[49] Similarly to the

---

47. Krueger, 1. The data in the study was drawn from a 1997–2013 National Health Interview Survey, which included data from almost 200,000 randomly sampled children. The authors identified seventeen outcomes of well-being (such as having asthma or ADHD and the number of days of school missed in a year) to see how prevalent these are for children in nine types of family structure.

48. The authors mention most of these limitations (ibid., 6). Although gay and lesbian families are not explicitly addressed, see "Government Policies to Support Families," in this chapter.

49. Robert D. Putnam, *Our Kids: The American Dream in Crisis* (New York: Simon & Schuster, 2015).

hypothetical case study in chapter 3,[50] *Our Kids* lays, side-by-side, the stories of American youth from upper-class families and lower-class families.[51] A child of the latter type is David, whose story is summarized by one reviewer of the book thus: "Kids like David are insecure, confused, and despairing. They believe that no one cares or helps or even notices them. They see the world as 'unpredictable, intractable, malign.' . . . Insecure bonds . . . leave kids unmoored, untrusting, and unready for the challenges of adult life."[52]

The challenges of family structure and parental commitment are both internal and external. There are economic, cultural, and political dimensions to the challenges, which demand economic, cultural, and political responses from those who are concerned about the common good.

*Economic challenges.* "Plummeting wages and lengthening work weeks, joblessness and mounting insecurity—these are the hallmarks of our age."[53] These are the sobering words of Sylvia Ann Hewlett, an economist, business expert, and author who writes about working parents, and Cornel West, a prolific author, social activist, and professor of philosophy, religion, and African American studies. In 1998, they coauthored *The War on Parents*, which addresses the challenges facing working families in the United States. Economic pressures are high on the authors' list of concerns. Not much has changed since their book appeared. After the economic recession that began in 2007, the vulnerable became more vulnerable. Even for families with steady jobs, wages didn't seem to stretch as they had in the past. Generally speaking, that perception is reality: American workers have seen their real wages (adjusted for inflation) stagnate since the 1970s. (Ironically, the productivity of American workers has soared during the same period.[54]) The situation is especially bleak for men, as two economists explain:

---

50. That case study compares Ellie, from a well-off, suburban family, to Robert, from an urban, working-class family. Putnam's book compares families like Ellie's to families who are financially and culturally *worse-off* than Robert's. In these families, "Fathers die, disappear, or end up in prison. Mothers take off as well, carried away by new boyfriends and by the powerful tug of drug addiction. . . . A stream of other adults . . . flow through kids' households" (Barbara Dafoe Whitehead, "Separated at Birth," review of *Our Kids* by Robert D. Putnam, *Commonweal* [June 12, 2015]: 26).

51. Putnam writes, "Roughly speaking, the educational attainment of Americans can be divided into thirds, with the top third college graduates, the bottom third no more than high-school-educated, and the middle third with some secondary education (*Our Kids*, 45). He applies the terms "upper class," "lower class," and "middle class" to the groups respectively. Another way to think about class is in terms of income distribution. In 2012, the bottom 20 percent of American households made no more than $20,600 annually, while the incomes of the top 20 percent started at $105,000. These two groups arguably count as "poor" and "rich" respectively (Tax Policy Center, "Tax Facts: Household Income Quintiles 2000–2012, updated June 25, 2014, *http://www .taxpolicycenter.org/taxfacts/Content/PDF/income_quintiles.pdf*).

52. Whitehead, "Seperated at Birth," 26.

53. Sylvia Ann Hewlett and Cornel West, *The War against Parents* (New York: Mariner Books, 1998), 59.

54. Steven Greenhouse, "Our Economic Pickle," *New York Times*, January 12, 2013, *http://www .nytimes.com/2013/01/13/sunday-review/americas-productivity-climbs-but-wages-stagnate.html?_r=0*.

When we consider all working-age men, including those who are not working, the real earnings of the median male have actually declined by 19 percent since 1970. This means that the median man in 2010 earned as much as the median man did in 1964—nearly a half century ago. Men with less education face an even bleaker picture; earnings for the median man with a high school diploma and no further schooling fell by 41 percent from 1970 to 2010.[55]

The growth in wages for women during the same time period was better, the authors note, but recently, women's wages have stagnated as well. Moreover, women's earnings still lag those of men: women earn 82 percent of what men earn[56] despite having steadily streamed into the workforce during the past fifty years. Currently, about half the American workforce is women.[57] Among heterosexual married couples, 54 percent have wages from both the husband and wife, the latter contributing, on average, 38 percent of the family income.[58]

There are many reasons women—single, partnered, or married—work, including personal and professional fulfillment. Yet the stagnation of wages means that many middle-class families see having two parents working full-time as a necessity, not an option. A 2009 report by the National Center for Children in Poverty specified what it really means "to make ends meet" by developing a Basic Needs Budget. The author of the report, Kinsey Alden Dinan, calculated that a two-parent family with two children requires at least $35,000 if it lives in a rural area and up to $67,000 if it lives in a large urban area. If one parent works part-time or stays home, the other parent's wage obviously must be higher, and the cost savings are not as great as might be supposed. Since median household income in the United States hovers at just more than $50,000, Dinan concludes:

> Millions of America's families scrape by on less than what it takes to cover their basic needs. Parents may find cheaper, but potentially less-reliable and lower quality, care for their children. They may live in over-crowded housing or in unsafe neighborhoods—or get behind on rent or utility bills. These are tough choices that jeopardize the well-being of our nation's children and families.[59]

---

55. Michael Greenstone and Adam Looney, "The Uncomfortable Truth about American Wages," Economix blog at the *New York Times*, October 22, 2012, *http://economix.blogs.nytimes.com/2012/10/22/the-uncomfortable-truth-about-american-wages/*.

56. U.S. Bureau of Labor Statistics (BLS), "Women in the Labor Force: A Databook," *BLS Reports*, February 2013, 1, *http://www.bls.gov/cps/wlf-databook-2012.pdf*.

57. Women constitute 51 percent of the managerial and professional workforce, and 47 percent of the total workforce (BLS, "Women in the Labor Force," 2).

58. BLS, "Women in the Labor Force," 3. The report does not address same-sex couples.

59. Kinsey Alden Dinan, "Budgeting for Basic Needs: A Struggle for Working Families," National Center for Children in Poverty, March 2009, *http://www.nccp.org/publications/pub_858.html*.

Dinan calculates that a family of four living in or near a high-cost city requires $52,000 to $67,000 to meet its basic needs. So the Jenkinses are "just making it" with a combined income of $74,000 for a family of five. In fact, they are doing a bit better than the average family in Niles, Illinois. However, the wages for their jobs, especially for teaching nursery school, tend not to rise much throughout time. Olivia, the eldest Jenkins child, is rightly concerned that it will be difficult to find a decent job even after graduating from college.

Parents like Robin and Dave have to work harder while receiving insufficient societal support. It would not be surprising if one of the parents wanted to take on a second job to provide additional income and more opportunity to save—but how would that affect the time they can spend with their children?

*Cultural challenges.* Another external challenge to families' flourishing is certain cultural influences that make it harder for parents to educate their children in virtue and steer them on a sensible path. Conservative commentators and politicians often blame the popular media for corroding values. Hewlett and West, although politically liberal, make a similar complaint. They say parents are portrayed as "dysfunctional and incompetent" in popular media.[60] Another topic of concern is the amount of graphic violence on television, in movies, and in video games. When it has been discovered that mass shooters have played violent video games or reveled in violent movies, calls for constraints on violent media rise—and then fade within weeks.

It is difficult to establish cause and effect, however. Do television programs showing rude children and self-centered parents *cause* children and parents to act badly, or do programs simply *reflect* what is already acceptable in the culture? Do violent images in the media make children more violent, or do they contribute to violence only among those who are already mentally ill or otherwise pushed toward violence by social and psychological stressors? Endless debates about causation versus correlation hamstring the social conversation over the best use of media. Even if there is no straight line of causation from media portrayals to viewers' actions, people should still care about what they watch and what their children watch. The virtue tradition has long argued that a person ought to be thoughtful about media consumption.[61] A constructive option, when the media presents unvarnished images of how people sometimes behave, is for parents to use these opportunities to talk with their children about serious matters, encouraging virtuous self-monitoring and modeling good decision making.

Perhaps it is not the *content* of media programming so much as the *quantity* of media Americans consume that is a problem. Today's American children have more screen time per week than in the past. At the same time, childhood obesity

---

60. Hewlett and West, *The War against Parents*, 127.

61. For example, Seneca, in *On the Shortness of Life* 14, speaks of how reading philosophy provides enriching thoughts and ever-dependable friends (that is, the authors), in contrast to rushing about in social activities, where acquaintances are bound to disappoint one.

rates have risen. Children's television habits and use of other electronic media, if poorly monitored and controlled, take time away from exercise and reading; children's activities become unbalanced and their flourishing suffers. The use of social media by children is a similar matter of debate. Is social media sucking teens into a virtual world, so they become incapable of holding a face-to-face conversation? Dave and Robin Jenkins likely face these issues. The two older children are likely to be heavily involved in social media and cell phone use; one or more of the children might spend significant time playing video games. It would not be surprising if Robin and Dave regularly find themselves nagging one or more of their children to "put the phone away" and asking, "Why don't you read a book, or go outside?" They may wonder if they are using the right parenting strategy on this matter.

*Political challenges.* Where should parents find support in their pursuit of flourishing for their families, and why are they not finding it? According to virtue ethics, government is part of a mix of necessary institutions that should support citizens and groups in their pursuit of flourishing. There are some things that only government can do or that government does best, such as building infrastructure, ensuring law and order, and ensuring universal schooling. Many think government does too much for Americans, yet Hewlett and West say, "The American government has largely gotten out of the business of supporting moms and dads."[62] They argue that politics needs to become more responsive to ordinary citizens, which would necessitate changes that politicians are loath to enact, such as making the practicalities of voting easier. In the 2000s, many U.S. states moved in this direction by implementing early voting and mail-in voting. Recently, though, some of these states have reduced early voting options and tightened voting regulations. In states where these laws have not been blocked by courts, some people have found it more difficult to vote or have been turned away from voting—particularly college students and poor and working-class citizens.[63]

Robin and Dave, the parents in the case study, vote. Their village maintains a well-organized website that provides meeting agendas and other documents. Yet Robin and Dave may not feel engaged in politics beyond the town level. Not uncommonly, citizens even feel that their town government is not as responsive as it should be. As for state and national politics, in every election cycle, more money is spent. The amount of money special-interest groups, corporations, unions, and wealthy individuals pour into campaigns is virtually unlimited. What voice, then, do the Jenkinses have, and how can they exercise it?

---

62. Hewlett and West, *The War against Parents*, 89.

63. See Steven Yaccino and Lizette Alvarez, "New G.O.P. Bid to Limit Voting in Swing States," *New York Times*, March 29, 2014, *http://www.nytimes.com/2014/03/30/us/new-gop-bid-to-limit-voting -in-swing-states.html*; Dana Liebelson "North Carolina Fights to Take Voting Site Away from Pesky College Kids," *Huffington Post*, October 23, 2014, *http://www.huffingtonpost.com/2014/10/23 /north-carolina-early-voting-college_n_6031670.html*.

The list of political challenges facing families points to a huge problem: American government is divided and seems not to be working for ordinary people—at least not all the time. Although this problem is widely acknowledged across the political spectrum, there is no agreement on how to remedy it. Each major political party blames the other, and each party focuses on different solutions. Liberals typically say the influence of corporations and wealthy political contributors needs to be reduced and that safety nets for families need to be strengthened. Conservatives typically say the government has taken too many responsibilities from local communities, so it is better to prevent the federal government from creating more programs and increasing the tax burden on families. One taking a character-and-community approach might suspect that there is some truth on both sides of this political divide, but that politicians have lost the virtue of collaboration.

## Responses to External Challenges

Life is not easy for families these days. As Hewlett and West emphasize, parents need help. The point is not that every challenge can or should be removed. Just as individuals do better at developing character and flourishing when they face difficulties, families do better at the same by facing obstacles—if the obstacles are manageable. The communities and institutions on which families rely bear some responsibility for clearing those obstacles and assisting families. By the same token, and as stated earlier, virtuous families with a high sense of mission are motivated to promote their own and society's flourishing, seeing both as inherently valuable. Given these mutual responsibilities, the recommended responses are organized in these areas: (a) government policies to support families, (b) government and business cooperation to promote family-friendly work, and (c) family practices to promote the common good.

### Government Policies to Support Families

The role of government in promoting families' flourishing is broad because government is involved in many dimensions of citizens' lives. For instance, maintaining highways helps families because it helps citizens in general. The focus here, though, is on the urgent, daily needs of families like the Jenkinses, the poor families of Putnam's hometown, and all families struggling to make ends meet and raise their children in a society that presents challenges to character-formation.

*Don't seek legal shortcuts to stronger families.* Can American families be strengthened through laws? Though conservatives have promoted this idea for some time, even the liberal authors Hewlett and West argued, in 1998, that laws should encourage marrying couples to take their responsibilities more seriously and make it harder to divorce. Three states enacted "covenant marriage" in the 2000s, an option in which a marrying couple promises to seek counseling if they are considering divorce (something many separating couples do anyway) and agrees to a waiting period. But there is no evidence that this legal option did anything to change divorce rates or improve a couple's satisfaction with, or commitment to, their marriage.[64] Putnam says, after two decades of trying, such legal experiments have not worked, and so, "other than a reversal in long-established trends in private norms, or a strong and sustained economic revival concentrated on the working class, I see no clear path to reviving marriage rates among poor Americans."[65]

*Cut through the culture wars.* The "culture wars" refer to the strident red-state-versus-blue-state debates that have characterized U.S. national politics increasingly since the late 1970s. The conservative political-cultural attitude in the United States is associated with restricting or outlawing gay marriage, abortion, and teen access to contraception in the name of "defending the family." The liberal attitude is associated with the opposite, not only in the name of "individual rights" but also as a new "family values" position that respects the diversity of American family structures. These issues are too complex to address here, but, in short, the character-and-community approach favors ratcheting down the culture-war debates.[66] It is worth following the evidence regarding social capital: Putnam notes that social media campaigns directed at getting teens to avoid pregnancy have made some difference; in fact, social norms can change, because U.S. teen pregnancy is now at a historic low in the modern era.[67] Finally, while those adopting traditional virtue-ethical theories based in Western religions have argued that government must defend traditional marriage, other virtue thinkers argue that the most important social goal is to promote families with committed spouses and parents, hence that virtue ethics is perfectly compatible with same-sex marriage.[68] Supporting the latter position

---

64. In the three states that have covenant marriage—Louisiana, Arkansas, and Alabama—fewer than one percent of marrying couples have chosen the option, so any effect on divorce rates has been negligible (Sheri Stritof, "Covenant Marriage Statistics," accessed June 1, 2015, *http://marriage .about.com/od/covenantmarriage/*). For research showing that opting for a covenant marriage does *not* correlate with the spouses having greater satisfaction in their marriages as time progresses, see Alfred DeMaris et al., "Developmental Patterns in Marital Satisfaction: Another Look at Covenant Marriage," *Journal of Marriage and Family* 74, no. 5 (2012): 989–1004.

65. Putnam, *Our Kids*, 244–45.

66. Hewlett and West say they are trying to do this. Two other books that focus on alleviating culture-war issues that relate to families are, from a theological perspective, Don S. Browning et al., *From Culture Wars to Common Ground: Religion and the American Family Debate*, 2nd ed. (Louisville: Westminster John Knox Press, 2000); and, from a legal perspective, Naomi Cahn and June Carbone, *Red Families v. Blue Families: Legal Polarization and the Creation of Culture* (New York: Oxford University Press, 2010).

67. Putnam, *Our Kids*, 245–46; Child Trends Data Bank, *Teen Pregnancy: Indicators on Children and Youth*, updated May 2014, *http://www.childtrends.org/?indicators=teen-pregnancy*.

68. A virtue-based argument against same-sex marriage is Matthew R. Frank, "Religion, Reason, and Same-Sex Marriage," *First Things* (May 2011): 47–52. Virtue-based arguments for same-sex marriage are William McDonough, "Alasdair MacIntyre as Help for Rethinking Catholic Natural Law Estimates of Same-Sex Life Partnerships," *Annual of the Society of Christian Ethics* 21 (2001): 191–213; and Stephen R. Brown, "Naturalized Virtue Ethics and Same-Sex Love," *Philosophy in the Contemporary World* 13, no. 1 (Spring 2006): 41–47.

are studies and arguments indicating that children fare well in committed-couple families, straight or gay.[69]

*Strengthen the resources families need for flourishing.* Based on the reasoning that laws and tax policies are unlikely to reverse marriage rates, Putnam directs his attention to what government can do to help financially at-risk children in all forms of families. Summarized briefly, these include: (a) *expanding safety nets*, including the child tax credit, the Earned Income Tax Credit, food stamps, housing vouchers, and child care support; (b) *improving the quality of education* for American children, especially poor children; (c) *investing in poor neighborhoods* through collaborations among government and the business and nonprofit sectors; and (d) *moving poor families to better neighborhoods*, along with "intensive counseling to support the families who move."[70]

## Government and Business Cooperation to Promote Family-Friendly Work

Parents' jobs are significant for both the material resources they provide families and the impact on parents' ability to spend quality time with their children. Hewlett and West conducted a survey and found that "mothers and fathers are desperately worried about the parental time famine. This is the number-one problem in their lives."[71] Both businesses and government can shape working conditions to be more family-friendly.

*Provide decent pay and benefits for working families.* Examples of government policies that should be enacted, according to Hewlett and West, are paid parenting leave for twenty-four weeks (federal law currently requires six-weeks of unpaid leave), a ten-day paid leave from work for new fathers, and an increase in the minimum wage to a living-wage level (in 2016, a living wage was estimated to be $19 to $27 per hour for one adult and one child, depending on geographic locale, yet the federal minimum wage has been $7.25 since 2009).[72] Such improvements are unlikely if citizens wait on governments to propose them, yet community coalitions have had success in prompting changes: in recent elections, voters in four states passed laws to raise the minimum wage,

---

69. In the June 26, 2015, U.S. Supreme Court decision legalizing same-sex marriage, Justice Anthony M. Kennedy argued in the majority opinion that the children of same-sex couples are harmed "without the recognition, stability, and predictability marriage offers" (*Obergefell v. Hodges, http://www.supremecourt.gov/opinions/14pdf/14-556_3204.pdf*, p. 15). The American Sociological Association filed a brief in the case presenting evidence that children of same-sex parents fare just as well as those of different sex parents (*http://www.scotusblog.com/case-files/cases/obergefell-v-hodges/*).

70. Putnam, *Our Kids*, 246–60 and the extensive corresponding endnotes that provide supporting research. Some of these strategies are examined in chapters 6–8 of this book.

71. Hewlett and West, 232.

72. Ibid., *The War against Parents*, 233, 236, and ch. 9 as a whole. For living wage rates, see Dr. Amy K. Glasmeier's Living Wage Calculator on the Internet at *http://livingwage.mit.edu*. See also the discussion, in this chapter, of Dinan's Basic Needs Budget, which is essentially the same as a living wage calculation.

and community organizers pushed Los Angeles to raise its minimum wage to $15 an hour by 2020.[73] For businesses to provide the best level of benefits that they can reasonably afford is warranted not only on the deontological grounds of justice, but as a way to enact their character and promote the flourishing of their workers—the strategy is both sensible and virtuous (ch. 7).

*Promote family-friendly working conditions.* A wide range of options, including flex-time, telecommuting, work-sharing, and so on, have been proposed. Some initiatives are led and implemented by corporations; others require encouragement from the federal government in the form of tax breaks for companies that adopt the initiatives.[74] Part-time workers need protections, such as knowing their schedules enough in advance that they can plan for transportation and child care.[75]

*Make child care broadly available and affordable.* The authors surveyed in this chapter agree that high-quality, affordable, and flexible child care options need to be available if American children are to flourish collectively given the realities of working families.[76] Indeed, child care is a concern across income brackets. Therefore, taking child care seriously as a public good could chip away at social segregation. Mickey Kaus says, "Unlike schools, day-care centers can be conveniently located near places of work rather than near homes. . . . Let the toddlers of secretaries mix with the toddlers of bank presidents. Let their parents worry and visit together."[77] Clearly, companies could do the same (and a small proportion of the larger corporations do), regardless of government initiative.

## Family Practices to Promote the Common Good

The final set of recommendations returns to what families can do in view of their mission as promoters of the common good. Though some are similar to or the same as internal practices like socializing, volunteering, and voting, these practices are considered from the perspective of how they address external challenges and connect the family, as a group, to other families and groups.

*Think carefully about where to live.* Choices parents make about where to live, with whom to socialize, how to use family time, and how to spend money not only affect the family's character and well-being, but the ethos and

73. Shaila Dewan, "Higher Minimum Wage Passes in 4 States," *New York Times,* November 5, 2014, *http://www.nytimes.com/2014/11/05/us/politics/higher-minimum-wages-prove-popular-in-fla-marijuana-is-less-so.html*; and Jennifer Medina and Noam Scheiber, "Los Angeles Lifts Its Minimum Wage to $15 Per Hour," May 19, 2015, *New York Times, http://www.nytimes.com/2015/05/20/us/los-angeles-expected-to-raise-minimum-wage-to-15-an-hour.html.*

74. Hewlett and West, *The War against Parents,* 234–35; Cahn and Carbone, *Red Families v. Blue Families,* ch. 12.

75. Renée Loth, "When 'Flexible' Schedule Means Unpredictability," *Boston Globe,* May 28, 2015, *https://www.bostonglobe.com/opinion/2015/05/28/work-when-you-need/cXG3IWgOHfJPIx50vONIaK/story.html.*

76. Hewlett and West, *The War against Parents,* 246–51; Putnam, *Our Kids,* 248–49; Cahn and Carbone, *Red Families v. Blue Families,* 195, 198, 201.

77. Mickey Kaus, *The End of Equality,* 2nd paperback ed. (New York: Basic Books, 1995), 95.

flourishing of their communities. These factors were discussed in this chapter as internal practices, but *location* is a new consideration—one that impacts the other practices. Where to live and what kind of home to seek are choices with more substantial implications for social flourishing than people may realize. If an individual's or couple's decision about where to live is largely guided by wishes for luxury, concerns about status, or narrow considerations about their own quality of life—which are not virtuous motives—the family's character and flourishing will likely remain cramped. The neighborhoods of the well-off U.S. suburbs offer many advantages, but also there are moral risks, including the pressures to socially compete, over-consume luxury goods, and want one's kids to excel at everything. On the positive side, there are moral rewards to be found in living intentionally and modestly—rewards like family bonding, psychological health, more opportunities for connecting with neighbors.

*Educate for justice.* To practice justice and instill justice in their children, parents can do several things. A family that enjoys financial security and other social privileges should strive to remain aware of its advantages in financial and social resources. The point is not to feel guilty about one's privileges, but, in line with the virtue of critical thinking, to be aware of one's advantages, practice charity in how one thinks and talks about people with fewer advantages, and teach children to be similarly aware. This critical thinking fuels the family's practices of charity and justice. As Rubio recommends,[78] families should discuss social concerns. They should make decisions as a family about how to eat more justly, conserve scarce resources, and reduce the household's carbon footprint. Parents should consider discussing the family budget with their children and involving the children in making decisions about priorities. Age-appropriate conversations of this sort teach children about the value of money and the responsible use of resources, and they honor the children's moral agency.

*Serve.* It almost goes without saying that helping one's neighbors and volunteering as a family—as the Jenkinses do in the case study—are excellent ways to display a family's love and strengthen its community. Rubio says, "Direct service works like nothing else to increase compassion, in part through encouraging a recognition of privilege."[79] Families may also bond with other families by doing service, as through a church or civic association; the connections they develop with like-valued families can benefit themselves and their community (ch. 8).

*Be civically active and build new communities.* Despite the obstacles to democracy mentioned earlier, parents should vote, for they certainly cannot make their political community any better by *not* participating in politics. Parents should expose their children to the political process in age-appropriate

---

78. Rubio, *Family Ethics*, 146–51 (discussed in the context of her chapter on eating) and 182 (on family budget).

79. Ibid., 205.

ways: bringing the children with them to the polls and talking to their older children about politic and political issues. With the ultimate goal of helping a child develop a mature worldview and the skill of critical thinking, parents should explain to the children *why* they believe what they do, patiently and fairly presenting other perspectives as well.

Throughout this book, the wide-ranging value of civic participation is indicated; so when families do just about anything of a civic nature (and for the children, of an extracurricular nature), they contribute to social capital in a way that bridges the gaps among members of their communities. For families, there are, however, two pitfalls in civic activity of which to be aware. First, there can be too much of a good thing: the family must take care not to overcommit itself and cause its members stress. But on the positive side of this coin, Rubio says, "I notice that among my students, the ones who are really extraordinary in their faith as well as in their social justice commitments often come from families who have stepped off that busyness track."[80]

The second pitfall is becoming too inwardly focused in one's civic activities. For example, in the same interview, in response to a question about how to get Catholic families involved in service through their parishes, Rubio answers in a way that has wider implications:

> Start by asking: Are we making service a regular part of parish life for families? Is it a part of the religious education program, for example? In most parishes I'm familiar with in the Midwest, what's really central to parish life is sports. But if that's what we're doing all weekend long, then how can we possibly have time to do other things? Could we come together to create community around a nursing home instead of the soccer field?[81]

Families who want to teach their children commitment to the common good and express this in the family's lifestyle should be cognizant of how the ethos and practices of their community can become problematic. There is nothing wrong with sports and other popular activities, but families striving to maintain character might need, at times, to resist the status quo and opt out of full participation.

This approach to life, which could be called "living counterculturally," can take many forms.[82] Yet whatever form it takes, living in such a way is easier to do with the support of other like-minded families. Therefore, as a final

---

80. "Don't Focus on the Family," interview with Julie Hanlon Rubio, *U.S. Catholic* (February 2011): 36.

81. Ibid., 36.

82. In addition to *Family Ethics*, chs. 6–7, Rubio discusses family lifestyle choices in "Does Family Conflict with Community?" *Theological Studies* 58 (1997): 597–617. See also the Recommendations for Further Reading and websites at the end of this chapter.

recommendation, families may explore ways to work together for the same goals and support each other in a character-based lifestyle. It could mean working with other families in associations to improve their neighborhood's safety and livability. It could mean working in a community garden and buying from local farms and small businesses. It could mean robust participation in an ongoing form of volunteerism or social change. It could mean participating in a religious community that helps the family live more authentically and serve others. More ambitiously, it could mean bringing families together in a pro-family political movement or participating in a form of intentional community in which families adopt a simpler lifestyle and share communal responsibilities. Any family that is questioning "the busyness track" and yearning for a deeper experience of community may explore these avenues, remembering that it is better to start small than not to start at all.

## Conclusion

The family, as the fundamental social unit, is essential to the development of character and the pursuit of flourishing for everyone in society. This statement is true on a deeply personal level, for everyone starts acquiring the capabilities that lead to a flourishing life at home—whatever home is. Aristotle wrote, "It is no small matter whether one habit or the other is inculcated in us from early childhood; on the contrary, it makes a considerable difference, or, rather, all the difference."[83] The statement about the essential role of the family is also true on a larger level, for families are major contributors to social capital. Families are educators, sources of economic initiative, and stabilizing forces in neighborhoods. They can also be promoters of positive change for the common good by taking their social mission seriously. By engaging in daily practices from virtuous intentions, families become communities of compassion, respect, and purpose that model what society should become. If families receive the social supports discussed in this chapter, they will be empowered to carry on that mission.

### Questions for Review

1. Why is the family the foundational group in society?
2. In what ways do families create capabilities in children?
3. How do families develop virtues in their members?
4. What is a "practice"?

---

83. Aristotle, *Nicomachean Ethics* (1103b22–25), trans. Martin Ostwald, reprint ed. (New York: Pearson, 1999), 34–35.

5. Based on the example of eating meals together, explain another family practice.

6. What are some internal challenges facing families? Can families of all types and backgrounds experience these challenges?

7. Summarize the trends in U.S. family structure from 1960 to the current day.

8. Describe some of the economic, cultural, and political challenges facing contemporary families in the United States.

9. How do tax policies impact families' flourishing?

10. What are the "culture wars," and what do they have to do with family flourishing?

## Discussion Questions and Activities

1. This chapter presents a number of ideas about what parents can do to help their children develop good character. What do you consider to be a few of the most important things parents can do? Put another way, if a parent wants to ensure he or she is raising a child well, what is the most important advice the parent should heed?

2. Should every family have a social mission? Does your family have one, even if it is not explicitly called such? If so, what are the features of that mission?

3. Write a mission statement for yourself, or join with others to write one for your family or a club to which you belong. Suggest that your church and your employer create mission statements if they do not already have them and offer to help in writing them.

4. Does the case study of the Jenkins family effectively capture the flourishing and difficulties of contemporary middle-class American families? Explain your response.

5. What are your thoughts about the family practices recommended? Which does your own family follow? Is there anything you would add or change in this set of recommendations?

6. There has been much debate in the United States about the role of "big government." Evaluate the government's role, as presented in the chapter, in helping families. Describe what you see as the best balance between government solutions on the one hand and personal and local solutions on the other.

## Recommendations for Further Reading

Farley, Margaret A. *Personal Commitments: Beginning, Keeping, Changing*. Rev. ed. Maryknoll, NY: Orbis Press, 2013.

Farley's approach is phenomenological, meaning she closely examines commitments as people experience them. Topics include the role of love, affection, emotion, and choice in commitments; the meaning of fidelity; what happens when commitments are violated; and the ethical principle of "just love."

Hewlett, Sylvia Ann, and Cornel West. *The War against Parents*. New York: Mariner Books, 1998.

A manifesto that describes and decries the many political, legal, economic, and cultural challenges facing American middle class families. The authors sum up their recommended social agenda in a Parents' Bill of Rights.

Roche, Mary M. Doyle. *Children, Consumerism, and the Common Good*. Lanham, MD: Lexington Books, 2009.

Employs the principle of the common good to analyze the impact of consumer culture on children, in the forms of advertising and child labor. Roche also presents families and schools as groups through which children can serve the common good.

Rubio, Julie Hanlon. *Family Ethics: Practices for Christians*. Washington, DC: Georgetown University Press, 2010.

Based in Catholic theology and ethics, Rubio takes a virtue-oriented approach to examining the ethical responsibilities of families and the ways they can flourish and help society flourish.

Tough, Paul. *How Children Succeed: Grit, Curiosity, and the Hidden Power of Character*. Boston: Houghton Mifflin, 2012.

A journalistic treatment of recent efforts toward understanding how children can succeed in the face of social and family deficits. Tough summarizes what is known about the psychology and neuroscience of such traits as persistence and curiosity.

Wall, John. *Ethics in Light of Childhood*. Washington, DC: Georgetown University Press, 2010.

Wall, a philosophical and religious ethicist, believes moral theory should no longer ignore the experience of one-third of humanity. A creative argument for "childism"—applying children's experiences to ethics to further humanize it.

Wallis, Jim. *Rediscovering Values: A Moral Compass for the New Economy*. New York: Howard Books, 2010.

Wallis, a public theologian and head of the Sojourners organization (*https://sojo.net*), addresses moral, religious, and political responses to the 2007 economic recession. He concludes with "twenty moral exercises" that families, congregations, and communities may adopt.

## Websites with ideas and support for socially minded families:

Families with Purpose. *http://www.familieswithpurpose.com.*

FranklinCovey. *http://msb.franklincovey.com.*

   Resources for family mission statements.

National Parent Teacher Association. *http://www.pta.org.*

The Simplicity Collective. *http://simplicitycollective.com.*

   Ideas about practicing a simple lifestyle.

Working Families Party. *http://workingfamilies.org.*

# Schools
## Education for the Good Society

The moral responsibility of the school, and of those who conduct it, is to society.

> —*John Dewey (1859–1952), philosopher and education reformer* [1]

The public schools are the public's schools, but even more important, the children in them are—and should be thought of—as the public's children.

> —*Anne Wescott Dodd and Jean L. Konzal, education professors* [2]

---

## Chapter Overview

- indicates the importance of lifelong education for virtue and flourishing, with a focus on schooling from kindergarten through high school
- describes the benefits of schools to their members and vice versa
- describes the benefits of schools to society and the assistance society provides schools
- examines challenges to education that arise in school communities and other challenges from external economic, cultural, and political sources
- recommends, for schools and individuals, virtuous practices that respond to challenges and promote social flourishing
- identifies the policies and resources schools need to fulfill their mission

---

1. John Dewey, *Moral Principles in Education* (Carbondale, IL: Southern Illinois University Press, 1975), 7.

2. Anne Wescott Dodd and Jean L. Konzal, *How Communities Build Stronger Schools* (New York: Palgrave Macmillan, 2002), 12.

## Education Matters

In a 2012 article, *New York Times* columnist Nicholas Kristof told the story of Olly Neal, an African-American who attended an all-black elementary school in Arkansas in the 1950s, during the era of segregated schools.[3] Neal was one of thirteen children whose father had only a second-grade education. By Neal's own admission, "I was not a nice kid. I had a reputation." He remembers causing his English teacher, Mildred Grady, to cry by mouthing off to her. One day, Neal went into the school library and saw a book with a somewhat risqué cover. Intrigued, but not wanting his friends to think he would voluntarily read a book, he stole it, read it at home, and loved it. Then he snuck the book back to the library and found another title by the same author at the same place on the shelf. He stole that, read it, and twice more returned the book to the library to find another book. Neal had become hooked on reading.

As an adult, Neal became Arkansas's first African-American district attorney; he was later elected as a circuit judge and appointed as a judge on the state court of appeals. Years later he attended a reunion of his elementary school, where he met the teacher whom he made cry—Mrs. Grady. She revealed that she had seen him stealing the book in the library. She was about to stop him but realized what was happening. Instead, she drove seventy miles to the nearest big city to search for another book by that author, and she placed it on the library shelf in the hopes that Neal would come back. He did, and she did the same thing twice more.

The story of Mrs. Mildred Grady and Judge Olly Neal illustrates the importance of teachers, mentors, and other caring adults for a young person's character development. The story suggests that education matters greatly for the pursuit of flourishing. Individuals, their families, and the communities in which they become productive members feel the impact of education. The story further suggests how the ripple effects of education are significant for the well-being of society. Certainly, a society that hopes to flourish cannot ignore its duty to educate young people to the best of its ability.

Schools of all sorts—public and private, religious and secular—render a great service to the common good, due in no small part to the commitment of their staff—and teachers like Mrs. Grady. Yet students need more than character education. Students who have encountered mental or physical abuse, low parental involvement, lack of role models, learning disabilities, poverty, racism, and negative peer pressure bring many deficits into the classroom. They may be poorly prepared for school, have difficultly learning, display inappropriate behavior, and have low motivation to learn. However, the challenge is not only to individuals. The collective problem represented by the story of Neal has been labeled "the achievement gap" in American education. This term refers to the

---

3. Nicholas D. Kristof, "How Mrs. Grady Transformed Olly Neal," *New York Times*, January 22, 2012, *http://www.nytimes.com/2012/01/22/opinion/sunday/kristof-how-mrs-grady-transformed-olly-neal.html.*

disparity in performance among groups of students, especially between (a) African American and Hispanic students on one hand, and white students on the other, and (b) between students from families of lower socioeconomic status and those of higher socioeconomic status.[4] The achievement gap negatively impacts the ability of schools to promote personal and social flourishing. Reducing the gap, and eventually eliminating it, will contribute greatly to the United States becoming a more just and flourishing society.

Technical solutions to the pedagogical, cultural, economic, and political factors of the achievement gap lie beyond the scope of an analysis based in virtue ethics. What virtue ethics directs about this issue is that social institutions are responsible for developing citizens capable of pursuing flourishing and possessing the character and motivation necessary to contribute to the common good. *Character education* can be defined as: any school-instituted program, developed in cooperation with other community institutions, (a) to shape, directly and systematically, the behavior of young people by influencing the values underlying their behavior and (b) to form and transform their characters so that (c) they may flourish as members of their various communities.[5] Virtue ethics offers six general guidelines for thinking about schooling:

1. Schools are socially situated, which affects both the opportunities they offer and the challenges they face.

2. Schools have many stakeholders. Families and the political community are essential partners. Other institutions, such as nonprofits and businesses, serve a valuable supporting role.

3. Schools and their members must respect all children's dignity and honor each child's ability to contribute.

4. The social mission of schools (which is not their only mission) is to educate their students to be civic-minded, responsible members of society and, as institutions, to model the common good in their operations.

5. Schools are essential to the common good, so they require substantial support from government, primarily, as well as from the business and philanthropic sectors.

6. The details of pedagogical practice and curricula are not dictated by virtue theory, except for the basic principles that (a) education should be an

---

4. Editorial Projects in Education Research Center, "Achievement Gap," *Education Week*, updated July 7, 2011, *http://www.edweek.org/ew/issues/achievement-gap/*. The racial-ethnic disparities are considered a function of socioeconomic disparity, although there are other issues that can hamper the achievement of minority students and that require educational intervention.

5. This definition, reflecting widely accepted ideas in the field, is based on James Arthur, "Traditional Approaches to Character Education in Britain and America," in *Handbook of Moral and Character Education,* ed. Larry P. Nucci, Darcia Narvaez, and Tobias Krettenauer, 2nd ed., (New York: Routledge, 2014), 43–60, at 53 (point [a] is from Anne Lockwood, quoted by Arthur, point [b] is from Arthur, and point [c] is this author's). Both editions of the *Handbook,* which is an excellent resource, are cited often in this chapter (1st ed. was edited by Nucci and Narvaez and published in 2008).

integrated activity directed to students' holistic flourishing and incorporating character education; (b) there is value in both tradition and innovation; and (c) educators must think critically and exercise humility and other virtues to develop effective educational practices.

These guidelines frame the discussion in this chapter, which addresses both character education and the role of educational policies in remediating socio-economic inequalities. Ethical challenges having to do with character are often interconnected with challenges arising from inequality. In contemporary American debates about the quality of public education, many people take positions that overemphasize one dimension. Some say, "The problem with schools is that there is no respect and discipline. Parents are not raising their kids with good character anymore." Others counter, "Poverty affects children so much before they even get into the classroom. Rather than blame the children or their parents, society needs to give them financial assistance." Likewise, some think the model of public schooling is broken because it fails to teach character and hold children to rigorous standards, while others claim private schools and charter schools "skim off" the good students with engaged parents, leaving the public schools to deal with everyone else. In contrast to these either/or positions, the character-and-community approach suggests that ethical and structural problems go hand-in-hand, as do their solutions.

## The Shape of Education: Settings, Types of Schools, and Philosophies

*Education* and *schooling* are related but distinct terms. Education is the broad process by which people work cooperatively to develop their own and others' knowledge, skills, and character throughout the lifespan—as through family, work, service, and other settings. Schooling is the formal setting in which much, but certainly not all, education occurs. Schooling deserves its own focus because, "In a democratic society, . . . public schools serve the common good by providing the knowledge, skills, and experiences children will need to function effectively as adults in a complex world."[6]

Education is a wide-ranging activity that occurs in many settings throughout one's life. It begins with the family, which influences a person throughout his or her lifespan. Education continues, for most young people, with preschool, elementary school, and high school (some children, a small percent, are homeschooled). Many students who complete high school then attend college or university (terms that are used interchangeably in this book). In the United States currently, around 65 percent of high school seniors go on to college, but only

---

6. Dodd and Konzal, *How Communities Build Stronger Schools*, 4.

some complete their studies.[7] An increasing number of college graduates are attending graduate programs, in part because, in a competitive economy, further education is necessary for a worker to get hired and advance. Finally, education continues for many adults on the job and in other formal and informal settings. For reasons of space and focus, this chapter focuses mainly on primary (grades K–8) and secondary (grades 9–12) schools.[8]

## Public and Private Schools

The schools that students attend are of two major types, *public* (paid for in whole or part by government through tax funds and available free or at low cost to attendees) and *private* (at which attendees pay tuition), but this basic division becomes more complex depending on the level of schooling.

- *Preschools* are largely nonprofit institutions that children from low-income families may attend for free or at low-cost through government programs combined with need-based discounts offered by the schools. Some pre-schools are philanthropic and make themselves affordable for families of limited means; others are geared toward well-off families, charging tens of thousands of dollars in tuition.
- *Elementary and secondary schools* are either public institutions, free for all residents, or private institutions. Some private institutions are secular and guided by a particular educational mission and philosophy, others are oper-ated by religious groups.
- *Magnet schools* are public schools, from preschool to high school, that draw students from across a school district and sometimes from multiple districts. Magnet schools occasionally adopt a particular theme that weaves through-out their curricula, such as technology, the arts, marine science, leadership, and so on. Families must apply for magnet schools; the application process is not competitive, but places may be assigned by lottery or similar methods.
- *Charter schools* are independent schools operated by nonprofit groups or for-profit companies under a charter from a state government. As of early 2014, there were more than 6,400 charter schools in forty-two states.[9] Students can attend charters as an alternative to assigned public schools, with the

---

7. Around 34 percent of Americans have a bachelor's degree and around 40 percent have com-pleted some college. These figures are from two *New York Times* articles: Floyd Norris, "Fewer U.S. Graduates Opt for College after High School," April 25, 2014, *http://www.nytimes.com/2014/04/26 /business/fewer-us-high-school-graduates-opt-for-college.html*, and Catherine Rampell, "Data Reveal a Rise in College Degrees among Americans," June 12, 2013, *http://www.nytimes.com/2013/06/13 /education/a-sharp-rise-in-americans-with-college-degrees.html*.

8. For more on the family, see ch. 5, and for some additional attention to college and graduate schooling as these relate to work, see ch. 7.

9. Center for Education Reform, "2014 Charter School Law Rankings and Scorecard," *https:// www.edreform.com/2014/03/2014-charter-school-law-rankings-scorecard/*.

tuition paid by the public school district. The rationale for charter schools is to offer more choices to families, often in locations where the assigned public schools are considered substandard. Examples of charter schools are the Knowledge Is Power Program (KIPP),[10] the Harlem Children's Zone, Achievement First—which are all nonprofit organizations—and Academica, a for-profit corporation that runs thousands of schools in several states.

- *Colleges and universities* are divided into public, private (religious or secular), and for-profit institutions. Students attending university typically pay tuition and fees, but the cost is much lower at public institutions. Per-student costs at private institutions vary widely, depending largely on the student's financial aid package. For-profit institutions, which are mostly trade schools and nationwide online universities, are among the most expensive options for students.

Neighborhood public schools, to which children are assigned based on residency, are the setting in which most American schooling happens. But magnet, charter, and private schools—schools that parents are able to choose—cannot be overlooked. More than one-quarter of the nation's students attend them (fig. 6.1). These schools and their proponents claim the schools do a better job than

## Types of Schools American Children Attend[11]

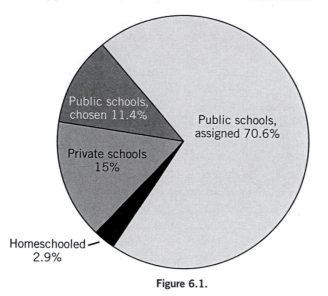

Figure 6.1.

---

10. For a profile of the KIPP schools, see Jay Mathews, *Work Hard. Be Nice.* (Chapel Hill: Algonquin Books, 2009).

11. This diagram reports the types of schools American children aged 5–17 attended in 2007. The data is from National Center for Education Statistics, "Digest of Education Statistics: Most Current Digest Tables," table 206.20, *http://nces.ed.gov/programs/digest/current_tables.asp*.

their public counterparts at educating for character *and* helping disadvantaged students overcome obstacles.

## Philosophies of Education

The ethical analysis undertaken here raises issues central to the philosophy of education. Those issues can be addressed without adopting any particular philosophy of education. There are two reasons to avoid privileging one philosophical approach. First, philosophies of education are so numerous it would be impossible to examine them in any detail in this chapter. The term "philosophy of education" refers to two groups of approaches:

1. *Comprehensive.* A comprehensive perspective on human nature, the nature of knowledge, ethics, and the nature of society support a systematic account of the nature and goals of education. The palate of options is almost as diverse as the field of philosophy itself, since most philosophers throughout the ages commented, at least briefly, on educational topics.

2. *Methodological.* This approach involves teaching practices, curricular content, and school organization. Examples include Montessori and Waldorf schools, classical "great books" education, Deweyan progressive education, Catholic parochial education, and so on.

Investigation of philosophies of education in both senses is a worthy enterprise, but it cannot be done justice here.[12]

The second reason to leave educational philosophies to the side is that, since contemporary society includes a diversity of educational options, there is no sense in trying to harmonize them. Diversity in fundamental philosophical perspectives is ethically acceptable, as long there is a general social consensus about the key features of a schooling approach. One of those features is that character education is a necessary part of schooling. Diversity in approaches to teaching and structuring schools is also ethically acceptable, as long as the essential tasks of education are done well and justly.

Therefore, virtue ethics is a perspective that can be combined with many philosophies of education by applying the six guidelines presented in the introductory section of this chapter. Among these guidelines, it is worth emphasizing

---

12. A commentary on the complexity of the field is D. C. Phillips and Harvey Siegel, "Philosophy of Education," *Stanford Encyclopedia of Philosophy*, Winter 2013 ed., *http://plato.stanford.edu/archives/win2013/entries/education-philosophy/*. For a good overview of philosophies of education in the primarily comprehensive sense, see Nel Noddings, *Philosophy of Education*, 3rd ed. (Boulder, CO: Westview, 2011). Philosophies of educational methodolody are surveyed in many education textbooks; see, for instance, Kevin Ryan and James M. Cooper, *Those Who Can, Teach*, 13th ed. (Belmont, CA: Wadsworth, Cengage Learning, 2012), ch. 9, which categorizes philosophies as primarily content-centered or student-centered.

two points that lie at the heart of the character-and-community approach. First, education should be an integrated activity directed to students' holistic flourishing, incorporating character education. Second, schools can be virtuous communities that contribute to the common good by developing virtues and capabilities in students, but they require the support of other civic groups and government to do their task well. In other words, schools are among the important institutions that mediate between persons and society.

## Schools and Their Members

The two main relationships in the community connections chart are of persons to groups and groups to society (fig. 6.2). A consideration of relationship number 1 involves describing the contributions of schools to character and flourishing. As in all the chapters, the description of the benefits that occur between groups and their members is not universal—for many schools are flawed—but is an indication of what is possible when the group and its members abide by ethical standards.

### Schools and Members

**Figure 6.2.** Community Connections: A School and Its Members

## Education Promotes Capabilities and Character

The word *education* is based on the Latin for "to lead out." A teacher draws out a student's inchoate skills, developing them and adding more skills to lead the student to greater knowledge and capability. This leading-out process is directed toward a goal: that a student becomes happier, healthier, and more capable of flourishing and contributing to society. Education must be directed toward developing the student's practical and conceptual reasoning; physical, mental, and emotional health; ability to relate to others interpersonally and socially; and character traits. In other words, education is directed to the four domains identified in chapter 3: mind, body, relationships, and character. Since persons are whole beings, these capabilities are overlapping and mutually reinforcing.

## Mind and Body

The most obvious capability that education targets is the intellect. Schooling helps students acquire the knowledge that makes them well-rounded persons who understand their world and appreciate the riches of their cultural tradition. The basic skills at the center of primary schooling have been popularly called "the Three R's": reading, writing, and arithmetic. Toward the end of the twentieth century, a slightly different "big three" skill set gained prominence as a way to assess American students in comparison to each other and to students internationally: reading, math, and science. These core subjects are part of a deeper tradition in Western culture, originating from the same Greco-Roman culture that generated virtue ethics. The "liberal arts" refer to an education that promotes a student's freedom (the meaning of the word "liberal" in this phrase) by giving him or her the knowledge and skills for thinking critically, developing insights, and being a mature participant in a free society. The classical liberal arts immerse students in literature, the arts, math, and science.[13] Today the liberal arts encompass these and similar subject areas (including history, social sciences, philosophy, theology and religious studies, and foreign languages) as well as fundamental skills of reasoning that traverse subjects: critical thinking, quantitative reasoning, public speaking, critical reasoning, and effective writing.[14] The goal of a liberal education is to gain a deep, effective understanding of truths about the world and human nature.

Some virtues focus on excellence in reasoning. Formal as well as informal education develops the five capabilities of reasoning that Aristotle examines in book 6 of the *Nicomachean Ethics*—"craft, scientific knowledge, prudence, wisdom, and understanding."[15] Common to all five virtues is that they are directed toward attaining the truth. While much could be said about the philosophical notion of moral truth, both in Aristotle's time and today, the bottom line for Aristotle is quite simple: making moral decisions must be based on good thinking that is responsive to the truths of the world. As philosopher Sarah Broadie puts it, "The truth of a choice is its distinctive excellence as an articulate product of thought."[16]

---

13. The seven subjects classified as liberal arts in the classical era were grammar, rhetoric, logic, arithmetic, geometry, musical theory, and astronomy.

14. For more exploration of the liberal arts, see Fareed Zakaria, *In Defense of a Liberal Education* (New York: W. W. Norton, 2015) and Mark William Roche, *Why Choose the Liberal Arts?* (Notre Dame, IN: University of Notre Dame Press, 2010).

15. Aristotle, *Ethics* 6.3 (1139b17). Space does not allow an explanation of these five virtues, but see ch. 2 for an explanation of prudence. Aristotle reduces these five to two master virtues: wisdom and prudence. For an explanation of his moves, which can be difficult to follow, see Anthony Kenny's commentary in the introduction to Aristotle, *Eudemian Ethics* (New York: Oxford University Press, 2001), xvii–xxii.

16. Sarah Broadie, *Ethics with Aristotle* (New York: Oxford University Press, 1991), 224 (italics removed). Her ch. 5, esp. 219–25, gives a good explanation of Aristotle's account of truth as it relates to ethics.

The body is a second domain of personal well-being. Schooling promotes physical health and skills in several ways—from recess to gym classes to health classes. Schools also pay attention to whether children are getting healthy meals and enough to eat. All states have programs to provide free or reduced-cost breakfast and lunch for low-income students.

## Relationships

Relationships are a third domain of flourishing. The ability to relate well to others, both peers and adults, is promoted throughout schooling, in part by programs for social-emotional intelligence. Schools set baselines for relationships through rules and codes that require respectful speaking, a prohibition on fighting, and so on. Students or employees who violate the rules can face various punishments. These deontological and consequentialist approaches work best when complemented by a virtue approach, which, arguably, should be foremost. For example, teachers must show respect in word and action to students if they want the children to do the same toward teachers and peers. School is also an important setting for creating friendships, learning how to maintain them, and dealing with their changing nature. Schools help students become better at being friends by ensuring that children are learning social-emotional intelligence and respect.

## Character

Education is properly directed to moral education as one of its goals; indeed, no method of education is free of moral implications. But what role do schools play as moral educators? Philosopher Robert Adams helpfully approaches this question by proposing that virtue-based moral education has three main "sets of tasks" that he characterizes as "elementary, modular, and integrative."

The elementary tasks "consist very largely in initiation into social practices and the conventions that govern them."[17] By conventions, Adams means the basic rules and virtues that govern any workable society. For example, it is generally wrong to lie, it is good to be kind, and so on. By social practices, he is thinking, in part, of the kinds of practices within which families engage, as discussed in chapter 5. He also means the process by which children learn to give reasons for their actions, accept the reasons of other people, pay attention to their own and other's feelings, and learn how to disagree with others.[18] Children's capacities for these tasks are developed at home but also in school, especially in preschool and early elementary school.

---

17. Robert Merrihew Adams, *A Theory of Virtue: Excellence in Being for the Good* (New York: Oxford University Press, 2006), 213.

18. Ibid., 214–16.

The second set of tasks is called modular, referring to the contexts and social roles—such as student, teammate, club participant, employee, or volunteer—in which people learn specific virtues. Adams comments, "If one is to learn virtue, Aristotle thinks, one must when young be led by one's teachers to perform, repeatedly, noble actions. In this way one is not only to learn how to do such actions; one is also to find pleasure in doing them and shame in failing to do them, and thus come to be autonomously motivated to do them."[19] This habituation—through repetition, under the guidance of adults, with praise and blame attached—is what much of the behavioral training of the early years of school is about. Children thus learn traits of respect, cooperation, timeliness, and so on. Even in high school and college, teachers strive to train students to do similar things at a higher level of sophistication and with more subtle inducements.

The goal of virtue-based education is that a person comes to unite his or her elementary and modular virtues into a comprehensive character. This is Adams's third, or integrative, task of moral education. It is also a particularly challenging goal, one that takes a long time and is perhaps never fully achieved. Adams says, "Moral integration is an inherently difficult task for which we have no 'sure fire' method. . . . We are unlikely to find *totally* integrated people."[20] Integration is largely in the hands of the individual, who must engage in ongoing self-examination with a willingness to work on the flaws in his or her character.

Though integration is a personal project, one's schooling can lend support for it. Some families enroll their children in religious schools for this reason, believing that such a school maintains a comprehensive culture that helps a student achieve an integrated character. It is true that religious schools strive to do this, but efforts at integrated character education are not limited to them. Although it may not be well known, public schools can and do teach moral development. Currently, thirty-six of the United States have laws mandating or encouraging character education.[21] These laws reflect what appears to be a large public consensus favoring that schools teach values such as honesty, respect, and democracy.[22] Whether or not a school explicitly thinks of itself as engaging in character education, every school, in fact, teaches its students virtues and lessons about character every day. Thus schools would do well make their character education formal and intentional, such as by following the principles recommended by the Character Education Partnership (table 6.1).

---

19. Ibid., 217.

20. Ibid., 230.

21. For updated information, see Character Education Partnership, "Character Education Legislation," accessed January 31, 2015, *http://character.org/more-resources/character-education-legislation/*.

22. More than 90 percent of the general public and nearly 80 percent of students support values education in surveys conducted by Public Agenda (*First Things First* [New York, 1994], 24–27, and *Getting By* [New York, 1997], 29, both at *http://www.publicagenda.org*).

**TABLE 6.1 The Character Education Partnership's Eleven Principles of Effective Character Education**

| |
|---|
| 1. promotes core values |
| 2. defines "character" to include thinking, feeling, and doing |
| 3. uses a comprehensive approach |
| 4. creates a caring community |
| 5. provides students with opportunities for moral action |
| 6. offers a meaningful and challenging academic curriculum |
| 7. fosters students' self-motivation |
| 8. engages staff as a learning community |
| 9. fosters shared leadership |
| 10. engages families and community members as partners |
| 11. assesses the culture and climate of the school |

## Schools Flourish because of Their Participants and Stakeholders

Not only do schools contribute to the well-being of their members, but individual members contribute to the well-being of the institution, making the dynamic of flourishing mutual and synergistic. There are several participants and stakeholders in a school, each of whom is crucial to the school's success.

*Teachers* are crucial because they spend significant time with children. It is not the time per se that is so important, but the personal encounter in which the student can come to know that the teacher is a knowledgeable guide who truly cares. Anecdotally, adults attribute significance to past teachers whom they found particularly committed and effective, as in, for example, the story of Neal and Mrs. Grady. Parents see that a committed teacher who connects with their child makes a difference in the child's enjoyment of school and willingness to learn. When teachers are able to improve student outcomes, the children are likely to do better down the road in many ways. Efforts to measure the effectiveness of teachers are controversial, but, of the factors under a school's direct control, the quality of teachers matters the most.[23]

*Staff and administrators* are another important part of the equation. Principals receive the greatest focus, as they hire and mentor teachers and set the overall tone and agenda for a school. "The simple fact is that without effective leaders most of the goals of educational improvement will be very difficult to achieve."[24] The principal plays a big role in setting the school's culture, certainly not by creating it single-handedly, but by encouraging everyone to take the school's culture seriously and inviting all into a process of improving it. Employees, from the front office to the library to the cafeteria, should be committed to the welfare of the children.

*Students*. Learning is a social activity, so the students have an ongoing influence on each other and the teacher. Children bring vitality, playfulness, and curiosity to the school day. Their impact on each other is significant—which is why their behavior has to be managed well by teachers and schools.

*Families*. As much as it is true that teachers are a major influence on the child's education, clearly the family is also—by influencing everything that happens outside the school day. The social skills, character, knowledge base, and emotional and physical health that a child receives from home greatly influence how he or she learns and behaves in school. Families are the key partners with teachers, so channels of communication must be open. Families help the school through attending meetings, communicating with teachers, volunteering for school events, and supporting fundraisers as their budget allows.

*Members of the local community* are also involved—adults and older students volunteer in the school, business owners donate goods and services, and so on. These persons and groups help the school carry out its multifaceted mission. As has been seen, character-education experts generally believe that community members are crucial partners with the schools in the task of moral education.[25]

## Schools and Society

Turning to relationship number 2 (fig. 6.3), schools contribute to society materially and ethically, and from society they receive assistance that makes their contributions possible.

23. RAND Corporation, "Teachers Matter: Understanding Teachers' Impact on Student Achievement," accessed January 23, 2015, *http://www.rand.org/education/projects/measuring-teacher-effectiveness/teachers-matter.html*.

24. The Wallace Foundation, "Five Key Responsibilities—The School Principal as Leader: Guiding Schools to Better Teaching and Learning," accessed January 23, 2015, *http://www.wallacefoundation.org/knowledge-center/school-leadership/effective-principal-leadership/Pages/key-responsibilities-the-school-principal-as-leader.aspx*.

25. Dodd and Konzal are one example; the definition of character education from Arthur and Lockwood is another. See also *Handbook*, ed. Nucci et al., 2nd ed., part 5, "Moral and Character Education beyond the Classroom."

## Schools and Society

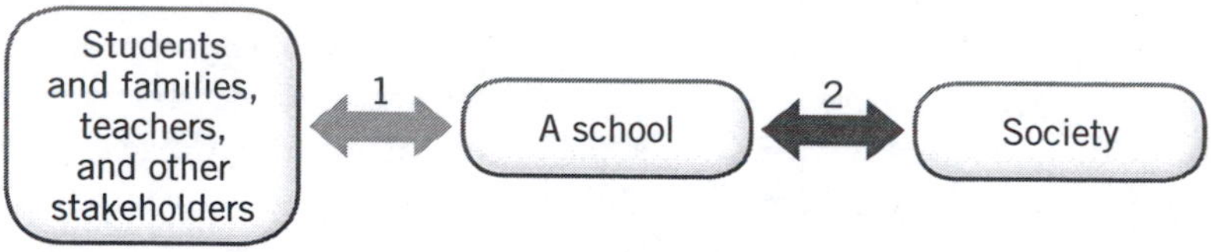

**Figure 6.3.** Community Connections: A School and Society

# Schools Contribute to Society, Increasing Social Capital for All

Good schools make a community a more enjoyable place to live. The quality of schools encourages families with children, or that plan to have children, to move to an area. Many positive ripples flow from this residential decision: a better property tax base, more jobs, and increased participation in community affairs. Families with children in local schools are likely to be concerned about traffic safety, the quality of parks, and other matters. Some families will make efforts to see that resources are in place by volunteering, voting, and attending public meetings. These comments are consistent with the theory of social capital presented by Robert Putnam, which indicates that when citizens are actively involved in groups and institutions, such as schools, they are more likely to contribute to society, and that the entire social fabric becomes stronger.[26]

Children whose schooling includes robust character education are more likely to be moral, contributing members of their communities. There is mounting evidence that students who participate in ongoing, integrated, evidence-based character education programs in schools show measurable, positive effects in their sexual behavior, knowledge of character, socio-moral cognition, problem-solving skills, and emotional competency.[27] "Comprehensive, high quality character education . . . is not only effective at promoting the development of good character, but is a promising approach to the prevention of a wide range of contemporary problems. These include aggressive and anti-social behaviors, drug use, precocious sexual activity, criminal activities, academic under-achievement, and school failure."[28] Moreover, students who participate in

---

26. Robert D. Putnam, *Bowling Alone* (New York: Simon & Schuster, 2000). See chs. 3–5.

27. Marvin W. Berkowitz et al., "What Works in Character Education: What Is Known and What Needs to Be Known," in *Handbook*, ed. Nucci and Narvaez, 1st ed., 422.

28. Victor Battistich, "Character Education, Prevention, and Positive Youth Development," white paper (Character Education Partnership, 2011), 1, *http://www.character.org/wp-content/uploads/2011/12/White_Paper_Battistich.pdf*.

community service[29] and extracurricular activities are more likely, as adults, to be active, constructive members of their civic community. Putnam points to a study showing that "regardless of the students' social class, academic background, and self-esteem, those who took part in voluntary associations in school were far more likely than nonparticipants to vote, take part in political campaigns, and discuss public issues two years after graduating."[30] It is likely that these students, as adults, will take at least some of the traits developed in their character education to their workplaces, churches, and civic associations.

Schooling is important for the overall health of a nation's economy. People who complete college (and those who complete any graduate schooling) develop advanced skills that financially benefit not only themselves but their employers and the economy. From an economic standpoint, a country wants (or should want) its citizens to attain a high school education.[31] That education should adequately prepare students for high-tech and well-paying jobs and for college. Since each level of schooling builds on the next, the economic implications of education filter down to the earliest years. According to the Paris-based Organisation for Economic Co-operation and Development (OECD), "There are enormous economic gains to be had by . . . countries that can improve the cognitive skills of their populations."[32] To fifteen-year-olds in countries around the world, the OECD administers a triennial exam on math, science, and reading (known as PISA) on which students in several Asian and Northern European countries perform well, and on which American students perform below the global average. OECD predicts that if all countries raise their average score by twenty-five points during the next twenty years—which means, for instance, that U.S. scores on math would match current scores in Austria, Ireland, Australia, and Vietnam—there will be a gain of $115 trillion in the countries' combined gross domestic products "over the lifetime of the generation born in 2010."[33]

---

29. Daniel Hart et al., "The Moral and Civic Effects of Learning to Serve," in *Handbook*, ed. Nucci et al., 2nd ed., 456–70. The authors present evidence of the benefits of service learning at the high school level as well as evidence that its effects may not be as long-lasting as proponents claim. Therefore, they say, more longitudinal studies are needed and character educators should be cautious about seeing service learning as a panacea.

30. Putnam, *Bowling Alone*, 339.

31. The national average for high-school completion reached 80 percent in 2012, and the rate continues to rise (Niraj Chokshi, "For the First Time, The U.S. High School Graduation Rate Tops 80 Percent, Report Finds," *Washington Post*, April 28, 2014). However, currently, only twenty-three states and the District of Columbia make education compulsory until age eighteen (National Conference of State Legislatures, "Upper Compulsory School Age," updated January 14, 2014, *http://www.ncsl.org /research/education/upper-compulsory-school-age.aspx*).

32. OECD, "Country Note: United States," 2012 PISA results, 7, *http://www.oecd.org/united-states/PISA-2012-results-US.pdf.* "PISA" stands for Programme for International Student Assessment. Those testing in the program are Russia, all the countries of Europe, most of the countries of North and South America, and most of the countries of East Asia.

33. OECD, "The High Cost of Low Educational Performance: The Long-Run Economic Impact of Improving PISA Outcomes," 2010, 27, *http://www.oecd.org/pisa/44417824.pdf.*

## Society Assists Schools Materially and Ethically

In the other direction, society supports schools through the material and ethical assistance given by a number of social institutions. Government figures prominently, since tax monies make the bulk of American education possible and, in the modern world, education is seen as a basic human right to be ensured by governments.[34] State, local, and federal governments fund, support, and structure education.

- Education laws start at the state level. State governments authorize public schools, set standards and policies for them, and decide what kinds of nonpublic schools can offer education under certain standards. State and local governments are the largest sources of revenue for public schools, at 44 percent each (fig. 6.4). States also supervise higher education and fund state universities, at which many of tomorrow's teachers are trained.

- Local governments create school districts and provide a large proportion of funding for public schools, through property taxes. Boards of education supervise district budgets, hire superintendents, oversee curricula, and set policies. Boards of education are elected, so public education is ultimately accountable to local citizens.

- The federal government has taken an increasingly prominent role in public education since the creation of the U.S. Department of Education under President Jimmy Carter in 1979. The Department establishes policies, distributes funds, conducts research, and leads policy conversations on America's schools. Congress provides funding to states for education and creates laws pertaining to education, such as Title IX (1972), which forbids gender-discrimination in education and school sports programs, and the No Child Left Behind Act (2001), which created standards for closing the achievement gap.

Government also directly supports citizens seeking education. For starters, public school is free from kindergarten through grade twelve. Some districts also have free part-day or all-day preschool. The federal program Head Start supports school-readiness through a variety of activities, including preschool, for children from poor families who are under age five. Districts often provide free busing for children who live some distance from school.[35] Public schools provide additional services for students with learning disabilities and

---

34. *The Universal Declaration of Human Rights* (1949) states, "Everyone has the right to education. Education shall be free, at least in the elementary and fundamental stages. Elementary education shall be compulsory. Technical and professional education shall be made generally available and higher education shall be equally accessible to all on the basis of merit" (Article 26.1, *http://www .un.org/en/documents/udhr/*).

35. Note that the ability of districts to provide preschool and busing varies; not every district can afford these services.

## Sources of Revenue for U.S. Schools[36]

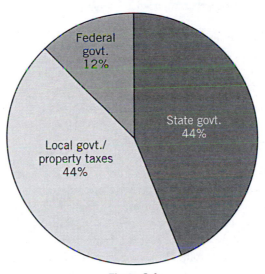

**Figure 6.4.**

other special needs, and sometimes more intensive and specialized services, following federal law.[37]

These services are all part of public education, whereas parents choosing private schools must pay tuition and fees. Under education reform efforts of the past twenty-five years, some states and districts have provided support to families choosing non-public options, like charter schools. Thirteen states and the District of Columbia have voucher programs that give families a tuition scholarship to take to any school, including a religious school. The eligibility standards vary, but all focus on students who are low-income, have certain disabilities, or go to a low-performing public school.[38] The programs have survived legal challenges but remain controversial.[39]

---

36. National Center for Education Statistics, "Revenues and Expenditures for Public Elementary and Secondary School Districts: School Year 2010–11," September 2013, *https://nces.ed.gov/pubsearch /pubsinfo.asp?pubid=2013344*.

37. The Individuals with Disabilities Education Act 1990 (IDEA) was a groundbreaking law to ensure that children with disabilities receive an equal education. IDEA is widely praised, but Congress is often criticized for failing to provide sufficient funding to cover the services mandated under IDEA. See Daveen Rae Kurutz and Patrick Varine, "Debate Brews over Formula to Pay for Special Education," *Trib Live Neighborhoods* (Pittsburgh), May 21, 2014, *http://triblive.com /neighborhoods/alleghenyneighborhoods/alleghenyneighborhoodsmore/6062976-74/special-education-state - axzz3kbtH9JgW*.

38. National Conference of State Legislatures, "School Voucher Laws: State-By-State Comparison," as of January 2014, *http://www.ncsl.org/research/education/voucher-law-comparison.aspx*.

39. Larry Abramson, "School Voucher Debate Heats Back Up," National Public Radio, May 6, 2011, *http://www.npr.org/2011/05/06/136055744/school-voucher-debate-heats-back-up*.

Each state runs a system of higher education, usually featuring major research universities, a range of other universities, and two-year community colleges. These options are more affordable for residents than private school tuition or out-of-state public tuition. (However, the share of college costs students pay has been rising throughout the past two decades.[40]) States have created investment plans called 529s that help families save for college. The federal government supports grants, low-interest loans, and tuition credits for college students and other family members. Some states have done an ambitious job of expanding college access to all residents regardless of income level; the model initiative here is Georgia's HOPE program.

Finally, and briefly, two other major sectors of society help schools flourish—business and philanthropy. Businesses often donate money and services to schools. Other connections may involve a company providing internships or a company's employees volunteering in a school, such as through tutoring. The philanthropic sector encompasses a range of nonprofit organizations—in addition to schools themselves—that support schools through direct service, such as tutoring and running afterschool programs; providing family services such as nutrition aid, health care, testing for special needs, and advising parents on educational services; conducting education policy analysis; and advocating for policy changes. Philanthropic organizations include local volunteer organizations, such as tutoring and mentoring organizations and PTAs; state and regional foundations; and national foundations such as the National Schools Foundation Association, the Wallace Foundation, Edutopia, and the Bill and Melinda Gates Foundation. Interesting and transformative collaborations between schools, businesses, and nonprofits have been developed (ch. 8).

It is clear by now that Dodd and Konzol's statement from the start of this chapter—"the public schools are the public's schools"[41]—is both a descriptive and a moral statement. Factually speaking, the public is heavily invested in the educational system, supporting it through taxes and charitable support. In return, all citizens, even those who do not have school-aged children, benefit from the work of schools. Ethically speaking, schools are at the service of society and, reciprocally, society, both its institutions and citizens, have a duty to support the schools. Since society gains much from its educational system, this duty ought not be seen as burdensome, but as a path to greater happiness and well-being for everyone.

---

40. Tim Haab, "Is It Time to Redefine 'Public' in Public Education?" *Environmental Economics* (blog), August 18, 2014, *http://www.env-econ.net/2014/08/is-it-time-to-redefine-public-in-public-education.html*, citing the Chronicle of Higher Education's *Almanac of Higher Education 2014.*

41. Dodd and Konzal, *How Communities Build Stronger Schools*, 12.

# Challenges within Schools and Virtuous Responses

Having examined the benefits of schools for their members and society, it is important to consider how education for character and flourishing can occur in the face of myriad challenges. Internal challenges are ones that, although influenced by external forces, must be primarily responded to within the school. It is worthwhile remembering that the internal and external can never be neatly separated; indeed, in education, the two realms impact each other continuously, as can be seen in the following case study.

## Resistant and Receptive Students—A Case Study

Makayla attends college on a suburban campus.[42] As a requirement of her course on ethics, she is participating in service learning by volunteering at Lincoln High School, located in the nearby city. Lincoln's student body is almost entirely of minority background, about half Hispanic or Latino and almost half African American with just a few students who are Asian or white. Makayla helps out in Ms. Bennett's freshman math classes as a tutor, helping small groups of students with problems after the teacher has taught the lesson to the entire class. Ms. Bennett is in her second year of teaching at the school, which is her first full-time job after getting her teaching degree. Makayla reflects on her experiences in journals that she writes for her professor, saying she believes she has led a sheltered life, because she was surprised at the attitudes of the students. "Many of them are reluctant to get help and would rather sit there alone and listen to music or talk with their neighbor about personal issues. Some of the students who are willing to receive help only want it because they think that I will do their work for them. Once they found out that's not my role, they suddenly have no interest in working." When Ms. Bennett warned one student that she should stop talking and pay attention because a test was coming up, the student responded by saying, "Miss, I don't care about what you're teaching. I don't want to learn and I don't care if I get an F."

By contrast, Makayla has found several students among Ms. Bennett's classes who are interested in being helped, so she focuses on them. During the semester, she saw the grades of one of her regular students, Jordon, move from C- to B. Makayla observed that Ms. Bennett did not have time in class to give enough individual attention to students such as Jordon. At the end of the semester, Jordon gave Makayla a note thanking her for all she did for him and expressing hope that she would come back to volunteer next term.

---

42. This case study is modeled on the service-learning experiences of the author's own students. Individual cases have been combined and names and identifying features changed, but the quotations are from actual students' papers and journals.

One afternoon in the middle of the semester, Makayla ate lunch in the faculty lounge with several teachers. The teachers were talking about their day so far, and all were frustrated. Makayla wrote, "They spoke of the disrespect and attitude problems they got from students. But, although they seemed upset about it, they were all willing to move on and try to make the students want to learn." These experiences left Makayla with conflicting thoughts and many questions. Before the semester started, she had been thinking about teaching as a career. She was inspired by Jordan's progress and felt good about the help she had given him. Yet, at the same time, she felt daunted by the resistance and resignation of other students. Makayla wonders how she could possibly survive a year as a teacher in a school like Lincoln High.

## Internal Challenges

The case study illustrates several challenges facing schools and their members. The following challenges are highly relevant in examining the relationship between character and community.

*Behavioral discipline and low academic performance.* Students bring the challenges of their home life and the deficits of their community to school, making the educational experience more challenging for all. Lincoln High is such a school. Makayla observed firsthand that many students in the classroom were not doing well in school and did not feel that they could do well. Though only freshmen, some had already given up, such as the girl who said, "I don't care if I get an F." Nationwide statistics on disruptive student behaviors in the classroom are hard to come by, but data does show that students who are suspended are disproportionately male, students of color, students with learning disabilities, and students who are not native English speakers.[43] These results suggest that low socioeconomic status (SES) is a risk factor for problematic behavior but, more so, is one that disposes a student to receive a more severe punishment.[44] Civil-rights and child-rights advocates are concerned that disadvantaged students are suspended and expelled to an unfair degree.[45]

---

43. U.S. Department of Education Office for Civil Rights, "Civil Rights Data Collection: Data Snapshot (School Discipline)," Issue Brief No. 1 (March 21, 2014), *http://ocrdata.ed.gov/Downloads/CRDC-School-Discipline-Snapshot.pdf.*

44. Sheryl A. Hemphill et al., "Are Rates of School Suspension Higher in Socially Disadvantaged Neighbourhoods? An Australian Study," *Health Promotion Journal of Australia* 21, no. 1 (April 2010): 12–18.

45. Russell J. Skiba, "Where Should We Intervene? Contributions of Behavior, Student, and School Characteristics to Suspension and Expulsion," research paper presented at "Closing the School Discipline Gap Conference," April 5, 2013, *http://civilrightsproject.ucla.edu/resources/projects/center-for-civil-rights-remedies/school-to-prison-folder/state-reports/copy_of_dignity-disparity-and-desistance-effective-restorative-justice-strategies-to-plug-the-201cschool-to-prison-pipeline.*

*Teacher support.* The job of teachers in schools like Lincoln is highly challenging. Young teachers such as Ms. Bennett have fewer options when seeking a job, so they are more likely than seasoned teachers to end up at schools like Lincoln High. Burnout is a risk, so there is a high turnover rate, and then more young Ms. Bennetts fill the gap. Thus schools are likely to put the most inexperienced teachers in the most challenging classrooms. Journalist Joe Nocera illustrates this problem when he interviewed three sisters who are teachers. The sisters, ranging in age from 28 to 38, had all started in urban classrooms but went on to teach in different settings—one in an urban primary school, one in an urban charter school, and one in a suburban primary school. Nocera was struck by a similarity among the sisters' diverse teaching careers: "All three sisters felt that they had been unprepared to stand in front of an urban classroom when they first became teachers."[46] They had not done enough student teaching in urban settings and had not received good preparation on how to manage the challenges they would face there. High-poverty schools hire an estimated seventy thousand new teachers every year, and 50 percent of all beginning teachers leave the profession within five years.[47] These trends indicate that the Ms. Bennetts of American public education need daily support within their schools, and the Makaylas of American colleges need to be reassured that they will be well prepared to enter classrooms like the one at Lincoln. Too many young teachers and prospective teachers are not finding this support.

*Character education.* It seems that the problem Ms. Bennett is facing is that some of her students have poor character. While this may be true, ethical analysis aims to understand why. Students who are not trying to learn have deficits of persistence, fortitude, and hope: They *don't believe* that they *can* learn. Such youth have received signals—perhaps from home, peers, or even teachers—that there is no point in trying. David Banks, the president of a charter school network, writes, "Parents who once struggled in school themselves may have lost faith that education can make a difference. . . . Teachers can be just as negative. I can't count the number of times I've been invited by a principal to speak at a struggling school, only to have the principal confide in me, *My teachers don't even believe in these kids.*"[48]

The question is whether schools can do something about these negative forces acting on children. Is character education the answer? Despite the claims made earlier, that most schools do teach moral development, rigorous studies of character education programs yield mixed results. Daniel Lapsley and David

46. Joe Nocera, "Three Sisters (Not Chekhov's)," *New York Times*, September 27, 2013, *http://www.nytimes.com/2013/09/28/opinion/three-sisters-not-chekhovs.html*.

47. Dana Goldstein, *The Teacher Wars: A History of America's Most Embattled Profession* (New York: Doubleday, 2014), 7–8.

48. David C. Banks with G. F. Lichtenberg, *Soar: How Boys Learn, Succeed, and Develop Character* (New York: Atria, 2014), 13.

Yeager evaluated the programs included in the Department of Education's What Works Clearinghouse (WWC), which "catalogs empirical evidence on the efficacy of a wide variety of educational curricula and interventions, including character education."[49] To be included in the WWC, a character education intervention must pass an exacting protocol. According to Lapsley and Yeager,

> The first thing to notice is that after decades of visibility as an educational priority, only 13 character programs make the evidentiary cut to be included in the WWC. The second thing to notice is how thin the evidence is for character education—only five of 13 programs are at least potentially efficacious in influencing knowledge, attitudes and values; only three influence behavior, and just one program influences academic achievement.[50]

This observation raises the question of whether public schools in high-poverty areas, under immense pressure to raise student test scores, have anything to gain by devoting precious instructional time to character education.

## Responses to Internal Challenges

The responses to internal challenges come from individuals within school communities and schools as institutions. Drawing upon virtues is at the heart of ethical practices that promote character and flourishing.

### Teachers

Recall Mrs. Grady. She engaged young Olly Neal in an instance of character education. Grady's action would have been welcomed by John Dewey, who wrote, "The introduction of every method that appeals to the child's active powers, to his capacities in construction, production, and creation, marks an opportunity to shift the center of ethical gravity from an absorption which is selfish to a service which is social."[51] Grady let Neal's curiosity drive him and let him take responsibility for his own learning. She couldn't be sure he wouldn't keep or read the book, but her hunch was right; he even brought the book back to the library. Grady's approach reflects a prudence that she likely showed regularly in her teaching.

This story suggests that educating for character is best accomplished when it is woven into regular educational practice. Lapsley and Yeager survey two main delivery mechanisms for character education—direct and indirect

---

49. Daniel K. Lapsley and David Yeager, "Moral-Character Education," in *Handbook of Psychology*, vol. 7, *Educational Psychology*, ed. William M. Reynolds and Gloria E. Miller (Hoboken, NJ: Wiley & Sons, 2013), 147–78, at 162–63.

50. Ibid., 164.

51. Dewey, *Moral Principles in Education*, 26.

methods.[52] Traditional interventions involve direct instruction; in these mechanisms, the teacher overtly tells students what character traits are valued and what actions are expected, on the assumption that children do not know how to behave. Indirect or "stealthy" interventions assume that children know, at some level, the right ways to act and are motivated to do so but encounter barriers that prevent them. There is good evidence that direct methods can backfire but that indirect methods are effective, especially with older children. Indirect methods "have the advantage of being 'small' and minimally invasive, which is useful for promoting internalization, avoiding stigmatization," and encouraging a teen to resist peer pressure. "By avoiding direct persuasion and instead harnessing and re-directing the forces already acting on an adolescent's behavior, they [teachers] may produce more lasting behavioral change."[53]

As applied by Ms. Bennett, the direct approach of telling a student that the student was risking an F was ineffective. An indirect approach could be one in which she shows the student the immediate, internal reward of mastering a particular skill, and in which she arranges student groups so students such as Jordon are modeling behaviors for the others. Lest teachers feel the task is overwhelming, Lapsley and Yeager give a helpful reminder, based in research: "Becoming an effective character educator does not require a substantially larger or different tool box of instructional practices than what is required to be an effective educator."[54]

## Schools and Administrators

Recent years have seen efforts to bring systematization and better research to the field of character education. Many scholars work on the topic, many professional organizations and foundations promote it, and many schools across the country have programs for it. In 2008, the *Handbook of Moral and Character Education* included a chapter arguing that many early and even recent efforts at character education lacked a solid research base.[55] However, this situation is changing for the better as more studies have been conducted on what approaches work. By the time the second edition of the *Handbook* was released in 2014, Marvin Berkowitz and Melinda Bier saw an exponential increase in studies and meta-analyses on character education methods, as approaches such as the Eleven Principles were adopted.[56] The recent research suggests schools

52. Lapsley and Yeager, "Moral-Character Education," 167–70.

53. Ibid., 169.

54. Ibid., 171.

55. James S. Leming, "Research and Practice in Moral and Character Education: Loosely Coupled Phenomena," in *Handbook*, ed. Nucci and Narvaez, 1st ed., 134–57.

56. Marvin W. Berkowitz and Melinda C. Bier, "Research Based Fundamentals of the Effective Promotion of Character Education in Schools," in *Handbook*, ed. Nucci et al., 2nd ed., 248–60 (compare Berkowitz et al., "What Works in Character Education," in *Handbook*, ed. Nucci and Narvaez, 1st ed., 414–31).

can undertake to teach specific virtues. The approach will probably be more successful when integrated into the curriculum and life of the school and when the mechanisms are indirect but nonetheless substantial. Schools should bring students together in collaborative activities, from school celebrations and field days to service projects. They should teach social-emotional intelligence, which encompasses the abilities to understand one's emotions, regulate how one reacts emotionally to others, and deal with social conflicts through conversation.[57]

The principal of the school and the superintendent of the district should lend strong support to these efforts. "Every character education program should have a clear mandate from the school authorities" and needs "the commitment of the entire school community, from the school principal to the bus drivers."[58] Successful programs likewise need to involve parents and community leaders. Through mechanisms such as town-hall meetings and meetings of the parent-teacher association, schools should listen to families to find out how they can best support them and invite them to partner in the effort. Since some of the challenges that Ms. Bennett and teachers like her encounter have to do with the problems students encounter at home, schools need to make a contribution, as best they can, to strengthening families' well-being; these efforts may need to be initiated at the district, city-government, or state-government level.

## Students and Families

Students are still learning and maturing, so they will make mistakes and cannot always grasp the meaning and consequences of their actions. Nonetheless, schools and parents should strive to help young people take responsibility for their behavior and their learning. Particular school programs are geared toward developing self-control, teamwork, and so on. For instance, mentoring programs run by the school or a local nonprofit organization in partnership with the school can give students support in their learning and involve them in activities that build social capital. Schools and families can make it a priority to involve every student in at least one extracurricular activity.

Parents have a responsibility to be involved in the school to the best of their ability. Their children's learning and character development is best helped if parents regularly communicate with teachers.[59] There is a Golden Mean to be achieved: parents should be involved in their children's education and advocate for their children, yet they should not be unrealistic, narrow, or demanding. There is a natural tendency for parents to be concerned about their child, while teachers and schools are concerned with all children. Both sides should

---

57. Jennifer Kahn, "Can Emotional Intelligence Be Taught?," *New York Times Magazine*, September 11, 2013, *http://www.nytimes.com/2013/09/15/magazine/can-emotional-intelligence-be-taught.html?pagewanted=all&_r=0.*

58. Ryan and Bolhin, 239.

59. Dodd and Konzal, *How Communities Build Stronger Schools*, 7.

be aware of this difference in perspective. When the school actively involves parents, the parents are more likely to see themselves as having ownership in the school, and the difference in perspective can be alleviated.[60] There is much that families can do to promote their children's education inside and outside of school, throughout childhood. The family practices proposed in chapter 5 are ways to do so.

## Challenges outside Schools and Virtuous Responses

The external challenges to schools and education are social, cultural, economic, and political forces that make the job of these organizations complex and sometimes controversial. Once again, there are many challenges that can be mentioned, yet not all can be addressed here.[61] The following four, in particular, are obstacles to character education in the context of the achievement gap.

### External Challenges

*Poverty in families and communities.* To the classroom, children bring deficits and challenges derived from, or exacerbated by, their early rearing, home life, financial resources, and neighborhood experiences. Now, although the associations between low socioeconomic status (SES) and academic attainment are well-documented, can it be said that low SES *causes* poor attainment? Proving causation is difficult, yet several studies have isolated family income and discerned that it is a causal factor in children's low academic attainment.[62] The precise mechanism apparently has to do with stress. Dr. Clancy Blair of New York University has conducted research supporting the contention that stress from a variety of poverty-related sources—"including crowded and chaotic home and classroom environments, for example, or problems with family or peers—impedes learning." He further comments, "Although parents in poverty can and do provide sensitive care, they are less likely to do so, given the realities of their situation and, potentially, their own high stress levels."[63] The challenges are about much more than home life: the racial and economic

---

60. Ibid., 18–24.

61. For instance, on the challenges presented by media and technology, see ch. 5.

62. Cecilia Elena Rouse and Lisa Barrow, "U.S. Elementary and Secondary Schools: Equalizing Opportunity or Replicating the Status Quo?," *The Future of Children* 16, no. 2 (Fall 2006): 104, *http://www.princeton.edu/futureofchildren/publications/journals/article/index.xml?journalid=35&articleid=89*. The authors discuss several studies, concluding that family income is *a* causal factor, but not the only one—genetics and family structure may be factors as well.

63. National Institutes of Health (NIH), "Stresses of Poverty May Impair Learning Ability in Young Children," news release, August 28, 2012, *http://www.nih.gov/news/health/aug2012/nichd-28.htm*.

segregation that exists in many parts of American society is reflected in many public schools, making the educational experience in them substandard, unequal, and unjust.[64]

*Inadequate funding for school districts.* Short-term problems occur for all schools when the economy is weak. The economic recession that began in 2007 caused states and localities nationwide to cut education budgets, freeze salaries or give low raises, and lay off employees. Unfortunately, the effects are not short-term. Although the recession officially ended in 2009, "at least 35 states are providing less funding per student for the 2013–14 school year than they did before the recession hit. Fourteen of these states have cut per-student funding by more than 10 percent."[65] A long-term structural problem is that, regardless of the strength of the economy, schools are funded to unequal amounts. As seen in figure 6.3, on average, 44 percent of public school revenues come from local government, which means from local property taxes, for the most part. With lower average family incomes and less valuable housing stock, poorer communities have a harder time funding their schools, even when state governments give additional help to these communities.

The results are seen in the data for disparate per-student funding across the United States. The national median for revenues per student was $12,054 in 2011. Five percent of school districts had revenues per student of $8,416 or less, while five percent had revenues per student of $23,997 or more.[66] Lincoln High, the school in the case study, could be in a relatively well-funded district if it is located in a large metropolitan area such as New York or Boston, but it will still be substantially underfunded compared to suburban districts with the highest-performing schools. Districts with more funding can pay teachers more, retain better teachers, and provide more extracurricular activities.

*Low-quality teacher-training programs.* One would think that teacher-education programs prepare educators for the challenging, real-world contexts faced by Ms. Bennett and the three sisters interviewed by Nocera, but, according to the National Council on Teacher Quality (NCTQ), programs have not done well in this regard. NCTQ started issuing annual reports on the state of teacher training programs at America's public and private universities. Its second annual report, the *2014 Teacher Prep Review*, examines 1,612 teacher preparation programs and rates more than half of them at the lowest quality level. By contrast,

64. Nikole Hannah-Jones, "How School Segregation Divides Ferguson—and the United States," *New York Times,* December 19, 2014, *http://www.nytimes.com/2014/12/21/sunday-review/why-are-our-schools-still-segregated.html.*

65. Michael Leachman and Chris Mai, "Most States Funding Schools Less than before the Recession," Center for Budget and Policy Priorities, May 20, 2014, *http://www.cbpp.org/research/most-states-funding-schools-less-than-before-the-recession.*

66. National Center for Education Statistics, "Revenues and Expenditures for Public Elementary and Secondary School Districts: School Year 2010–11" (Washington, DC: September 2013), 3, *https://nces.ed.gov/pubsearch/pubsinfo.asp?pubid=2013344.*

"only 26 elementary programs and 81 secondary programs make NCTQ's lists of Top Ranked programs. Seventeen states and the District of Columbia are without a Top Ranked program in either elementary or secondary education."[67] Moreover, "District superintendents tell us that elementary teachers simply don't know the core subjects of the elementary curriculum."[68] Thus NCTQ finds that there is a lot of work to be done.

*Education reform efforts that are controversial and yield mixed results.* "Education reform" refers to efforts to change public policies to improve the quality of public education, especially in the past quarter century through such initiatives as these:

- establishing high standards in the structure and content of curriculum and the delivery of instruction
- using statewide standardized tests to assess student learning at several grade levels and to compare schools' and districts' performance nationally and internationally
- providing increased merit-pay for teachers who perform well, while requiring poorly performing teachers to get additional training and mentoring—and perhaps firing them if they do not improve
- holding schools accountable for student performance, as measured by test scores, by placing on probation schools that do not make adequate yearly progress, and perhaps closing them
- allowing other schooling options for families, such as magnet schools, charter schools, and tuition vouchers for private schools
- reforming or ending some protections enjoyed by teachers

It is reasonable to assume that some of these activities could be beneficial—and, indeed, some benefits are being demonstrated. However, several of these initiatives are highly controversial, and critics have charged that the rationale behind them is not to improve education but to punish teachers. The political challenge is that public debate can generate more anger than answers, obscuring grassroots and cooperative efforts. It is worth noting that education reform is nothing new: Dana Goldstein's *The Teacher Wars: A History of America's Most Embattled Profession* "demonstrates that almost every idea for reforming education over the past 25 years has been tried before—and failed to make a meaningful difference."[69] This is not to say that public education cannot be improved, but Goldstein

---

67. National Council on Teacher Quality (NCTQ), *2014 Teacher Prep Review* (February 2015), 2, *http://www.nctq.org/dmsView/Teacher_Prep_Review_2014_Report.*

68. Ibid., 3.

69. Claudia Wallis, "Progress Report," book review of *The Teacher Wars*, by Dana Goldstein, *New York Times*, August 22, 2014, *http://www.nytimes.com/2014/08/24/books/review/the-teacher-wars-by -dana-goldstein.html.*

makes a plea for realism: "America loves to dream an impossible dream when it comes to education."[70]

## Responses to External Challenges

This chapter is not the place to address, in any complete and systematic way, the professional and political challenges just described. Still, some summary suggestions can be ventured from a character-and-community approach focused on promoting character. Recommendations should flow from the six guidelines presented at the beginning of the chapter and should seek a Golden Mean—a balance between the competing extremes in policy debates.

### Practices for the Education Profession and Local Communities

*Improve teacher training.* In its second annual review, NCTQ notes, with satisfaction, that the issue of teacher preparation is finally receiving serious attention and that several universities are making concerted efforts to improve their training programs in just one year's time. NCTQ specifically noticed attention to the problem entailed in the case study of Lincoln High:

> The most promising sign of progress is in the training teacher candidates receive in how to manage classrooms—an area that new teachers perennially describe as their most difficult challenge. Of the institutions that submitted new materials [for the 2014 review], 15 percent made important improvements to the guidance they give to their student teachers about how to set rules, how to minimize classroom disruption, and how to apply consequences to misbehavior fairly and effectively.[71]

Teacher training has also been invigorated by alternative models, such as Teach for America (TFA), a nonprofit organization that recruits bright college students to become teachers in high-poverty schools. Goldstein notes TFA's model in a positive tone: "Teach for America offers one model for challenging the status quo in teacher education, by quickly providing its corps members with an intensely practical and prescriptive set of classroom strategies."[72] However, others are suspicious of that model. In the words of a former TFA teacher, "Five weeks of training was not enough to prepare me for a room of 20 unruly elementary-schoolers."[73] TFA is a nonprofit organization filling what it sees as an unmet need: there are

---

70. Ibid.

71. NCTQ, 4.

72. Goldstein, *The Teacher Wars*, 249.

73. Olivia Blanchard, "I Quit Teach for America," *The Atlantic*, September 23, 2013, *http://www.theatlantic.com/education/archive/2013/09/i-quit-teach-for-america/279724/*.

not enough good, committed teachers willing to take on the toughest teaching assignments. The need is undoubtedly real and demands serious attention from citizens and officials.

*Reinvigorate teaching practices.* Goldstein offers three examples for how to do this. The first is a simple, daily one: teachers need to watch each other teach. She says, "The classroom should not be a black box closed to outside scrutiny, especially for novice teachers."[74] Novice teachers need to see veteran teachers in action and vice versa; it would not be too difficult for schools and districts to make adjustments to the workday and to the duties of veteran teachers to make this happen. Another recommendation is to keep teaching interesting by creating opportunities for experienced teachers to practice new skills that help their schools in other ways, such as writing curricula and mentoring younger teachers.[75] Third, and more ambitiously, Goldstein says, creating "communities of practice" would get educational professionals collaborating in new ways. For example, "teacher prep programs and kindergarten through grade twelve schools would work in alliance. They would select a school of thought to emphasize and develop evidence-based best practices that can be shared among researchers, working teachers, and trainee teachers."[76]

*Use knowledge of the research on children's development to create educational strategies.* Dr. Blair, the researcher on the effects of poverty on learning, says the facts about stress are daunting but that they also allow policymakers and educators to find ways to thwart those effects.[77] Responses at the policy level are initiatives to reduce poverty and promote family health. Responses at the classroom and school level are pedagogical strategies such as those recommended by educators Eric Jensen, Ruby Payne, and Doug Lemov.[78] Jensen's classroom-level strategies, for instance, are organized by the acronym SHARE: Standards-based curriculum and instruction; Hope building; Arts, athletics, and advanced placement; Retooling students' mental processing skills; and Engaging instruction.[79]

*Adopt a family-school-community partnership model.* Dodd and Konzal commend a "community center" model in which the school is seen as a resource for the whole community—a location for cultural programming and

74. Goldstein, *The Teacher Wars*, 270.

75. Ibid., 266–67.

76. Ibid., 265. The scholars who made the proposal are Harvard sociologist Jal Mehta and Johns Hopkins political scientist Stephen Teles.

77. NIH, "Stresses of Poverty."

78. Eric Jensen, *Teaching with Poverty in Mind* (Alexandria, VA: ASCD, 2009) and *Engaging Students with Poverty in Mind* (Alexandria, VA: ASCD, 2013); Ruby K. Payne, *A Framework for Understanding Poverty: A Cognitive Approach*, 5th ed. (Highland, TX: aha! Process, Inc., 2013); Doug Lemov, *Teach Like a Champion 2.0: 62 Techniques That Put Students on the Path to College* (San Francisco: Jossey-Bass, 2015).

79. Jensen, *Teaching*, 107.

public meetings.[80] Schools, citizens, and local institutions would continually collaborate, guided by a central question: "What can all of us together do to educate our children well?"[81] A few character education programs explicitly engage community partners, but this approach can be expanded.[82] Service is important in both directions: community members and institutions help the school by volunteering there, while the school and its students can help the community. Most schools are eager to have volunteers for help with tutoring, extra-curricular activities, school functions, and so on. Universities often make major contributions to local public schools through student service and service learning, as illustrated in the case study. There are also substantive partnerships in which a university sends teachers-in-training to work in a school and conduct educational and psychological research to benefit young people.

## Initiatives for Policymakers and Opinion Leaders

*Pay teachers more.* Goldstein notes, "In 2012, the median income of an American teacher was $54,000 per year, similar to the salary of a police officer or librarian," but significantly less than that of other professionals, such as nurses, accountants, computer programmers, and lawyers.[83] In South Korea, where teaching is highly respected, educators are paid on par with engineers and doctors. The comparatively low pay in the United States "is undoubtedly one reason why some ambitious people leave or never enter the profession, and why teaching is less culturally respected than it should be."[84] It is not easy to know how pay could be increased, but presumably federal and state governments would have to pour more resources into education, since local governments are already strapped. It is also important to recruit more male and minority teachers.[85] Introducing innovative variations to the structure of the job, as mentioned in the previous section, might entice such candidates.

*Provide more funding for school districts under a more equitable funding system.* Since a large proportion of school funding comes from local property taxes, school funding varies widely depending on the wealth of the community. Matt Miller, a senior fellow at the Center for American Progress, argues that a strong federal role is required. First, the federal government would "bring all states up to a certain guaranteed baseline of funding per pupil. . . . States would have to tax themselves at a certain minimal

---

80. Dodd and Konzal, *How Communities Build Stronger Schools*, 129–32.

81. Ibid., 126.

82. Jim Lies et al., "The Community Contribution to Moral Development and Character," in *Handbook*, ed. Nucci and Narvaez, 1st ed., 520–36.

83. Goldstein, *The Teacher Wars*, 263–64.

84. Ibid., 265.

85. Ibid., 270.

rate." Then the federal government would give addition aid to states that still fall short in their tax resources.[86] Miller proposes the federal government offer states money earmarked for substantially raising teacher salaries in high-poverty schools, in exchange for state-level policy changes for education reform. Making increased funding available to encourage states to adopt education reform policies is the model used in President Barack Obama's Race to the Top initiative. Like all efforts in education reform, Race to the Top has proven controversial. The difference with Miller's proposal is that he would direct the funds specifically for teacher salaries, whereas Race to the Top funds have been used for a variety of activities.[87]

*Return tests to their rightful role as diagnostic tools.* This recommendation by Goldstein is likely to be greeted with approval from parents and teachers, many of whom have bemoaned the amount of classroom time spent preparing for annual tests and the rigid nature of the teaching that is required to prepare students for the tests. Indeed, parental and student backlash against overreliance on standardize tests has become a notable trend, one to which states now feel beholden to respond.[88] Tests are helpful for identifying strategies that improve student learning, teachers who need more training, and masterly teachers who can serve as mentors—but not, Goldstein argues, for evaluating, paying, and firing teachers.[89] Putting tests back in their place might help rescue other pieces of education reform, such as the Common Core Standards. These curriculum standards—intended to set high, nationwide expectations for students' competency in math and language arts—have been tainted, in the public's eye, by their association with unpalatable high-stakes tests.

*Practice good faith in policy debates.* What constitutes "good faith" is in the eye of the beholder, but it is an important goal for which to strive, since the waters around education reform are murky. While there are political leaders whose partisan agendas are driving at least some education reform initiatives, most of the politicians and foundations involved in education reform should be taken at their word when they say they are concerned about students suffering from the achievement gap. Reformers can prove the authenticity of their

---

86. Matt Miller, *The Tyranny of Dead Ideas: Revolutionary Thinking for a New Age of Prosperity* (New York: Holt Paperbacks, 2010), 211.

87. See the White House's Race to the Top website at *https://www.whitehouse.gov/issues /education/k-12/race-to-the-top*. Once supported by many politicians, both Democratic and Republican, Race to the Top has come under increasing fire from both sides of the political spectrum. On the potential abuse of the program's funding, see Emma Brown, "Ed Tech Company Folds after Receiving Millions in Race to the Top Funds," *Washington Post*, May 6, 2015, *http://www .washingtonpost.com/local/education/ed-tech-company-folds-after-receiving-millions-in-race-to-the-top -funds/2015/05/06/c637e5aa-f310-11e4-b2f3-af5479e6bbdd_story.html*.

88. "More Students Revolting against Standardized Tests," CBS/Associated Press, February 20, 2015, *http://www.cbsnews.com/news/more-students-revolting-against-standardized-tests/*.

89. Goldstein, *The Teacher Wars*, 269.

concerns by refusing to demonize teachers. Teachers ought to be more respected for the value they give to society. By the same token, teachers should not demonize the education reform movement. Some teachers and teacher unions could be more willing to embrace their accountability to society and enact virtues of flexibility, innovation, and risk-taking. In this light, one of Goldstein's modest recommendations is to end certain outdated union protections, primarily the strict seniority rule dictating that, when layoffs are necessary, the last person hired by the district is the first to be laid off. Overall, the character-and-community paradigm supports education reform efforts in which teachers and their unions work as partners with politicians and families.

*Respect private schools and charter schools as part of the mix of options, but keep them accountable to the wider public.* Private schools and homeschooling should neither be overemphasized nor underemphasized, but rather, respected as a choice that some families make. At the same time, elected officials can ensure public schooling is of good quality so families do not feel the need to leave the system so their children can receive a decent education. One of the rationales for the creation of charter schools was to introduce competition into public education. The belief is that, when parents have more options from which to choose, regular public schools will have to raise their quality to entice families. Whether this competition has been useful is unclear. Despite the success of some charters, with the KIPP schools among the most lauded, there have been plenty of problems in the young movement.[90] One major concern is that, in states where it is easy to create charter schools, such as Florida, for-profit companies have opened thousands of schools, taken vast sums of public money, and lobbied officials for sweetheart deals.[91] Despite the claims of some reformers that few strictures should be placed on charters, it is the responsibility of government to ensure that charter schools are institutions that serve the common good. When they are accountable, charter schools can be appreciated as places that incubate creative ideas about teaching and that bring new models forward.[92]

*Attack poverty.* This final initiative is essential for the improvement of American education. Although much of this work goes beyond education policy, the implications are evident. High-quality schooling is one of the solutions to poverty, since education helps young people attain the skills needed to secure decent-paying jobs. Poverty must be battled across a child's lifespan, from birth to college.[93] On the latter end of that spectrum, two of President Obama's policy

90. See Bruce Feller, ed. *Inside Charter Schools: The Paradox of Radical Decentralization* (Cambridge, MA: Harvard University Press, 2000).

91. See Alec MacGillis, "Testing Time: Jeb Bush's Educational Experiment," *The New Yorker,* January 26, 2015, 42–53.

92. Goldstein, *The Teacher Wars,* 266.

93. James J. Heckman, "Lifelines for Poor Children," *New York Times,* September 14, 2013, *http://opinionator.blogs.nytimes.com/2013/09/14/lifelines-for-poor-children/.*

recommendations are sensible: states should require adolescents to remain in school until age eighteen, and community college should be free for low-income citizens.[94] By promoting housing policies that encourage neighborhoods to retain a mix of low-income and middle-income families, states would encourage socioeconomically integrated schools, with positive implications for closing the achievement gap. A school district in Atlanta, Georgia, provides a model that is now being copied in other cities.[95]

## Conclusion

After families, schools are the most significant influence on children's character. The schools carry the public's anxieties and hopes. Part of the angst about public schools comes from the fact that teachers are ordinary people doing a job on which the future of American society and the futures of its children depend. Dewey said, "Education is, and forever will be, in the hands of ordinary men and women."[96] Instead of wishing it were otherwise, virtuous citizens can help these ordinary men and women do their job well by supporting them and collaborating with them. Citizens should work together to ensure schools are places where children flourish. Then schools will not merely be microcosms of society, but models of what society can become.[97]

## Questions for Review

1. What is the achievement gap?
2. What is character education, and why is there a lack of agreement about it within schools and society?
3. Besides intellectual skills, what capabilities of the mind does education promote?
4. What does Robert Adams mean by the elementary, modular, and integrative tasks of education? Which of the tasks does formal schooling develop especially well?

---

94. In his 2012 State of the Union address, Obama stated the goal of age eighteen, which would require legal mandates by the states, while in his 2016 budget he proposed a ten-year, $60 billion plan to make community college tuition free for some students (Allie Bidwell, "Obama 2016 Budget Boosts Funding for Early Ed, Community College," *U.S. News & World Report*, February 2, 2015, *http://www.usnews.com/news/articles/2015/02/02/obama-2016-budget -boosts-funding-for-early-ed-community-college*).

95. Sarah Garland, "Rich Kid, Poor Kid: How Mixed Neighborhoods Could Save America's Schools," *The Atlantic*, July 25, 2012, *http://www.theatlantic.com/national/archive/2012/07 /rich-kid-poor-kid-how-mixed-neighborhoods-could-save-americas-schools/260308/*.

96. Quoted in Goldstein, *The Teacher Wars*, 9.

97. Compare the epigraph of ch. 5 by Julie Hanlon Rubio.

5. What is the relationship between a country's educational achievement and its economy?

6. What are the major sources of funding for American public schools? Why is the reliance on local funding considered problematic?

7. Briefly describe the forms of support for education made by the three levels of government.

8. What are the challenges—internal and external—to education when students come from a low socioeconomic status?

9. What is education reform, and why is it controversial?

## Discussion Questions and Activities

1. Think about one of your teachers, from any level of schooling, who had an important influence on you. Tell that story, in speech or writing. What were that teacher's notable qualities? What were his or her teaching strategies? Relate points in your story to points made in this chapter.

2. Describe your primary, middle, high school, or other educational experience, such as being homeschooled. Try to describe the ethos of the school (its overall ethical character and climate) as you experienced it then and as you see it now. What factors, internal and external to the school, helped or harmed that ethos?

3. Give a description of a school you attend, or have previously attended, related to concepts in this chapter—its socioeconomic situation, whether it engages in character education, and the internal and external challenges it faces. (The same exercise can be done with a school you did not attend, but have observed, such as in a service-learning project.)

4. After reviewing this chapter's case study on resistant and receptive students, how would you explain the attitude of the freshman who said, "I don't care if I get an F"? How would you respond to the student if you were Ms. Bennett? What should be the role of the family in addressing the student's attitude?

5. Teachers are important, but some say that education reformers place too many expectations upon them. Guided by ethical concepts and virtue theory, take a position in this debate: should the primary focus be on improving teachers, reforming curricula, getting parents to take more responsibility, alleviating poverty, or some combination of these approaches?

6. This chapter contains strategies for the education profession to respond to external challenges. Assess one or more of these strategies. Do the same for the policy initiatives presented. Your answers should be guided by ethical concepts and virtue theory.

## Recommendations for Further Reading

Baird, Katherine. *Trapped in Mediocrity: Why Our Schools Aren't World-Class and What We Can Do about It.* Lanham, MD: Rowman and Littlefield, 2012.

An economist diagnoses the shortcomings of the American education system in a strong but even-handed manner.

Dewey, John. *Democracy and Education.* Simon & Brown, 2012.

One of the most important books on educational philosophy by "the father of American public education."

Goldstein, Dana. *The Teacher Wars: A History of America's Most Embattled Profession.* New York: Doubleday, 2014.

A journalist's 175-year history of American public education, showing how the profession has been under intense public scrutiny from the beginning and how virtually all of the ideas touted under current education reform have been tried in earlier decades.

Kozol, Jonathan. *Fire in the Ashes: Twenty-Five Years among the Poorest Children in America.* New York: Broadway Books, 2013.

The most recent in a series of books that began with *Savage Inequalities* (1991), *Fire in the Ashes* brings the story of a poor Bronx neighborhood, its children, and its schools up to date. Kozol believes that poverty is the greatest source of educational problems and that well-off Americans have failed to meet their obligation to provide avenues of opportunity to poor children.

Noddings, Nel. *Caring: A Relational Approach to Ethics and Moral Education.* Berkeley: University of California Press, 1984; revised 2003 and 2013.

The central work by a preeminent contemporary philosopher of education, in which she offers a theory known as "the ethics of care."

Nucci, Larry P., Darcia Narvaez, and Tobias Krettenauer, eds. *Handbook of Moral and Character Education.* 2nd ed. New York: Routledge, 2014.

An excellent compendium on all aspects of character education. The chapters, written by experts in the field, are based on up-to-date research on the effectiveness of various approaches and programs.

Ryan, Kevin, and Karen E. Bohlin. *Building Character in Schools: Practical Ways to Bring Moral Instruction to Life.* San Francisco: Jossey-Bass Publishers, 1999.

This readable book gives a rationale for character education and offers many approaches, examples, and tips.

**Websites for information and examples of character education programs:**

Character Counts! *https://charactercounts.org.*

Character Education Partnership. *http://character.org.*

The Jubilee Centre for Character and Virtues. *http://www.jubileecentre.ac.uk.*

U.S. Department of Education, Partnerships in Character Education Program. *http://www2.ed.gov/programs/charactered/index.html.*

### Websites for a range of perspectives on education reform and the achievement gap:

The Center for Education Reform. *https://www.edreform.com.*

The Annie E. Casey Foundation. *http://www.aecf.org.*

The Bill and Melinda Gates Foundation, Measures of Effective Teaching Project. *http://collegeready.gatesfoundation.org.*

The Common Core State Standards Initiative. *http://www.corestandards.org.*

Diane Ravitch. *http://dianeravitch.com.*

Edutopia. *http://www.edutopia.org.*

The National Education Association. *http://www.nea.org.*

The Wallace Foundation. *http://www.wallacefoundation.org/pages/default.aspx.*

# Work
## Meaning on the Job, Responsibility in the Economy

The most beautiful fate, the most wonderful good fortune that can happen to any human being, is to be paid for doing that which he passionately loves to do.

—*Abraham Maslow (1908–1970), psychologist* [1]

The first principle of business ethics is that the corporation is itself a citizen, a member of the larger community, and inconceivable without it.

—*Robert C. Solomon (1942–2007), philosopher and business ethicist* [2]

---

## Chapter Overview

- explains why work as a value-creating activity matters for flourishing and character
- describes the reciprocal benefits between businesses and their employees, customers, and other stakeholders and the benefits of businesses to society and the assistance society provides to businesses
- examines challenges facing workers and companies—both internal challenges to company culture and external challenges from social forces, such as economic recessions and the changing nature of capitalism

*Continued*

---

1. Quoted in Tal Ben-Shahar, *Happier: Learn the Secrets to Daily Joy and Lasting Fulfillment* (New York: McGraw Hill, 2007), 101.

2. Robert C. Solomon, *Ethics and Excellence: Cooperation and Integrity in Business* (New York: Oxford University Press, 1993), 148.

204 Toward Thriving Communities

> **Overview** *Continued*
>
> - recommends, for workers and businesses, practices that promote character and flourishing through work
> - explores the possibility that businesses and other institutions can collaborate to promote a renewal of civic virtue

## Work Matters

While playing soccer in high school, James suffered a tear in the anterior cruciate ligament (ACL) of his knee, for which he required surgery. He greatly appreciated the assistance of his physical therapist, not only because the therapist helped his knee improve but also because his conversations with the therapist made James feel better about what was happening. Although this ACL injury scuttled James's dreams of playing professional soccer, his positive experience in rehab gave him the idea of pursuing a career in physical therapy. "I want to help people who have faced obstacles like I did," he says.

A recent college graduate with a degree in physical therapy, James now works at the practice where he interned during his senior year. During a typical workday, James sees patients of all ages who are rehabbing after surgeries and injuries. He enjoys working with these patients, talking with them about their lives, and seeing them achieve increased physical function. His coworkers and manager have helped him learn how to do his job better, and he enjoys the camaraderie and teamwork he experiences in the office. Although his workday is fast-paced, and sometimes a little stressful, James thoroughly enjoys his job. "No matter how hectic the office gets, every day I get to see people make improvements in their lives because we are working with them," he says. "I love my job!"[3] Not everyone can speak as positively about their work as James does, but nearly everyone hopes that their work can increase their happiness and flourishing.

While some people's career aspirations are focused on money and success, many veteran workers testify that money and titles do not equate with happiness. Rather, argue virtue ethicists, people are most satisfied by doing their work according to high standards of quality and of ethics and with the well-being of others in mind. As David Brooks, author of *The Road to Character*, puts it, there are two sets of virtues, the résumé virtues and the eulogy virtues. "The résumé virtues are the skills you bring to the marketplace. The eulogy virtues are

---

3. The character of James is based on many of the author's own students who have spoken similarly about their reasons for choosing their planned career paths.

the ones that are talked about at your funeral—whether you were kind, brave, honest or faithful."[4] Most people would agree that the latter set of virtues is the one that really matters in the end. "But our culture and our educational systems spend more time teaching the skills and strategies you need for career success than the qualities you need to radiate that sort of inner light. Many of us are clearer on how to build an external career than on how to build inner character." The workplace is a setting that naturally prods a person to develop his or her résumé virtues. During one's career, though, one has to continue nurturing the other set of virtues, lest one discover, perhaps in the twilight of life, that one is not satisfied with the person he or she has become.

This chapter explores what makes work meaningful and moral—that is, how work contributes to flourishing, character, and the common good. Particular attention is paid to the setting where most Americans do their work: the for-profit business enterprise.[5]

## Meanings of Work

"Work" can mean different things to different people. Work can be defined descriptively, emotionally, or philosophically. First, a descriptive, dictionary-style definition of work is: an activity that a person does for pay and to provide a product and/or service to others. People often think of work as one's job (employment for pay) and as one's career (the line of work for which one has trained and that one performs for many years). Second, there are varied emotional meanings of work. In some situations, work is seen as toil and drudgery (e.g., "Ugh, I have to go to work now"), while in others, work is seen as enjoyable, even fun. When James says, "I love my job," many listeners can relate—even though the work is hard, sometimes stressful, and even though he is doing it partly for the pragmatic purpose of getting a salary, James finds his work engaging and meaningful. Third, there are philosophical definitions of work. Within this category, a virtue-oriented definition of work is: something that draws upon one's skills, virtues, knowledge, and

---

4. David Brooks, "The Moral Bucket List," *New York Times*, April 11, 2015, *http://www.nytimes .com/2015/04/12/opinion/sunday/david-brooks-the-moral-bucket-list.html*. The article is a précis of *The Road to Character* (New York: Random House, 2015). See also his TED talk, "Should You Live for Your Résumé . . . or Your Eulogy?" *https://www.ted.com/talks/david _brooks_should_you_live_for_your_resume_or_your_eulogy?language=en*.

5. Roughly 6 percent of American workers are self-employed, 10 percent work for nonprofits, and 15 percent work for the local, state, or federal government. Therefore, approximately 69 percent of workers are employed by for-profit enterprises. Statistics compiled from the U.S. Bureau of Labor Statistics, "Employment by Major Industry Sector," December 2013, table 2.1; "Self-Employment in the United States," September 2010, *http://www.bls.gov/emp/ep_table_201.htm*; and Lester M. Salamon et al., *Holding the Fort: Nonprofit Employment During a Decade of Turmoil*, Center for Civil Society Studies at Johns Hopkins University, January 2012, *http://ccss.jhu.edu/wp-content/uploads /downloads/2012/01/NED_National_2012.pdf*.

passion to create a valuable result that helps oneself and others in an extrinsic and intrinsic fashion.

The virtue-oriented definition of work is key for this chapter, and it offers the critical foundation on which the facts and emotions about the world of work can be assessed. In the virtue approach to work, the distinction between extrinsic and intrinsic value is important. *Extrinsic value* refers to the practical benefits to the worker and others, such as financial gain, products, services, and prestige. *Intrinsic value* refers to the potential of work for being good and meaningful for the worker regardless of any practical benefits it produces. Examples of intrinsic value are the worker's sense of being engaged in the work, the worker's exercise of virtues while working, the aesthetic value of the work, and the worker's attempt to benefit others, directly or indirectly.

Extrinsic values are neither immoral nor amoral. There is nothing wrong with workers being motivated by decent pay and praise. But good work is work that incorporates extrinsic benefits in the pursuit of intrinsic value. A virtue-ethical approach holds that it is desirable and possible for work to be good in three simultaneous senses: (1) good according to moral standards, (2) good for a person's deep happiness, (3) and good for others in society. The phrase "good work" will be used in this chapter to convey this threefold goal of all forms of labor and employment.

## The Promise and the Problems of Work

Work matters for persons and society. For people work yields practical benefits, such as income, but it also has a large effect on one's psychological and moral well-being. Who doesn't want to be able to say, "I love my job"? People wish for this, not only because they spend so much time at work, but also because something deep in human character makes people yearn for purpose.

Work also contributes mightily to the health and vitality of society. The economic implications come to mind first: the work of individuals and their businesses makes a society prosperous. In addition, work is communal most of the time, so it is a context in which people can help each other, create friendships, and build social capital. Most paid work occurs in the context of a business, an organization in which people collaborate to create goods and/or deliver services that other people find useful. Business activity is part of social well-being: the happiness, stability, and flourishing of a nation largely rises and falls with its economic health. It is obvious, but not unimportant, to say that work allows humans to survive and makes society possible.

In contrast to the positive, work also can harm flourishing and character. Some people might not know what kind of work will make them deeply satisfied; indeed, family members, peers, teachers, or the media might have discouraged them from inquiring about the deeper meaning of work. These factors may be why only 50 percent of employees in the United States are satisfied with their work.[6] In addition, some people are underpaid or out of work, so it would be a luxury for them to consider the intrinsic benefits of work—they need the pay before all else. At any workplace, one's coworkers, boss, or the organization itself might have ethical flaws that hinder well-being. Office politics, savage competition among coworkers, and pressures to act unethically create moral challenges for workers. Sometimes it is the worker who lacks character and undermines coworkers and the company.

On the social side, businesses are subject to the same problems facing organizations and communities as recounted in chapter 4. In their internal workings, businesses can hamper the flourishing of employees, customers, and other stakeholders by failing to respect them or by developing operational habits that are unhealthy and shortsighted. Businesses might not do enough to ensure that employees are doing their best work and flourishing in their daily tasks. Some employees might have vices that diminish the flourishing and ethical aspirations of their company. Looking externally, as businesses operate in society, they might fail to contribute as much as they could to the common good and, in some cases, they might actively undermine it.

Compare the story of James to that of Liz Guidone, age 22, who is profiled in a book about the enduring negative impacts of the recent economic recession on the millennial generation (that is, Americans currently in their twenties or thirties). Liz graduated from an Illinois college in 2011 with a degree in music business. During her studies, she had four unpaid internships, "mostly organizing details for events and retrieving hot cups of coffee. . . . In return, she received a college credit, which she paid for, and her employers offered her no training or field experience."[7] Liz was able to get a job in public relations after graduating, but it paid meagerly and quickly became unsustainable. At the time she was interviewed, Liz had moved back in with her parents and was working full time as a receptionist at a spa. "Life sucks at the moment," she said. The book's author, Riva Froymovich, comments: "Like many 20-somethings, Liz is willing to work hard for very little in order to gain experience, but her employers aren't giving her the training she needs to get ahead. None sought to retain Liz as a full-time employee after her internship ended. They just went on to the next free or low-paid millennial worker."[8]

Liz's case, like others to be explored later, suggests that an employee's pursuit of flourishing is strongly conditioned by the character of the company and the ethos of society. Virtue ethics has much to say about the promise and problems

---

6. From a February 2005 survey by the Conference Board, "Take This Job and . . . ," cited in Ben-Shahar, *Happier,* 98.

7. Riva Froymovich, *End of the Good Life* (New York: Harper Perennial, 2013), 79.

8. Ibid., 80

of work. Virtue thinkers can identify, in James's case, the practices that make work meaningful and moral and then recommend such practices to other workers. Virtue thinkers can identify, in Liz's case, obstacles to flourishing and evidence of weak character among businesspeople, and they can endorse virtue-based strategies to address these challenges. Because the experience of work is almost always communal, the social principles that fall under virtue ethics can and must be brought to bear on business activity and on the economic structures and political policies that guide business activity.

## Businesses and Their Members

The two main relationships in the community connections chart (ch. 4) are of persons to groups and groups to society. Looking at relationship number 1 (fig. 7.1), the purpose is to understand the contributions of a business to its members' characters and flourishing, as well as the members' contributions to the effective operation and well-being of the organization. In all versions of the chart in this book, the members of a group are those who belong to the group, participate in its activities, and help form the identity and character of the groups. A business also has "members" in this sense, but they are not normally called that. Rather, they are referred to according to their diverse roles: employees, managers, owners, customers, boards, investors, stakeholders,[9] and so on. In the "members" area of the work version of the community connections chart, these roles are indicated. Because this chapter's focus is on the activity of working, the primary focus is also on employees, who do the lion's share of a company's work. But other "members" are important to a business, so many will be mentioned along the way.

### Business and Members

**Figure 7.1.** Community Connections: A Business and Its Members

---

9. "Stakeholders" refers to those who are affected by a business and have a legitimate interest in its operations. Stakeholders can thus include local communities, subsidiary businesses, schools, professional organizations, labor unions, the national government, the international community, even the natural environment and future generations. See R. Edward Freeman et al., *Stakeholder Theory: The State of the Art* (New York: Cambridge University Press, 2010).

## Flourishing as Using Skills and Achieving Flow

Working tends to promote one's skills; acquiring and using these skills is beneficial for the worker as a person. The psychologist Mihaly Csikszentmihalyi claims that an engaging, enriching experience called "flow" is often best achieved when one is practicing skills. Flow refers to the experience of being fully engaged and fully enjoying a particular moment. Flow is not a superficial emotion of happiness; rather, it occurs when a person concentrates deeply and is in control of both the body and the mind, which are functioning in harmony.[10] Flow can be experienced in many ways, but some representative instances are when a person is playing a musical instrument, creating art, participating in a sport, praying or meditating, or doing a particular complex hobby or type of work. Flow-creating activities are ones that people enjoy and at which they are skilled. People do not have to be experts at the activity to experience flow, but they do have to invest themselves in a quest for greater mastery.

> A good flow activity is one that offers a very high ceiling of opportunities for improvement—playing the piano, for example, provides almost infinite challenges. Thus it invites growth. If one wants to stay in flow, he or she must progress and learn more skills, rising to new levels of complexity.[11]

Work is one significant setting in which people can experience flow, says Csikszentmihalyi, *if* the challenges presented by the job are balanced with the worker's skills. "Basically, the more a person feels skilled, the more her moods will improve; while the more challenges are present, the more her attention will become focused and concentrated."[12] One cannot be in flow all the time, but having regular opportunities for it is ultimately the reason some people are able to say, "I love my job!"

The concept of flow makes sense of the experience that work at its best doesn't feel like work but more like play. When a worker is in flow, his or her labor moves higher up a scale of quality and meaning: it moves away from being "toil" and becomes an expression of "vocation"—one's calling to do the work for its own sake. Play has a similar dynamic, as it moves from extrinsic and limited purposes, when it could be called "mere leisure," and becomes a flow experience, when it takes the character of "re-creation," a word conveying both the playful aspect (recreation in the everyday sense) and the creative, rejuvenating aspect of the activity. Imagine these scales as two sides of a step

---

10. Mihaly Csikszentmihalyi, *Good Business: Leadership, Flow, and the Making of Meaning* (New York: Penguin, 2003), 42–56 for a detailed account of flow.

11. Ibid., 63.

12. Ibid., 71.

ladder. The lower sides of the ladder are separate from each other, but at the top, they are joined, because, at their best, work and play are very similar: they both create flow and promote excellence.

Csikszentmihalyi believes that one can place oneself in a setting and in a frame of mind where opportunities for flow are regularly available. James, the young physical therapist encountered at the beginning of the chapter, has such a setting and mind-set, so his work is truly a vocation for him: he feels called to it, enjoys it, takes pride in it, and knows that he is doing some good for the world through it. Liz, on the other hand, is not in such a setting—yet. Notice that she has the same goal as James. She knows what good work is, and she yearns for it. She also wants to be paid decently and achieve financial independence from her parents. In the image of the ladder, the higher, intrinsic levels of work and play incorporate the lower, extrinsic levels. Someone who has a vocation for his or her job (or sport, or music, etc.) doesn't mind being paid for it or achieving recognition for it, but that is not what motivates the person to do it.

## The Connection of Thinking and Doing

Skills are just the first step in the way that work develops a person. Aristotle discerns a parallel between the dynamics of skills and virtues, according to philosopher Julia Annas, who expands some clues in the *Nicomachean Ethics* into an analogy between mastering a skill and growing in virtue. Virtues are similar to complex skills such as playing soccer, playing the piano, writing computer code, and building furniture. In both cases, says Annas, "we find not only the need to learn but the drive to aspire, and hence . . . the need for articulate conveying of reasons why what is done is done."[13] Notice that the final step in the process is explaining to others. Skills and virtues are not private matters. Being involved in them tends to involve one in a community that is pursuing excellence in a practice.

Annas's analogy does more than illustrate how virtue is developed; it entails that maturation in one's work contributes to the development of one's character. Matthew B. Crawford's *Shop Class as Soulcraft* illustrates the influence of work on character, by blending his study of philosophy with the life-lessons he has learned from riding and repairing motorcycles. He opens the book with the major problem he sees in the contemporary world of work—that "thinking has been separated from doing."[14] He traces the roots of this separation to early twentieth century developments in the business world ("scientific management" and the assembly line) and in contemporary consumer culture. He finds the separation entirely unhealthy: it degrades the work of manual laborers and demeans

---

13. Julia Annas, *Intelligent Virtue* (New York: Oxford University Press, 2011), 20.

14. Matthew B. Crawford, *Shop Class as Soulcraft: An Inquiry into the Value of Work* (New York: Penguin, 2009). The remainder of the current paragraph summarizes Crawford's discussion in ch. 2.

so-called "knowledge workers," who are often forced to work on a figurative assembly line. The separation disempowers most contemporary Americans, who do not know how to repair and take care of the stuff they own. When something is broken, often it is just thrown away. A related problem is that the American economy has shifted away from manufacturing during the last half-century.[15] The shift to a service economy has made the United States reliant on other nations for manufactured products, and it means the nation has fewer good-paying middle-class jobs on which, in previous generations, workers without a college education could support their families.

Work can be better—more engaging, meaningful, and useful—if the separation of thinking from doing is resisted. For inspiration and a model, Crawford looks to the "manual arts," that is, to crafts and trades. He writes, "This book grows out of an attempt to understand the greater sense of agency and competence I have always felt doing manual work, compared to other jobs that were officially recognized as 'knowledge work.' Perhaps surprisingly, I often find manual work more engaging *intellectually*."[16] Crawford understands that many people are involved in office work, computer work, and other jobs without a manual or craft-oriented dimension. Much of this work still has value, and much of it needs to be done. Crawford hopes that approaching one's work, whatever work it is, with the right mind-set can help one find greater meaning and satisfaction. "My point, finally, isn't to recommend motorcycling in particular, nor to idealize the life of a mechanic. It is rather to suggest that if we follow the traces of our own actions to their source, they intimate some understanding of the good life."[17]

## Character at Work

The potential contributions of work to the worker's body, mind, relationships, and character have been mentioned: all four of these domains of flourishing (ch. 3) are enhanced by flow experiences. Character deserves additional attention, because workers' characters are not only a source of their happiness, but the ethical compass by which they help others flourish.

Work is a practice, as described by Alasdair MacIntyre: it is a cooperative social activity embedded in a tradition, involving the pursuit of intrinsic goods, and requiring and promoting virtues that allow the participants to achieve those

---

15. In 1950, 30 percent of jobs were in manufacturing and 63 percent in services. Now only 12.5 percent are in manufacturing. See Hank Robison, "The Biggest Threat to Service-Sector Wages: The Service Sector," *The Desktop Economist* (blog), March 8, 2011, *http://www.economicmodeling .com/2011/03/08/the-biggest-threat-to-service-sector-wages-the-service-sector/*, and the Bureau of Labor Statistics, "Employment by Major Industry Sector."

16. Crawford, *Shop Class as Soulcraft*, 5.

17. Ibid., 197.

goods in an excellent manner.[18] Therefore, when one participates in work as an intentional practice, with like-minded people, in an institution that wants to pursue internal and external excellence, then the worker has substantial opportunities to grow in such virtues as

- *practical reasoning*, which is involved in every sensible decision at work; the reflective worker is prudent in figuring out how to achieve his or her goals amid challenges;
- *self-control (temperance), persistence, and courage*, which are inherent in flow experiences and are the qualities of a person that enable him or her to achieve flow;
- *critical and creative thinking*, which can be strengthened by engagement in one's work, including in the manual trades;
- *social-emotional intelligence, communication skills, and collaboration*, which are necessary for effective teamwork and can be improved as one cooperates well with coworkers;
- *purpose and vitality*, which are stoked when one is passionate about one's work and is employed in a context that matches skills with challenges; and
- *integrity*, which, in the sense of being true to oneself, is achieved when a worker is doing good work and enjoying regular opportunities for flow at work.

Additional virtues are prominent in the for-profit business sector, because that setting has particular goals and practices. For instance, Robert Solomon discusses the virtue of "toughness" that is often lauded by businesspeople:

> [Toughness] is often conflated with ruthlessness, or with stubbornness, or with general hardheadedness. As a business virtue, however, toughness makes sense and is successful only within a context more broadly defined by cooperation and congeniality. A business is not a slave ship. Toughness, as a business virtue, presupposes other virtues as well.[19]

Generosity is one of the virtues that makes toughness take the shape, not of ruthlessness, but of the ability to conduct business prudently, persistently, and

---

18. Alasdair MacIntyre, *After Virtue*, 3rd ed. (Notre Dame, IN: University of Notre Dame Press, 2007), 187–88. See also the discussion in ch. 5. MacIntyre has been much discussed in business ethics literature because his famous concept of a practice seems to relate well to business. Yet, interestingly, MacIntyre is reluctant to say that contemporary business as led by managers *is* a practice. His criticisms of office-based work in a capitalist, consumerist society are similar to Crawford's. For a discussion and critique, see Dennis McCann and M. L. Brownsberger, "Business Ethics after MacIntyre," in *Religious Perspectives on Business Ethics: An Anthology*, ed. Thomas O'Brien and Scott Paeth (Lanham, MD: Rowman and Littlefield Publishers, 2007), 179–98.

19. Robert C. Solomon, "Business Ethics and Virtue," in *A Companion to Business Ethics*, ed. Robert E. Frederick (Malden, MA: Blackwell Publishers, 1999), 30–37, at 35.

with the courage of one's convictions.[20] Therefore, those participating in a business, or in any form of work, require the cardinal virtues of love and justice to guide their overall habituation in, and practice of, role-specific virtues.

## Businesses Flourish because of Their Members and Stakeholders

In the relationship between employees and other members of a business (fig. 7.1), it is those members who enable the business to flourish; their character shapes the character of the institution. Each type of member does so in specific ways:

- *Supervised employees.* Employees in the lower rungs of the organizational hierarchy do the bulk of a company's work. Without these employees, a business could not thrive. They also carry out the small but crucial daily tasks that ultimately typify the company as an ethical or unethical one, as one that cares about its customers or doesn't, and so on.

- *Middle managers.* These managers play a crucial role as a conduit of communication and values in the firm. They feed the experiences and insights of the workers they supervise and throughout the ranks to higher levels of management. They train and guide workers in line with the goals of the company and the directives of management. However, because they are in the middle, their role is a challenging one.[21] Managers with strong character and good skills can help the company avoid internal clashes and miscommunication.

- *Leaders and owners.* Top-level managers and owners set the tone for an organization. In a flourishing business, they lead based on ethical standards; they are humble; they are realistic about the demands being placed on workers; they communicate well; they prudently plan for the future and invest in their employees; and they show respect for all members and stakeholders.

- *Customers.* Similar to employees, customers and clients make a business possible in a fundamental way; if people do not purchase the goods or services, the business will not exist. Loyal customers help a business thrive, and they will only be loyal if the business gives them good value and treats them with respect.

20. Solomon discusses toughness further in *A Better Way to Think about Business* (New York: Oxford University Press, 1999), 108–11.

21. Sociologist Robert Jackall conducted an ethnographic study that is now famous in the business ethics literature, *Moral Mazes: The World of Corporate Managers* (New York: Oxford University Press, 1988). He conducted fieldwork at two large corporations and a large public relations firm, at which he interviewed managers to understand how they experience their work and its moral meaning. He found that "bureaucratic work shapes people's consciousness in decisive ways," among the results of which is that people "bracket" their personal moralities at work "to follow instead the prevailing morality of their particular organizational situation" (5–6).

- *Communities.* The community in which a business operates helps a company in many ways. The relationship must be one of mutual respect, based on recognition of each other's needs and contributions.
- *Investors.* Individuals who invest in a business (those large enough to have investors) make a business possible. The same requirements of mutual respect and recognition of mutual value apply.

All participants contribute to a business's flourishing, including its financial bottom line, reputation, and longevity. By their actions, they help shape the character of the organization.[22] Finally, these members make it possible for a business to carry out its mission and contribute something of value to society.

## Businesses and Society

The organizations that employ people are variously called firms, companies, businesses, and—especially when they are large—corporations. The catch-all term in this chapter is a *business.* Businesses come in all sizes, from one employee to more than 10,000. Looking at businesses as distinct establishments, most U.S. businesses are small.[23] Yet looking at where people work, most Americans are employed at large businesses: approximately 50 percent of Americans work for companies with more than 500 employees, and one-third of those people work for companies with more than 10,000 employees.[24] Whatever their size, businesses contribute to society both materially and ethically, as portrayed in the second relationship in the community connections chart (fig. 7.2).

### Businesses and Society

**Figure 7.2.** Community Connections: A Business and Society

22. However, Jackall's study suggests that lower-level employees and middle managers in a large firm will find it an uphill battle to change a corporate culture without strong support from the firm's leaders.

23. Fifty-five percent of all business establishments in the United States have one to four employees. Bureau of Labor Statistics, "Distribution of Private Sector Firms by Size Class," 2014, *http://www.bls.gov/web/cewbd/table_g.txt.*

24. U.S. Census Bureau, "Statistics about Business Size (Including Small Business)," data from 2007, site updated August 2012, *http://www.census.gov/econ/smallbus.html.*

## Businesses Contribute to Society Materially

Work adds goods, services, and new ideas to a society. Under the virtue-oriented definition of work, *all* work adds value to society. Under the everyday definition, one gets paid to work in a way that adds measurable value to the economy. For most people, paid work occurs through businesses, so these institutions and their employees are the creators of measurable value. In fact, 87 percent of the U.S. gross domestic product is generated by private-sector industries.[25] Therefore, without businesses, the United States, like every other nation, would be highly impoverished.

All businesses pay taxes and many of them provide health and retirement benefits to workers. These activities contribute to the functioning of society. A business pays corporate income taxes at rates ranging from 15 to 35 percent, depending on its level of income; the top rate applies to taxable income over $18.3 million.[26] Corporate taxes make up 13 percent of the U.S. federal budget (with most of the rest coming from taxes on individuals). Notably, the proportion of the federal budget coming from corporate taxes has declined steadily throughout the decades, from a high of 40 percent in 1944.

Businesses provide benefits for their workers. Sixty percent of Americans receive health insurance and 45 percent receive retirement benefits through their jobs.[27] The proportion of people receiving retirement benefits through their employers has remained steady since the late 1970s (though the type of plan most workers receive has shifted from a guaranteed pension to contributions to a retirement fund), but the proportion of Americans receiving health insurance this way has declined by 10 percent in the past fifteen years. For both types of benefits, government programs (Social Security, Medicare, Medicaid, etc.) are meant to cover gaps in the employer benefits and provide for those who are unable to work. The Affordable Care Act of 2010 was enacted to get more people covered through their employers or, when that is not possible, through markets of insurance programs established by the states or federal government. While businesses' provision of health and retirement benefits is undoubtedly

---

25. U.S. Department of Commerce, Bureau of Economic Analysis, "Gross-Domestic-Product-(GDP)-by-Industry Data," data file on "GDP by Industry/VA, GO, II," 2013 figures, *http://www.bea.gov/industry/gdpbyind_data.htm*.

26. These and the other figures in this paragraph are based on projections for fiscal year 2015 as presented by the National Priorities Project, "Federal Revenue: Where Does the Money Come From," accessed March 7, 2015, *https://www.nationalpriorities.org/budget-basics/federal-budget-101/revenues/*.

27. Robert Wood Johnson Foundation, "Number of Americans Obtaining Health Insurance through an Employer Declines Steadily Since 2000," April 11, 2013, *http://www.rwjf.org/en/library/articles-and-news/2013/04/number-of-americans-obtaining-health-insurance-through-an-employ.html*; Employee Benefit Research Institute, "What Are the Trends in U.S. Retirement Plans?" accessed March 7, 2015, *http://www.ebri.org/publications/benfaq/index.cfm?fa=retfaq14*. The rest of the data in this paragraph also comes from these sources.

a benefit to society, it is an open question as to whether this arrangement is the fairest and most efficient. Later in this chapter, the issue of the division of responsibilities between business and government is revisited.

## Businesses Contribute to Society Ethically

The economist Milton Friedman famously claimed, "There is one and only one social responsibility of business—to use its resources and engage in activities designed to increase its profits so long as it stays within the rules of the game."[28] This is an inadequate doctrine in light of virtue ethics. Businesses are members of society. Since they claim rights and since they participate in every sector of social life, they also have responsibilities to the rest of society that go beyond playing by the rules of the game. A business has an interest in adopting the broader view of responsibility because, by taking a collaborative approach with other institutions in working for the common good, a business helps itself flourish along with others.

Michael Novak, an independent scholar at the American Enterprise Institute who has written voluminously on economic philosophy, business ethics, and theology, summarizes these contributions in the following points that emphasize the moral good that businesses can do in society.[29]

*Businesses create invention, ingenuity, progress, jobs, and wealth for the benefit of society.* Businesses need to be innovative and adaptable to achieve their economic purpose. In a free society under the rule of law, businesses can innovate and adapt to create new products, services, and technologies. The well-being of society depends, in significant measure, on the vitality of its business sector.

*Businesses exemplify respect for law.* Or they should, of course, as this duty is fundamental. Laws are established so that the rights of all persons and institutions are respected. Like all institutions in society, businesses are expected to play by the rules. Businesses do, most of the time. Novak points out that businesses can flourish only when they respect the laws. Businesses that are upstanding contribute to a cultural ethos of lawfulness, which is one of the hallmarks of American culture. In some other societies, corruption reigns.

*Businesses foster social justice.* This duty is also fundamental, as it follows directly from the previous point. Social justice refers, first of all, to a fair economic system; ethical businesses are essential to the pursuit of justice in this sense. Social justice, second, refers to remedying such harms as poverty, lack of

---

28. Milton Friedman, "The Social Responsibility of Business Is to Increase Its Profits," *New York Times Magazine*, September 13, 1970, and reprinted in many anthologies on business ethics.

29. These contributions are drawn from Michael Novak, *Business as a Calling: Work and the Examined Life* (New York: Simon & Schuster, 1996), combining and recasting some of the fourteen duties he presents at 138–53.

opportunity, and the deficits created by the business operations. Economic activity in a free market inevitably causes some adverse impacts on others—what economists call negative externalities. For example, companies in some industries cause pollution as a byproduct of their operations. It is only fair, then, that companies that contribute to pollution also contribute to its remediation through taxes and fees. These companies further promote justice by taking action and investing in new technologies to avoid pollution in the first place.

*Businesses contribute to making society a better place.* A business is a member of society. Depending on its size and nature, a business may participate in several communities, from local to national to international. Wherever a business or a part of a business is located, it stands in relationship with the people and groups in that area. The business relies on this social network and should contribute to it. For most businesses, this engagement comes naturally, especially in the local community.

*Businesses promote political and social liberty.* Businesses ought to promote political and social liberty. American society benefits ethically from the vitality of business activity in a free market, a belief similar to Tocqueville's (ch. 4). Companies are mediating institutions in Tocqueville's sense: voluntary communities that serve the common good. By their participation in free trade, businesses encourage an ethos of freedom in society. Even though businesses naturally protect their interests, they need not be selfish. Business has a vested interest in seeing that society is both politically and socially free. For these reasons, public policy should be premised on seeing businesses not as selfish but as moral enterprises.

## Society Assists Businesses Materially and Ethically

A free and economically vibrant society is the responsibility of all its citizens and institutions. Novak would say that the business sector only does its job well when it cooperates with the other sectors of society, and when all the sectors respect each other's freedom. Government and nonprofit institutions help—and ought to help—businesses thrive.

### Government

"Businesses are plants that do not grow in just any environment," writes Novak. "They depend on a certain sort of political environment."[30] Government helps establish that environment in several ways:

* Government services relating to education are essential for preparing citizens with the knowledge and skills that make them valuable members of the workforce.

---

30. Ibid., 147.

- Together, all branches and levels of government guard democracy and enforce the rule of law. Businesses operate best in a system of democratic capitalism, in which competition is open but fair. Businesses rely upon such laws as protection of patents and trademarks, protection against crime, and being able to have their contract disputes resolved in courts.
- Government gathers taxes to fund the operation of those legal protections and provide infrastructure, such as the highway system, air traffic safety, the energy grid, and so on.
- Government regulations constrain business activities in the interests of maintaining a fair market and protecting the public good.

Through such contributions, government helps individual companies and the whole business sector to flourish. Companies that participate in a free and fair society and that are held accountable to legal standards are encouraged to act in ways that reinforce their character as institutions and make them more inviting places to work.

Some people, such as Friedman, believe that businesses do so much for society by their economic activity that they should have to abide by only a bare minimum of regulations and tax obligations. Others believe that businesses, especially large corporations, have received enormous benefits from society for which they have not paid enough in taxes; these people believe that corporations have been able to use their clout to keep taxes and regulations too low. The complexities of this debate are beyond the scope of this chapter; however, the fundamental claims of a virtue-ethics perspective in this debate are: (a) government should be recognized as a set of institutions and activities that support businesses in diverse and sometimes underappreciated ways; (b) government has the responsibility of setting limits on business in the interests of the common good; and (c) in the spirit of achieving a Golden Mean, the limits must be reasonable, balanced, and established with the participation of the business community.[31] An example of putting these principles into action was when President Obama raised the fuel efficiency standards in 2012, almost doubling the average miles-per-gallon standard (to 54.5 mpg) that new cars and trucks would have to meet by 2025. While some commentators criticized the action as an unreasonable constraint on American automakers, the standards were established with the support of the automakers during lengthy negotiations with the White House.[32]

---

31. Relevant to this claim are the facts that (a) corporate tax rates in the United States are comparable to the rates in other rich countries and (b) current U.S. corporate tax rates are at historically low levels. See Thomas L. Hungerford, "Corporate Tax Rates and Economic Growth since 1947," Economic Policy Institute, June 4, 2013, *http://www.epi.org/publication/ib364-corporate-tax-rates-and-economic-growth/*.

32. Bill Vlasic, "U.S. Sets Higher Fuel Efficiency Standards," *New York Times*, August 28, 2012, *http://www.nytimes.com/2012/08/29/business/energy-environment/obama-unveils-tighter-fuel-efficiency-standards.html*.

## The Nonprofit Sector

Nonprofit philanthropic organizations can shape a social environment that promotes the flourishing and character of businesses. Some nonprofits work to ensure that citizens are well-educated and have the skills to attain good jobs. The primary goal of these nonprofits is to lift people out of poverty; while doing so, they also help businesses hire and retain good workers. University departments and professional schools (business schools, nursing schools, journalism schools, etc.) are other types of educational organizations that prepare people to enter careers and educate them in ethical and social responsibilities. Other nonprofits serve as watchdogs to hold businesses accountable for living up to their social responsibilities, such as protecting the environment and making safe products.

Yet another nonprofit category includes organizations focused on supporting workers, professionals, or businesses. Professional societies of those who work in a given field help those professionals do their work well and ethically. The efforts of professional societies and industry organizations are not without controversy. Since these institutions are established for the welfare of members, their perspectives can be limited. These organizations claim to work for the common good of society by promoting ethical economic activity, but not everyone sees it that way. For instance, a union speaks for the interests of workers in an industry, while companies and their related associations speak for corporate interests. Clashes in viewpoints are not uncommon; in fact, they are expected. The common good is honored when free groups advocate for their members' interests, as long as (a) the groups do so guided by virtues such as honesty, justice, and prudence, and (b) they communicate, negotiate, and collaborate with the other groups to achieve a result that is reasonable for all involved.[33]

The ethical relationship of business and society can be summarized thus: businesses add to the ethos of society when they conduct their work well and live up to their social responsibilities. In turn, businesses need the assistance of citizens and other social institutions. From a virtue-ethics viewpoint, the business sector cannot be considered a world unto itself. As Solomon claims, "The first principle of business ethics is that the corporation is itself a citizen, a member of the larger community, and inconceivable without it."[34]

# Challenges within Businesses and Virtuous Responses

The following case study features challenges that an employee might encounter within a business and raises considerations of the ethical responsibilities of a

---

33. Yves R. Simon, *A General Theory of Authority* (original ed., 1962; reprint ed., Notre Dame, IN: University of Notre Dame Press, 1991) contains a classic defense of the idea that the common good actually requires the individual members of a community or society to advocate for their own interests.

34. Solomon, *Ethics and Excellence*, 148.

business toward its members and society. The case serves as a touchstone for the internal and external challenges examined in the remainder of the chapter.[35]

## Corporate Social Responsibility Internship in India— A Case Study

The summer before entering her junior year as an undergraduate student at a university in California, Laura was selected to work for two months on a Corporate Social Responsibility (CSR) project in southern India. Laura's participation was part of a social entrepreneurship program coordinated by a large, Indian corporation and Laura's university. The internship goal was to assess the impact of one of the corporation's CSR projects: a community college that had been built in a rural Indian fishing village shortly after the village was destroyed by a 2004 tsunami. The project's aim was to develop the vocational and English-language skills of the young adults living in the region.

Laura was to spend two months gathering data about the participating students, documenting the project's progress and setbacks, and giving recommendations for improvement. She would then present her findings at the company's headquarters and answer questions about her experiences at the site. Laura had never been to India before and did not speak the local language, Tamil. Once she arrived in India, she met the CSR project's coordinator, Ravi, a young Indian social worker who had been working there for about three years. She soon discovered that Ravi would also be her supervisor, translator, and main local contact person. There were no other interns or Americans working at Laura's site.

From the start of her internship, Laura encountered several problems. Ravi did not make or was late for many of their appointments. Relying on other translators to conduct her interviews, Laura began learning of the problems that the community college faced. The students and staff confirmed her suspicions that, in the past, Ravi had spent little time at the college and that he had not conducted the weekly meetings and interviews with the college's staff and students that he claimed he had. After gathering student attendance data and conducting in-depth interviews with the students, teachers, and the director of the community college, Laura discovered that there had also been financial mismanagement of student tuition fees by the college's former director, a rapid staff turnover, and a sudden drop in female college attendance figures.

---

35. Luisa Beck, "Corporate Social Responsibility Internship in India," revised January 5, 2014, Giving Voice to Values (GVV) Curriculum at Babson College, *http://www.babson.edu/Academics /teaching-research/gvv/Documents/Student/Corporate-Social-Responsibility-Internship-in-India_A_S .pdf*, in the "Individual Cases and Modules" package. This case was inspired by an actual internship experience, but Beck changed the names and situational details to protect confidentiality. The original case has been lightly edited to shorten it for this chapter. It is used with the kind permission of the author and of the GVV director, Professor Mary Gentile.

Laura reported her findings to Ravi. He told her that he was glad that she had found out about these problems; however, he would not admit his part in any of them. Ravi encouraged her not to mention these problems in her report. When Laura replied that it was her responsibility to document the project's setbacks, he told her that the company's headquarters were too disconnected from the project to make valuable improvements. He explained that a full report might have negative consequences for the college's staff and students, but that he and she could work together to find more fitting and immediate improvements. Ravi's statements gave Laura pause, because she was a newcomer to this context and did not wish to harm the college and its students. However, she knew she had done her investigation well and she recalled her obligation to write a thorough report.

## Internal Challenges

There are several potential challenges to character and flourishing within business, as illustrated by Laura's case.

*Unethical colleagues create pressure on workers to act similarly.* Sometimes the problem is an isolated instance of one coworker's or supervisor's bad behavior prompted by poor decision-making or the perceived need to cut corners. Often the problem is more systemic in the person's character and, sometimes, the culture of the business. Ravi is such a supervisor. He didn't make just one poor decision; the evidence indicates that he is not living up to his responsibilities. He often does not show up for scheduled meetings with Laura or with students and staff at the college. He seems unconcerned about Laura's findings of financial mismanagement, staff turnover, and a drop in female student attendance. Laura would be justified in concluding that Ravi is irresponsible and that he shows a lack of honesty and integrity when Laura raises these issues. He does not admit any fault; instead, he subtly points the finger at Laura, suggesting that her lack of knowledge about the language and culture means that her concerns are off base. As Laura's supervisor, Ravi is supposed to support Laura in her work, to make it possible for her to do her job effectively and ethically. By not doing so, he is failing to show Laura the respect she deserves.

*Business cultures that encourage silence.* Some contributing factors include a flawed system of internal communication and weak procedures for protecting whistleblowers. The problem often exists at the grassroots, when workers fear that their coworkers will ostracize them or their immediate supervisor will punish them for speaking up. Business ethicist Marianne Jennings reports that, according to workplace surveys, about half of employees say they would *not* report on coworkers' illegal or unethical behavior. The explanation given by these employees is, almost universally, that they want to keep being seen as "a team player."[36] Ravi plays on Laura's sympathy for the community college's staff, which, he asserts, might be harmed by her report, and he tries to cajole Laura by criticizing the supposed aloofness of the corporation. Company leaders must be aware that a culture of fear will burgeon if they fail to communicate— forcefully and consistently—that they want employees to report anything that violates the company's ethical code and legal obligations.

*Lack of a robust, ethical mission.* Chapter 4 introduced the concept of teleopathy. This "sickness over goals" can derive from several sources, one of which is that key leaders in a company are narrowly focused on the financial bottom line. A company's mission statement might pay lip service to its ethical values, but if the leaders, through action or inaction, send the message that the company's social and ethical responsibilities are an afterthought, managers and employees tend to follow suit. In the case study, Laura does not know what the leaders of the Indian corporation would think about Ravi's actions. Presumably, the corporation cares about social responsibility since it created the program in which Laura is working and established the college as part of that program. However, so far, the corporation has not paid close attention to the problems occurring at the college. The financial mismanagement of the former director apparently went unnoticed, and the corporation allowed both that director and Ravi to hold their positions. The problem is not necessarily that the corporation is unethical, but that it is removed from the daily life of the community college and has not made the strength of that college a priority.

*Overt, systemic unethical actions by a company.* This arises when teleopathy runs rampant. Employees' fear of reporting illegal and unethical activities is one of seven signs that a company is headed for "ethical collapse," in the words of Jennings. She has in mind corporations such as Enron, Tyco, and WorldCom that imploded from systemic unethical and illegal behavior. Several of the warning signs reflect the teleopathy of these corporations, beginning with "pressure to maintain those numbers," that is, privileging rampant growth, focusing solely on the financial bottom line, and developing a business model inordinately dedicated to creating products and services that promise rapid profits. These companies' ethical sicknesses were exacerbated by overly ambitious CEOs, weak boards of directors, and pervasive conflicts of interest. When a company is approaching ethical collapse, it takes on a vicious character that becomes impervious to the virtuous behaviors of solitary employees. The community college in the case study is not yet a casualty. The corporation is neither in collapse nor seriously ill, but it has a sore in one part of its large body. If Laura turns a blind eye to what she has observed or if the corporation is not responsive to what it learns, this sore could turn into a large wound, harming many good people in the process.

---

36. Marianne M. Jennings, *The Seven Signs of Ethical Collapse* (New York: St. Martin's Press, 2006), 61.

# Responses to Internal Challenges

As mentioned earlier, a practice is a cooperative social activity that requires certain habits and develops those habits in the people participating. Practices are usually discussed in terms of the virtuous habits they instill, but some practices can promote vicious habits. The ultimate antidote to vicious practices is virtuous practices. The following practices of employees and companies are virtuous responses to the challenges identified. These practices can assist Laura and others in their quests to do good work.

## The Employees' Role in Creating a Virtuous and Flourishing Workplace

First, an employee must be virtuous. This may sound like a platitude, but it is not: if a business does not contain a sufficient number of broadly virtuous members, there is no hope of the business being virtuous. Virtuous employees have many of the virtues described earlier, such as social-emotional intelligence, collaboration, critical thinking, and persistence. If the virtuous employee's character is underdeveloped in some ways—which is true of everyone—the person is open to discovering those deficits and making efforts to improve. This employee will also rely upon coworkers who have the character strengths that he or she lacks. Given the challenge of silence based in fear, it is important for a virtuous employee to have wisdom, integrity, and courage.

Laura, with apparent virtues of honesty and integrity, knows that going along with Ravi's suggestions is improper. She has the humility to acknowledge to herself that some of her observations might be flawed because she is new to the local culture; she knows she is not as wise as someone who has worked in this field for many years. Yet she reasons that she has been careful in her investigations, that she has support for her findings, and that the university has placed trust in her. Both virtue ethics, which reflects her character, and deontological ethics, which reasons from her duties, converge in her decision to write an honest report. Consequentialist reasoning, which aims to promote the best results overall, also supports Laura's full disclosure.[37] However, her situation is delicate, because she is far removed from her support system and Ravi is not only her supervisor but also her only local contact for the program. It might be tempting for her to avoid the negative consequences of a conflict with Ravi and to work with him, somehow, toward modest improvements. If this were a long-term job, Laura would have to decide if her best choice might be to look for another job.

Virtue thinkers point out that, to be happy and ethical, one has to choose a career and a job carefully. Edwin Harman says that, for many college students, choosing an employer or a career "will in effect be choosing which desires to

---

37. Consequentialism should not be misunderstood or misapplied. Ravi's rationalizations about the possible results of Laura's honesty do not reflect how philosophical consequentialist ethicists think.

cultivate, hence choosing a character." As a professor of business ethics, Harman says he and other faculty should "help students understand the importance of that choice and not make it thoughtlessly."[38] Unfortunately, when someone needs a job, taking into consideration the ethical quality of the company seems like a luxury. Moreover, often one cannot tell that a business has ethical flaws or problematic coworkers until one has already been hired and worked there awhile. Virtuous employees must be ready to confront such problems as they arise throughout their working careers.

Finally, workers should support each other in doing good work. Virtuous employees should seek each other out and strive to create communities of good practice within the business. Virtuous people tend to find each other, although this may be difficult in some settings where there are few like-minded coworkers nearby. In India, Laura feels isolated with Ravi as her main contact. Fortunately, there are other people and other institutions involved in her internship, ones that are probably interested in seeing ethical improvements made. One is the community college and the other is her sponsoring university. Laura's first step could be to call or email her academic advisor or the program director in the United States to seek that person's advice.

## The Employer's Role in Creating a Virtuous and Flourishing Workplace

The importance of having virtuous employees entails that managers and leaders in a firm must hire the right kinds of employees and train them so they are most likely to be virtuous. Jennings and other commentators assert that it is imperative for company leadership to set an ethical tone and lead by example.[39] In business, as in any organization, role models are valuable tools in implementing virtue ethics. Many larger corporations have ethics programs, sometimes called compliance programs. The purpose of such programs is to make the employees aware of the company's mission and values, educate them about ethical problems that might arise in their work, inform them of relevant laws and ethical norms, and show them how to handle or report problems. The term "compliance program" is more common in industries that do contract work for the government, such as defense and aerospace. Compliance with laws is important, but ethics programs are flawed when they are focused mostly on legality or when they are perfunctory or merely distribute information. Regardless of its size, a company should have the following programmatic features to promote ethics:[40]

---

38. Edwin M. Harman, "Can We Teach Character? An Aristotelian Answer," *Academy of Management Learning and Education* 5, no. 1 (2006): 68–81, at 79.

39. Jennings, *The Seven Signs of Ethical Collapse*, 234–36 on leadership in the face of peer pressure, ch. 4 on CEOs, and ch. 5 on boards. Jagidsh N. Sheth, *The Self-Destructive Habits of Good Companies* (Upper Saddle River, NJ: Pearson Education, 2007), 14–17 makes a similar point.

40. See Herb Genfan, "Formalizing Business Ethics," *Training & Development Journal* 41, no. 11 (November 1987): 35–37; and Dan Rice and Craig Dreilinger, "Rights and Wrongs of Ethics Training," *Training & Development Journal* 44, no. 5 (May 1990): 103–8.

- a strong, meaningful mission statement and strategic plan that integrates ethical values and goals
- clear, respected policies requiring ethical behavior and encouraging reporting of violations
- frequent communication of the company's ethical values and expectations by the leaders
- regular ethics training for all employees using examples that are true to the company's experience
- solicitation of honest feedback from employees about the challenges they face when trying to behave ethically
- a process for making adjustments to policies and procedures in light of employee feedback
- regular audits of the company's compliance with laws and ethical norms

Ethics initiatives must address not only *people* but also *systems*. This is the argument of Daniel Terris in a book analyzing the ethics program at defense contractor Lockheed Martin. The program's "exclusive emphasis on lived individual experience is appealing and in many ways effective. But the impact of a corporation like Lockheed Martin is not simply the accretion of millions of acts of fundamental decency undertaken by 130,000 workers. It is also the impact of the corporation as a very powerful organization."[41] To address the systemic dimension, Terris recommends that ethics training address the complexities encountered by senior executives, the ethics office be given the charge of advising and monitoring the actions of top executives, experts in corporate ethics be appointed to the board of directors, and corporations "be more courageous and transparent about framing and publicly tackling emerging ethical issues, such as executive compensation."[42] A business that establishes ethical practices and policies helps its members do good work, helps society, and, indeed, helps itself.

## Challenges outside Businesses and Virtuous Responses

Companies can respond to internal challenges, in large measure, through their own initiative. But internal challenges are influenced by the cultural, economic, and political contexts in which the work of individuals and businesses occur. These contexts are not simply forces that work on businesses, for businesses themselves are cultural, economic, and political actors. Therefore, the large,

---

41. Daniel Terris, *Ethics at Work: Creating Virtue in an American Corporation* (Waltham, MA: Brandeis University Press, 2005), 117.

42. Ibid., 128–29.

external challenges to good work can be partly caused or exacerbated by business itself. But neither business, nor any other institution alone, can remedy them; collaboration is needed.

## External Challenges

*Economic forces hampering individuals' financial self-sufficiency.* These forces are always a threat to some citizens, but their deleterious effects are felt more widely when the economy is stagnant. The economic recession of the late 2000s exacerbated problems of unemployment, underemployment, and personal debt.

- *Unemployment.* The U.S. unemployment rate skyrocketed from 4.4 percent in May 2007 to 10.0 percent in October 2009. From that peak it gradually shrank to 5.4 percent by May 2015.[43] As Harvard economist Jeffrey Sachs notes, "In all, 8.6 million jobs where shed from the peak employment of 2007 to the trough of 2009. Even before the current crisis, the 2000s had the lowest growth of jobs in any decade since World War II."[44]

- *Underemployment.* The number of citizens who were underemployed or gave up looking for work also rose during the recession.[45] Liz Guidone, the recent college graduate described at the start of this chapter, who is frustrated by a series of unpaid internships, is an example of how even well-educated people are vulnerable. Despite having a college degree, she finds it difficult to land a full-time job in her field.

- *Debt.* Guidone's other major problem is her student-loan debt. Two in three college students graduate with debt, and for many of them, it remains a financial burden into their 30s and 40s.[46] In 2013, the average student graduating from a public university had $25,600 in debt, while one graduating from a private university had $31,200. Many millennials report that their debt requires them to delay marrying and starting families and makes

---

43. Federal Reserve Bank of St. Louis, "Graph: Civilian Unemployment Rate," FRED research database, accessed May 20, 2015, *https://research.stlouisfed.org/fred2/graph/?id=UNRATE*.

44. Jeffrey D. Sachs, *The Price of Civilization: Reawakening American Virtue and Prosperity* (New York: Random House Trade Paperbacks, 2012), 15.

45. Bureau of Labor Statistics, "Ranks of Discouraged Workers and Others Marginally Attached to the Labor Force Rise During Recession," *Issues in Labor Statistics,* April 2009, *http://www.bls.gov/opub/ils/ils74abs.htm*. For a more recent update of the statistics, see James Shrek, "Not Looking for Work: Why Labor Force Participation Has Fallen During the Recovery," The Heritage Foundation, September 4, 2014, *http://www.heritage.org/research/reports/2014/09/not -looking-for-work-why-labor-force-participation-has-fallen-during-the-recovery*.

46. Sources for the rest of this paragraph: Froymovich, *End of the Good Life*, 27–49; Bobby Brannigan, "A Student Debt Crisis Is Looming, according to Alarming Trends," *Huffington Post,* May 4, 2013, *http://www.huffingtonpost.com/bobby-brannigan/a-student-debt-crisis-is-_b_3195036.html*; and the College Board, "Trends in Higher Education: Loans," tables 13A and 13B, accessed March 18, 2015, *http://trends.collegeboard.org/student-aid/figures-tables/loans*.

it difficult to pay bills and buy homes. Total student debt is also a problem for the U.S. economy, as it has increased 511 percent since 1999, now totaling more than one trillion dollars and occasioning fears of a crisis if too many young people default on their loans.

*The tenuous experience of work in modern capitalism.* Sociologist Richard Sennett describes the problem powerfully in *The Corrosion of Character.* Sennett suggests that "no long term"—referring to an attitude of flexibility and lack of commitment—could serve as the motto of contemporary capitalism. Sennett heard the phrase from an executive at AT&T, who embraced it as the way that corporations need to conduct business these days. But Sennett argues that everyone is harmed by this situation. "'No long term' disorients action over the long term, loosens bonds of trust and commitment, and divorces will from behavior."[47] To illustrate, he profiles Rico, a technology advisor to a venture capital firm. Although Rico earns a much better income and has a higher social status than his father, who worked as a janitor, it becomes clear to Sennett that the father flourished in his work more than the son. For instance, Rico moves his family four times to pursue new job opportunities. When his job requires stressful, extended workdays for weeks at a time, Rico says, "It's like I don't know who my kids are."[48] Of Rico and his wife, Jeannette, who is also a full-time professional, Sennett writes, "Both husband and wife often fear they are on the edge of losing control over their lives. This fear is built into their work histories."[49]

For Sennett, the source of the parents' stress is not that both are working full-time. Rather, the transformed nature of time, place, and work in contemporary capitalism creates "a conflict between character and experience."[50] Workers in bureaucratic enterprises have a hard time exercising control over their work lives and telling a story about who they are and where the meaning of their work lies. Rico and Jeannette are casualties of the business culture of uncertainty. Rico feels he has to look out for himself, because he cannot trust that his employer will do so. But his attitude means that his employer loses the benefit of his loyalty. To the extent that uncertainty and lack of commitment reign in the modern economy, many people and institutions suffer.

*Cultural and economic pressures on businesses.* In recent decades, companies have been under financial pressures to downsize, lower labor costs, keep pace with rapid technological changes, and stay ahead of their competitors. Business leaders do not like to think of their firms this way, but too many examples have shown how real the risk is. Business leaders also point to additional

---

47. Richard Sennett, *The Corrosion of Character: The Personal Consequences of Work in the New Capitalism* (New York: Norton, 1998), Sennett, 31.

48. Ibid., 21.

49. Ibid., 19.

50. Ibid., 31.

financial pressure they face, such as taxes, competition from cheaper imports, competition from companies in countries with cheaper labor and fewer regulations, and the ballooning costs of employee health insurance and pensions. All of these pressures make it easy for companies to slip into teleopathy—concentrating so much on their financial returns that they ignore the humanity of their employees and skirt their long-term obligations to society.

*Insufficient business ethics education.* Business leaders and society look to business colleges and graduate programs to develop professionals with character and the skills to handle internal and external ethical challenges. This expectation on business programs is significant and perhaps unfair; after all, character is formed by many factors, the biggest of which is probably the family. Nonetheless, business ethics education is important, and business schools recognize this by incorporating ethics into their curricula. Yet whether ethics is a required and substantial element in *all* programs is difficult to determine.[51] How business schools implement the open-ended stipulations of the main accrediting body[52] varies widely. A much-cited news item from 2004 reported that only one-third of accredited business schools require a stand-alone ethics course."[53] A stand-alone course might not be necessary if ethics were integrated throughout the business curriculum, which is the approach most business professors prefer. However, a study of accounting professors who teach ethics determined that the number of classroom hours spent on ethics in the throughout-the-curriculum approach adds up to less than one course.[54]

In addition, the effectiveness of current efforts has been questioned. A group of researchers assessing multiple programs concluded, "Very few studies have shown effectiveness in changing an individual's ethical reasoning development through programmatic ethics training."[55] Further, there does not, as yet, seem to be consensus on the educational methods that work best. The most promising methods are intensive, requiring far more than lectures, tests, and papers. Business schools might see it as a difficulty to devote the needed time and effort.[56]

---

51. The lack of available nationwide data suggests that no well-known academic or corporate think tank is conducting a regular audit of business ethics education. It would render a great service to the academic and business communities if some institution took up this task.

52. Association to Advance Collegiate Schools of Business, "Eligibility Procedures and Accreditation Standards for Business Accreditation," April 8, 2013, updated January 31, 2015, *http://www.aacsb.edu/en/accreditation/standards/2013-business/*.

53. Kevin Breaux et al., "Ethics Education in Accounting Curricula: Does It Influence Recruiters' Hiring Decisions of Entry-Level Accountants?," *Journal of Education for Business* 85 (2010): 1, citing a 2004 article on Bloomberg News.

54. Cindy Blanthorne et al., "Accounting Educators' Opinions about Ethics in the Curriculum," *Issues in Accounting Education* 22, no. 3 (August 2007): 355–90, at 384.

55. Christopher Drees Schmidt et al., "Applying What Works: A Case for Deliberate Psychological Education in Undergraduate Business Ethics," *Journal of Education for Business* 88 (2013): 127–35, at 132.

56. Ibid., 132–33. These authors discuss the promising approach that will be returned to later.

*The U.S. political culture is insufficiently oriented to the common good.* American corporations and corporate leaders wield great power while workers and ordinary citizens have been increasingly disempowered. Political leaders have been charged with lacking the vision or will to nurture a virtuous economy. As Sachs puts it,

> At the root of America's economic crisis lies a moral crisis: the decline of civic virtue among America's political and economic elite. A society of markets, law, and elections is not enough if the rich and powerful fail to behave with respect, honesty, and compassion toward the rest of society and toward the world. America has developed the world's most competitive market society but has squandered its civic virtue along the way. Without restoring an ethos of social responsibility, there can be no meaningful and sustained economic recovery.[57]

Sachs backs up this strong statement with a great deal of data, including evidence of the growth of income inequality since the 1970s. "The wealthiest 1 percent of American households today enjoys a higher total net worth than the bottom 90 percent, and the top 1 percent of income earners receives more pretax income than the bottom 50 percent. The last time America had such massive inequality of wealth and income was on the eve of the Great Depression, and the inequality today may actually be greater than in 1929."[58]

## Virtuous Responses to External Challenges

Sachs issues a clarion call for a reawakening of civic virtue, a call that meets with approval from virtue ethicists. Although many recommendations can be made in response to the call for civic virtue—none of which are without controversy—the recommendations that can be developed from a virtue-based social ethic have a better chance of securing agreement in a pluralistic society.

### Practices for Workers and Businesses

*Practice purpose.* Csikszentmihalyi says that both workers and businesses must actively seek the "soul of business." His description of "soul" is virtually identical to the virtue of purpose as described in chapter 2: the trait of reaching for meaning beyond oneself. Soulful workers and soulful businesses strive to contribute to others and create lasting value.[59] Opportunities abound for practicing

---

57. Sachs, *The Price of Civilization*, 3.

58. Ibid., 22–23. These trends are not limited to the United States: compare the much-discussed work of French economist Thomas Piketty, *Capital in the Twenty-First Century*, trans. Arthur Goldhammer (Cambridge, MA: Belknap, 2014).

59. Csikszentmihalyi, *Good Business*, ch. 7.

purpose, although obstacles stand in the way. High school and college students can take advantage of the opportunities their schools provide for considering the meaning of good work and making thoughtful choices about their career paths. Workers at any stage of their careers can take a deliberative approach by clarifying their priorities, working on their characters, developing their skills, associating with the most virtuous coworkers and mentors they can find, and engaging in practices outside of work (such as prayer and meditation, exercise, community service, and connecting with family and friends) that enhance flourishing.[60] Managers and business leaders can practice "mindful leadership" by creating business environments that respect the ingredients of flow and character, adopting such practices as those mentioned in this chapter concerning businesses' internal responsibilities.[61]

*Give renewed attention to the human factor in business.* A business is a community that lives alongside other communities within a society, which is itself a large community. Every community is composed of people. Respect for people—in the form of love and justice as bedrock virtues (and principles)—must govern social relationships. The human factor can be kept front and center in management decisions, business plans, and economic policies. Managers and business can do so by following the practices that promote flow and character in their institutions, as already recommended. Policymakers would do well to keep in mind that "the quality of the labor force will be the most important single determinant of American prosperity in the decades to come."[62] Thus resources are needed for the education of citizens across the lifespan.

*Develop a cooperative approach internally and externally.* Many of the authors quoted in this chapter warn of the dangers of an excessively competitive mind-set. Competition is necessary in business, but it must be channeled by such virtues as compassion, justice, and humility. Unfettered competition is morally risky and self-destructive.[63] In the global economy, unrestrained competition leading to growing income inequality within and between countries is an unsustainable formula. Such competition also rapidly depletes natural resources and accelerates environmental degradation, which results in everyone being hurt. "Achieving the benefits of globalization," says Sachs, "therefore requires active international cooperation as well as internal cooperation."[64] Businesses would be wise to see themselves as partners with governments, nonprofits, and other businesses in establishing sustainable economic growth.

---

60. For specific suggestions, see Csikszentmihalyi, *Good Business*, ch. 8, and Ben-Shahar, *Happier*, ch. 7.

61. See also Janice Marturano, *Finding the Space to Lead: A Practical Guide to Mindful Leadership* (New York: Bloomsbury, 2014).

62. Sachs, *The Price of Civilization*, 19.

63. See Sheth, *The Self-Destructive Habits of Good Companies*, ch. 6, and Jennings, *The Seven Signs of Ethical Collapse*, 204.

64. Sachs, *The Price of Civilization*, 96.

*Promote social entrepreneurship and social businesses.* Social entrepreneurship, a much-discussed phenomenon in the past few decades, is the process of working for social change through innovative nonprofits and socially responsible businesses. Social entrepreneurship holds the promise that someone with a passion to make the world a better place can make a decent living while doing so by creating a business or nonprofit geared to a particular social cause.[65] Specifically within the business world, companies can decide to operate as "social businesses." Development economist Muhammad Yunus says, "A social business is designed and operated as a business enterprise, with products, services, customers, markets, expenses, and revenues—but with the profit maximization principle replaced by the social-benefit principle. Rather than seeking to amass the highest possible level of financial profit to be enjoyed by the investors, the social business seeks to achieve a social objective."[66] An example is Grameen Bank, a community development bank that Yunus founded in his native Bangladesh in 1976. Grameen provides small-business start-up loans, known as microloans, to poor entrepreneurs in developing nations under favorable terms. The number of social businesses is growing, and the scope of possibilities for them is extensive.[67] Whatever form they take, Yunus argues that they are essential to eradicating global poverty and ensuring the future of capitalism by creating a viable space within it for the social-benefit principle.

## Practices for Other Institutions

Many groups in society engage in practices that help businesses promote good work. Nonprofit organizations, educational institutions, and government have been discussed in this chapter and throughout the book. Some valuable practices have not been described here because they are treated in other chapters. One is that nonprofits and businesses could engage in innovative collaborations (ch. 8). Another is that businesses and government could partner with schools to close the educational achievement gap (ch. 6). Yet there are other educational and political strategies as well, disscussed in the following paragraphs.

*Make post-secondary education affordable and reduce student debt.* As the cost of college education has skyrocketed, many students graduate with massive debt and struggle to repay their loans. Froymovich, the author who

---

65. See ch. 8, where a nonprofit called buildOn is presented as example. For more details, see David Bornstein and Susan Davis, *Social Entrepreneurship: What Everyone Needs to Know* (New York: Oxford University Press, 2010) and Rupert Scofield, *The Social Entrepreneur's Handbook* (New York: McGraw-Hill, 2011).

66. Muhammad Yunus, *Creating a World without Poverty: Social Business and the Future of Capitalism* (New York: PublicAffairs, 2007), 23. For pioneering the practice of microfinancing, Yunus and Grameen won the Nobel Peace Prize in 2006.

67. See also Bill Saporito, "Making Good, Plus a Profit," *Time,* March 23, 2015, 22, on the trend of U.S. states allowing businesses to register as "benefit corporations," or B Corps.

demonstrates the employment woes of her own millennial generation, presents several innovative responses, some of which have already been tried. She praises a group of students at the University of California who authored a proposal that the university would "pay for all accepted students' education up front and allow graduates to repay the institution later, after securing employment."[68] This proposal would universalize what some state and federal government programs do: forgive a portion of a student's loans if that student performs substantial post-graduation community service or works in a job serving a greatly needed role. Froymovich also argues for improvements in the 529 college savings plans, as they do not generate sufficient savings for lower-income families, and for reforms to fix the loan-payback system so students are not burdened by debt. She expresses hope that online education will soon provide new, low-cost opportunities for earning a college degree. Just one year after her book was published, the University of the People, a tuition-free online university with a mission of making college accessible globally, was accredited and began offering four bachelor's degrees.

*Bring business ethics to a new level of seriousness and sophistication.* Diane Swanson is one of a number of business ethics professors who have been highly critical of the business college accrediting body, the Association to Advance Collegiate Schools of Business (AACSB International), for not requiring at least one course devoted to ethics in business curricula. She argues that both a required foundational course, delivered by knowledgeable faculty, and further teaching of ethics integrated into the curriculum are essential to address the "crises of legitimacy" in business education.[69] Moreover, the field of business education should improve the sophistication of its research to find the educational practices that are most effective. Pedagogies that have shown promise in enhancing moral development are those that attend as much to the method of course delivery as to course content. The teaching methods should be based on psychological insights about how students "construct knowledge through experience" and develop ethical awareness and skills "within a supportive and progressively challenging context."[70] Such an approach, based in cognitive developmental theory, fits well with virtue ethics.

*Renew the meaning of civic virtue for the twenty-first century.* Sachs spoke of the recovery of civic virtue as an antidote to economic forces of stagnation and stratification. To practice civic virtue, businesses must take seriously their obligations to the common good, while other members of society must respect

---

68. Froymovich, *End of the Good Life*, 163.

69. Diane L. Swanson, "Business Ethics Education at Bay: Addressing a Crisis of Legitimacy," *Issues in Accounting Education* 20, no. 3 (August 2005): 247–53. See also Larry A. Floyd et al., "Ethical Outcomes and Business Ethics: Toward Improving Business Ethics Education," *Journal of Business Ethics* 117 (2013): 753–76.

70. Schmidt et al., "Applying What Works," 128.

the constructive role that businesses can and do play. The following goals are ways to imagine, "What would a good society look like?" and then to think about what kinds of economic and political practices might move society in that direction.

* *Businesses and the wealthy could pay their fair share.* Sachs devotes a chapter of his book to analyzing the U.S. federal budget deficit and the possible solutions for eliminating it or reducing it to a reasonable level. He makes the case that there are little savings to be found in cutting the programs that are mentioned in this regard: foreign aid, Medicaid, Medicare, Social Security, and even the military. And so, "with a chronic budget deficit of around 6 percent of GDP, tax revenues will have to rise. It is high time that super-rich taxpayers picked up this cost."[71] He illustrates that there is both prudence and fairness in reversing the historically low tax rates on the wealthy and corporations. He clarifies, "My point isn't to bleed the rich but to call upon them to pay a decent and responsible share of the national needs."[72]

* *Government could relieve business of its outdated role in the social safety net.* If Sachs's proposal seems like it would burden businesses, it can be paired with another idea that does the opposite. Businesses face heavy financial burdens paying for employees' health-care costs, not to mention managing the paperwork and worrying about shifting regulations and ever-higher costs. Employees are likewise worried about keeping their health insurance, which hampers their ability to start their own businesses or work part time, because they would lose coverage. To date, business leaders have not warmed to the idea that government should institute a national health plan, but Matt Miller, a senior fellow at the Center for American Progress, believes that it is "a destined idea," one that would free businesses to do what they do best and that would put responsibility for the public's welfare where it properly belongs—in the government's portfolio.[73]

* *Business executives and organizations could take leadership in fostering conversation about the public agenda.* Miller argues that another destined idea is that businesses will take the leading role in forging a new public agenda for bold reforms in economics, education, and politics. He believes this will happen because political leaders will never be able to break out of the cycle of pandering to the public to win elections. "Business is poised to fill this void [of political leadership]. By instinct and temperament the sector is clear-eyed and unsentimental. It prefers pragmatic results to ideology, and it has the clout to be heard."[74] What Miller means is not that business executives will

71. Sachs, *The Price of Civilization*, 229.

72. Ibid., 235.

73. Matt Miller, *The Tyranny of Dead Ideas: Revolutionary Thinking for a New Age of Prosperity* (New York: Holt Paperbacks, 2010), 157–68.

74. Ibid., 228.

or should become the top leaders in society, but that they have a particular character that suits them for raising the uncomfortable questions that others do not want to ask.

- *Political officials could ensure all voices are heard in the public conversation.* Paired with the previous practice, it is high time to rebalance the power dynamics in the public conversation. The wealthy—both corporations and individuals—have the vast sums of money at their disposal to get their "voices" heard in the public square. The voices of the wealthy should not overwhelm those of middle class and poor citizens. When Miller speaks of the voice of business as important, he means in policy discussions, not elections. Sachs says, "The role of big money in politics has completely sidelined competent public administration."[75] Thus, he argues, campaign financing should be reformed, corporate lobbying sharply curtailed, and other reforms instituted so the government becomes, once again, the people's agent.

- *Citizens and government could adopt flourishing as their goal.* Sachs and Csikszentmihalyi commend Aristotelian virtue and Buddhist mindfulness.[76] The ethical, philosophical, and religious traditions based on these two sages extol a balanced view of material success: it is, at best, only a minor part of flourishing. This attitude needs to be adopted by citizens and society if they hope to flourish. Ultimately (and with many qualifications), citizens will get the government, economy, and culture that they foster through their daily practices. In the economic realm, if people purchase products heedlessly, if they take little thought about the impact of their choices on the environment, if they are uncritical of the media they consume, and so on, businesses will meet their wants. But if people live mindfully, eventually businesses and other institutions will respond to demands based in a deeper appreciation of the difference between what people may *want* and what they truly *need*.

## Conclusion

Businesses are communities with distinctive practices, one of which is to nurture the work of their employees. The pursuit of personal and social flourishing can come together in a person's work. Virtue ethicists propose that "good work" is not an empty dream. People can achieve work that is morally good, good for their own deep happiness, and good for others in society. Enjoying good work is not easy and often it is only partly achieved. It is, instead, an ongoing pursuit—one that virtuous workers believe to be worth the effort. In this pursuit, businesses, professional fields, and similar organizations can help workers. Businesses have

---

75. Sachs, *The Price of Civilization*, 238.

76. Ibid., ch. 9, and Csikszentmihalyi, *Good Business*, ch. 7.

not only the duty but also the great privilege of helping employees achieve good work. Practices based in virtue, flow, mindfulness, and social responsibility make good work a realistic dream for anyone.

## Questions for Review

1. What is meant by the "extrinsic" and "intrinsic" value of work, and how are they related?
2. What is "flow," and what factors contribute to it?
3. What can be learned about flow at work by examining flow during play?
4. How is the development of skills similar to the development of virtue, according to Annas?
5. What does Crawford mean by "the separation of thinking from doing" as it applies to work?
6. What is the moral bind that middle managers face, according to Jackall?
7. In what ways, according to Novak, do businesses promote political and social liberty?
8. Describe a contribution of government to business that is also controversial in some people's eyes. Do the same for a contribution that nonprofits make to business.
9. What are key ingredients for a successful company ethics program?
10. What is a "social business"?

## Discussion Questions and Activities

1. Describe one of your best work experiences, then list the features that made it great. Do the same for a bad work experience you have had, listing the features that made it problematic. Relate these features to concepts in the chapter, such as flow, extrinsic and intrinsic benefits, pressures to separate thinking from doing, teleopathy, pressure to conform to peers, and the company's code of ethics and ethical training (or lack thereof).
2. Describe someone you know whose work, during a period of time, developed his or her virtues (or vices). Be as specific as you can about how the person's character was influenced by (a) the person's own decisions, (b) the work activity itself, (c) common practices in this field or business, and (d) other people in the organization.
3. The greatest obstacle preventing employees from whistleblowing on unethical and illegal behavior is fear of "not fitting in." Can virtue ethics provide a strategy for diminishing this obstacle? Why or why not?

4. Does the idea of "no long term" portray your current or past job in any way, or the jobs of others you know? Explain and evaluate.

5. If you are in college, what ethics education have you received related to your planned career? Evaluate the quality of this education using ideas and information from the chapter. What additional ethics education have you received at college, and how could it be relevant to your work life?

6. Sachs claims that economic problems that have been brewing since the 1970s (e.g., stagnant wages, growing income inequality, weaknesses in public education, and the increasing political power of the wealthy) indicate a loss of civic virtue. Do you agree? Evaluate the civic practices recommended by Sachs and Miller.

## Recommendations for Further Reading

Ciulla, Joanne B. *The Working Life: The Promise and Betrayal of Modern Work.* New York: Three Rivers Press, 2000.

A historical, cultural, and ethical exploration of the meaning of work. Cuilla, a professor of leadership and ethics, considers how modern work, with its technological and bureaucratic features, makes it difficult for workers to find meaning.

Crawford, Matthew B. *Shop Class as Soulcraft: An Inquiry into the Value of Work.* New York: Penguin, 2009.

Crawford diagnoses the core problem of modern work as the separation of thinking from doing. He presents the possibilities for good work by drawing lessons from his own work as a motorcycle mechanic. See also his TEDx talk, "Manual Competence" at *https://www.youtube.com/watch?v=xdGky1JZovg.*

Csikszentmihalyi, Mihaly. *Good Business: Leadership, Flow, and the Making of Meaning.* New York: Penguin, 2003.

The psychologist who popularized the concept of flow discusses the obstacles to, and the conditions for, fully engaging work.

Froymovich, Riva. *End of the Good Life: How the Financial Crisis Threatens a Lost Generation—And What We Can Do about It.* New York: Harper Perennial, 2013.

The author powerfully presents the crisis afflicting millennials and offers specific policy recommendations, but she gives only brief, generic suggestions for how young people can find engagement in their work.

Meilaender, Gilbert, ed. *Working: Its Meaning and Its Limits.* Notre Dame, IN: University of Notre Dame Press, 2000.

An anthology of readings from history, philosophy, theology, poetry, fiction, and the Bible about varied understandings of work, such as work as vocation, work as irksome, etc. Useful in academic courses that consider the personal and social meanings of work.

Sachs, Jeffrey D. *The Price of Civilization: Reawakening American Virtue and Prosperity.* New York: Random House Trade Paperbacks, 2012.

A Harvard economist's wide-ranging analysis of the problems of economic stagnation and income inequality, with solutions ranging from the cultural to the political.

Solomon, Robert C. *Ethics and Excellence: Cooperation and Integrity in Business.* New York: Oxford University Press, 1993.

Solomon (1942–2007) was a virtue thinker highly influential in business ethics. This is one of his most comprehensive treatments of the topic, with substantial use of Aristotle.

Walker, Rebecca L., and Philip J. Ivanhoe, eds. *Working Virtue: Virtue Ethics and Contemporary Moral Problems.* Oxford: Clarendon Press, 2007.

This anthology applies virtue ethics to a variety of current social and professional contexts, such as medicine, psychiatry, military service, business, the environment, and race relations.

### Websites for business ethics and professional ethics:

Business Ethics: The Magazine of Corporate Responsibility. *http://business-ethics .com.*

Center for the Study of Ethics in the Professions at the Illinois Institute of Technology. *http://ethics.iit.edu.*

Corporate Social Responsibility Newswire. *http://www.csrwire.com.*

Ethics & Compliance Initiative. *http://www.ethics.org.*

Giving Voice to Values Curriculum at Babson College. *http://www.babson.edu /Academics/teaching-research/gvv/Pages/home.aspx.*

# 8
CHAPTER

# Service
## Groups That Promote Charity, Justice, and Purpose

Everybody can be great, because everybody can serve. You don't have to make your subject and your verb agree to serve. You don't have to know about Plato and Aristotle to serve. You don't have to know Einstein's theory of relativity to serve. You don't have to know the second theory of thermodynamics in physics to serve. You only need a heart full of grace, a soul generated by love. And you can be that servant.

—*Rev. Martin Luther King Jr.*[1]

---

## Chapter Overview

- defines service as a virtuous activity of individuals and volunteer organizations
- describes the benefits of volunteer groups to their members and vice versa as well as the benefits of volunteer groups to society and vice versa
- examines challenges facing people and groups that aim to serve by considering challenges within the groups and obstacles in society
- identifies the policies and resources that nonprofits need to fulfill their missions
- recommends practices, for volunteer groups and individuals, that promote social flourishing through service

---

1. Martin Luther King Jr., "The Drum Major Instinct," sermon at Ebenezer Baptist Church, Atlanta, Georgia, February 4, 1968, The Martin Luther King, Jr. Research and Education Institute, *https://king institute.stanford.edu/king-papers/documents/drum-major-instinct-sermon-delivered-ebenezer-baptist-church.*

# Service Matters

Service generates ethical and social benefits. Participating in service is a way for people and groups to express virtues, develop character, and help communities become more compassionate and just. In other words, service promotes personal and social flourishing. The personal, communal, and social expressions of service are integrally linked as is seen in this chapter.

# Volunteers

At the individual level, service demonstrates personal virtue and is a way to pursue personal meaning. *Service* is defined as doing something to help another person out of concern for that person's well-being. While it can involve various virtues, service is especially aligned to love, since service is an expression of compassion and kindness. People can serve in various ways: helping a friend with homework, shoveling a neighbor's sidewalk, donating to a food drive, tutoring a child in an afterschool program, volunteering at a school event, making calls to raise money for one's alma mater, helping on a house-building project, or getting signatures for a petition to reduce industrial pollution. Such activities range from ordinary ways of helping one's family and friends to activities coordinated through organizations.

Most people recognize that service is valuable, but the academic and political worlds have not always paid it the serious attention it deserves. Robert Payton and Michael Moody, scholars specializing in philanthropic studies, say, "Philanthropy deserves attention because everyone has some experience with it. Not all the experience is positive, nor is everyone actively engaged in philanthropy, but the experience of giving and receiving assistance is for practical purposes universal."[2] How many people actively engage in volunteer service? More than 62 percent of Americans report volunteering informally, as indicated by answers to a survey question about doing favors for one's neighbors.[3] As for formal service conducted through organizations, 62.8 million Americans volunteered at least once between September 2013 and September 2014. This represents 25.3 percent of Americans age sixteen and over and is little changed from the previous year. This volunteer rate is a few percentage points lower than in 2002, the first year the statistic was recorded. The main types of activities volunteers performed included collecting, preparing, distributing, or serving food (10.8 percent), fundraising (10.3 percent), tutoring or teaching (9.3 percent), engaging in general labor such as supplying transportation to people (8.2 percent), and providing professional or management assistance (7.1 percent).

---

2. Robert L. Payton and Michael P. Moody, *Understanding Philanthropy: Its Meaning and Mission* (Bloomington, IN: University of Indiana Press, 2008), 14.

3. The statistics in the rest of this paragraph are from the Corporation for National and Community Service, "Volunteering and Civic Engagement in the United States," 2013 data, *http://www.volunteeringinamerica.gov/national*, and the U.S. Bureau of Labor Statistics, "Volunteering in the United States, 2014," February 25, 2015, *http://www.bls.gov/news.release/pdf/volun.pdf.*

Volunteering usually makes the volunteer feel good; this is one of the pleasant aspects of service. There are other substantial benefits to the flourishing of volunteers, as are seen in this chapter. Virtue ethicists, given their interest in flourishing, are intrigued by these benefits, which should not be sought for their own sake as that defeats the essence of service. The paradox of service, similar to the paradox of love, is captured in an anonymous saying: "The best way to find yourself is to lose yourself in the service of others." Service is a practice with the power to develop excellence of character in the giver as it builds a relationship between the giver and the receiver. Philosopher André Comte-Sponville writes,

> Generosity elevates us *toward others*, as it were, and toward ourselves as beings freed from the pettiness that is the self. He who is not at all generous, our language warns us, is low, cowardly, petty, vile, stingy, greedy, egotistical, squalid. Which we all are, but not always and never completely; generosity is what sets us apart—or, sometimes, frees us— from these impulses.[4]

Service is appealing, then, for many reasons, one of which is that it leads persons to character and communities to the common good. Says Comte-Sponville, "Love is the goal, generosity the road to it."[5]

## Volunteer Groups

Service by groups is often called *charity* or *philanthropy*. Payton and Moody define philanthropy as "voluntary action for the public good."[6] Groups that engage in such action go by several names. *Volunteer groups* and *clubs* denote smaller, less formal gatherings of people around a service activity, while *philanthropies, charities,* and *volunteer organizations* are terms used for institutions with a budget and paid employees. Examples of the small, informal type are clubs and committees in high schools, colleges, and churches whose members engage in service. Examples of formal volunteer organizations include the Boy Scouts, Girl Scouts, Habitat for Humanity, Big Brothers Big Sisters, Save the Children, Catholic Charities, Lutheran Services in America, American Jewish World Service, the American Red Cross, the International Red Cross, and buildOn—an organization profiled later in this chapter. Often an individual volunteer participates in a small and fairly informal group that is part of a large organization. For instance, a church or school group might organize a handful of people to help on a Habitat for Humanity house-building project for a day. The church or school group might not have a budget, permanent organizers, or long-term plans, so

---

4. André Comte-Sponville, *A Small Treatise on the Great Virtues,* trans. Catherine Temerson (New York: Metropolitan Books, 2001), 102; italics in the original.

5. Ibid., 101.

6. Payton and Moody, *Understanding Philanthropy,* 6.

its service is made possible by the organization, professionalism, and budget of Habitat for Humanity, a charitable organization.

What links these disparate groups is that they are voluntary and nonprofit. *Voluntary* indicates that individuals freely choose to participate in such organizations and *nonprofit* means that these organizations do not earn a profit for owners or shareholders; instead, they redirect earnings (after expenses and savings) toward additional charitable programming. These organizations, small or large, are instances of *mediating institutions*, because they are conduits between individuals and the larger society; they facilitate the social participation of individuals and filter resources from the large structures of society to individuals.[7]

Volunteer organizations are a major presence in the United States. There were 1.44 million nonprofit charities registered with the Internal Revenue Service (IRS) in 2012.[8] This figure does not include three types of unregistered organizations: (1) those with less than $5,000 in annual revenue, (2) religious congregations, (3) organizations that still operate but stopped filing IRS paperwork. Adding these together, Payton and Moody estimate the total number of American charities as approximately two million.[9] Religious, educational, and social service organizations constitute three-quarters of the charities where Americans serve (fig. 8.1).

## Types of Organizations Where Americans Volunteered in 2013[10]

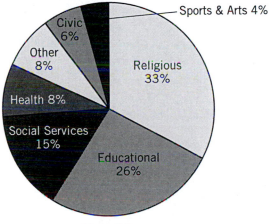

**Figure 8.1.**

7. See ch. 4, "The Art of Association," for further discussion.

8. National Center for Charitable Statistics (NCCS), "Quick Facts about Nonprofits," 2012 data, *http://nccs.urban.org/statistics/quickfacts.cfm.*

9. Payton and Moody, *Understanding Philanthropy*, 16. It is estimated that there are roughly one-quarter million unregistered nonprofits and another one-quarter million religious congregations engaging in charity. Adding these numbers to the registered organizations yields the estimate of two million.

10. Corporation for National and Community Service, "Volunteering and Civic Engagement in the United States," 2013 data, *http://2013.volunteeringinamerica.gov/national.*

## Funding the Service

While this chapter focuses mainly on service in the form of giving one's time and skills for the benefit of others, it is important to note that financial giving makes service possible. As with their time, Americans are generous with their money: they gave an estimated $358 billion to charity in 2014—a 7.1 percent increase over the previous year.[11] Individuals, who account for 72 percent of all giving to charity, were responsible for the majority of the increase. The remainder of charitable giving comes from foundations at 15 percent, bequests at 8 percent, and corporations at 5 percent (fig. 8.2).

### Sources of Charitable Giving in 2014[12]

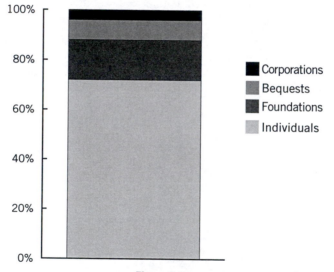

**Figure 8.2.**

Individuals are an indispensible source of charitable giving, and even though volunteerism has been on a slight decline in recent years,[13] individual giving was 4.2 percent higher in 2013 than in the previous year. Interestingly, while wealthier individuals (those making more than $100,000) account for a major share of the charitable giving (roughly one-quarter), the amount of income these individuals gave decreased 4.6 percent from 2006 to 2012, while those making less than $100,000 gave 4.5 percent more of their income during

---

11. The Giving Institute, *Giving USA 2015 Highlights*, 1, *http://givingusa.org*.

12. Ibid.

13. The Bureau of Labor Statistics data ("Volunteering in the United States, 2014") show a decline from a 27.6 percent volunteering rate in 2002 to 25.3 percent in 2014.

the same period.[14] It is worth noting that surveys suggest that two-thirds of U.S. households give at least some contributions to religious and/or charitable causes annually.[15] Charitable giving by individuals is not the only source of funding for nonprofit organizations. Rather, it represents roughly 13 percent of these organizations' revenues, while the largest portion, 73 percent, comes from fees for services paid for by clients, private sources, or the government.[16]

The aggregate of volunteers, groups, and funding is impressive. As Payton and Moody comment, "Philanthropy is a force of major significance in the United States when we consider its scale. . . . It is much bigger than most people think."[17]

## Volunteer Groups and Their Members

The two main relationships in the community connections chart are of persons to groups and groups to society (fig. 8.3). Looking at relationship number 1, the purpose is to understand the contributions of nonprofit organizations to their participants' character and flourishing, as well as the participants' contributions to the well-being of the organization.

### Volunteer Group and Members

**Figure 8.3.** Community Connections: A Volunteer Group and Its Members

## Volunteering Promotes Capabilities

Volunteering helps those who volunteer to flourish by developing their capabilities. Volunteers can gain practical skills, live with more meaning and happiness, and develop abilities that enhance individual effectiveness in work and other

---

14. Alex Daniels, "As Wealthy Give Smaller Share of Income to Charity, Middle Class Digs Deeper," *Chronicle of Philanthropy*, October 5, 2014, *https://philanthropy.com/article/As-Wealthy-Give-Smaller-Share/152481*.

15. The figure is 67 percent from a 2006 survey by *The Nonprofit Almanac*, as reported by NCCS, "Charitable Giving in America: Some Facts and Figures," *http://nccs.urban.org/nccs/statistics/Charitable-Giving-in-America-Some-Facts-and-Figures.cfm*.

16. Brice S. McKeever and Sarah L. Pettijohn, *Nonprofit Sector in Brief 2014*, Urban Institute, October 2014, figure 2, *http://www.urban.org/sites/default/files/alfresco/publication-pdfs/413277-The-Nonprofit-Sector-in-Brief--.PDF*.

17. Payton and Moody, *Understanding Philanthropy*, 16.

settings. First, volunteering promotes practical skills, especially those related to the organization's activities and the clients' needs. At a soup kitchen, volunteers learn to prepare food and work effectively in a large kitchen. On a home-building project, they learn carpentry skills. Other volunteers learn about budgeting, fund-raising, and organizing social activities.

Second, volunteers grow in happiness—the happiness of positive emotions and the happiness that comes from experiencing meaning.[18] As explained in chapter 3, ethicists in the Aristotelian tradition are comfortable lauding the practical and psychological benefits of being virtuous, as long as these extrinsic benefits do not become the primary reason for volunteering. Studies confirm the commonsense belief that money doesn't make one happier; in fact, giving does. In one experiment, researchers randomly approached people in public places and gave them small amounts of money. They told half of the people to spend the money on themselves that day and the other half to spend it on someone else. When the researchers later interviewed the subjects, the people who had given the money away reported much higher levels of happiness. "That leads to a fascinating possibility: that we mislead ourselves into thinking that we'll be happier spending on ourselves and acquiring material objects, while actually we may be wired to gain more pleasure from giving to others."[19] As for service, studies have shown that those engaging in volunteerism and civic engagement enjoy not only positive emotions, but also an increased sense of meaning and more robust social relationships.[20]

Third, volunteers develop capabilities that enable them to be more effective team members in work and other settings. They learn to work with different people within the volunteer setting, carrying these relational skills outside the setting. Volunteers develop know-how for respectful, non-condescending interactions with people in need of assistance. In working with fellow volunteers, employees, and leaders of the organization, volunteers hone skills needed for collaboration including listening, communicating orally and in writing, brainstorming, being proactive, and participating. Volunteering also helps individuals develop skills such as fundraising, public relations, and political advocacy.

---

18. These are two elements of Martin Seligman's account of well-being discussed in ch. 2.

19. Nicolas D. Kristof and Cheryl WuDunn, *A Path Appears: Transforming Lives, Creating Opportunity* (New York: Knopf, 2014), 239. The same study is commented on by Shankar Vedantam, "Research Suggests Generosity Is Hardwired Into Our Brains," National Public Radio, December 24, 2014, *http://www.npr.org/2014/12/24/372837173/research-suggests-generosity-is-hardwired-into-our-brains*.

20. See the Corporation for National and Community Service, Office of Research and Policy Development, *The Health Benefits of Volunteering: A Review of Recent Research*, 2007, *http://www.nationalservice.gov/pdf/07_0506_hbr.pdf*; Constance Flanagan and Matthew Bundick, "Civic Engagement and Psychosocial Well-Being in College Students," *Liberal Education* 97, no. 2 (Spring 2011): 20–27; Fengyan Tang et al., "Organizational Support and Volunteering Benefits for Older Adults," *Gerontologist* 50, no. 5 (October 2010): 603–12; and Irene Miles et al., "Psychological Benefits of Volunteering for Restoration Projects," *Ecological Restoration* 18, no. 4 (Winter 2000): 218–27.

Finally, volunteering promotes practical wisdom. As volunteers try, fail, and succeed during a period of time, they learn problem solving. They learn from the wisdom of seasoned volunteers. For example, anyone who has spent time teaching young people—such as in a religious education class, a Boy or Girl Scout meeting, or tutoring—knows that there is a lot to learn about becoming a good teacher. Volunteers learn to explain concepts to children, keep them engaged, and balance serious work with fun. While this prudential learning is at first specific (e.g., "This approach works for my tutee, Sam"), throughout time, the volunteer develops skills working with people of all ages.

Volunteers also develop prudential wisdom, coming to understand the complexity of some problems and how to act effectively despite limitations. Following is the blog of Mariel Klein, a young volunteer at St. Joseph the Worker in Phoenix, a center that assists homeless people in finding permanent employment. At the time she wrote this entry, Mariel was three weeks into her service with the Jesuit Volunteer Corps, a post-college program akin to a domestic Peace Corps.

> One thing I'm beginning to realize is that justice, and the pursuit of it, is at once incredibly complicated but also incredibly simple. It doesn't take a neurosurgeon to figure out what makes a human being thrive, and it shouldn't take a rocket scientist to realize that all human beings have inherent worth and all deserve at least the basic necessities of life in today's world. It all seems so mind-blowingly simple, until you are trying your hardest to help out Christopher, who was just released from jail, cannot get a bed or even begin to look for a job because he doesn't have an ID card, which he can't get because he can't get a bus pass because he doesn't have any money. He didn't lose his ID card or neglect it, or trade it away for drugs; it was stolen from him, along with all of his other belongings, in the supposed safe haven of the homeless shelter, and he just desperately wants to look for a decent job but missed his appointment to meet with a job developer because he was in prison.[21]

Klein had to deal with these multiple obstacles as she tried to help clients like Christopher secure the practical resources that might get them on the path to self-sufficiency. Klein could not change everything that was frustrating her clients, but her later blog posts suggest that she learned how to help them navigate their options.

---

21. Mariel Klein, "Brick by Brick," *And She Wandered 365 Days and 365 Nights in the Desert* (blog), August 27, 2013, *http://marielkleinjvc.blogspot.com/2013/08/brick-by-brick.html.*

## Can One Person Change the World?—A Case Study

In his memoir, *Walk in Their Shoes: Can One Person Change the World?*, Jim Ziolkowski narrates his quest for a meaningful life and promotes effective strategies to break the cycles of poverty. Ziolkowski grew up in a fairly typical middle-class family in Michigan. His parents' solid values, work ethic, and Catholic faith gave him and his four siblings a strong foundation in life. At twenty-four, Ziolkowski embarked on a high-powered corporate career when he was accepted into a management training program at General Electric (GE). But Ziolkowski was wary of the constraints of corporate life, not only because he loved adventure, but because he had already had eye-opening experiences travelling in Thailand, Nepal, and India. His sense of altruism, spirituality, and his quest for deeper meaning in life left him uneasy: "I couldn't reconcile the intense work in the comfortable [GE] offices in Connecticut with the hard suffering I had seen in those overwhelmed cities in India."[22] He dreamed of starting a nonprofit that would combat poverty through education.

Jim discussed these dreams with his younger brother, Dave, which led the two of them, with the help of a few friends, to found a charity called Building with Books in August 1991. Ziolkowski's initial dream was to build "three schools on three different continents while engaging students from three American high schools in intensive service and youth development programs. It struck me as the right combination of compassion, idealism, and social change."[23] Six months later, Ziolkowski decided he had to choose between Building with Books and the GE management program. He quit GE. Although initially worried that his fledging organization would never survive, Ziolkowski and his team gradually succeeded in raising money and achieving their goals. During the first two years, they started afterschool youth programs in three U.S. high schools and built a school in Brazil. After they constructed the second planned school in Malawai and the third in Nepal, Ziolkowski and other staff decided to keep going.

In 2008, the organization's name was changed to buildOn. By mid-2015, it had built more than 720 schools in seven countries and enabled more than 5,400 American youth to volunteer for a total of 1.5 million hours.[24] These facts suggest that many people's lives have been changed for the better by buildOn. In his book, Ziolkowski illustrates the powerful effects of philanthropy on buildOn's volunteers, students, and partnering communities in developing countries. The organization's leaders see their ultimate goal as creating a movement to break the cycle of poverty. When a local community takes the education of its children into its own hands, it gains control of its destiny and its charity needs decline.

---

22. Jim Ziolkowski with James S. Hirsch, *Walk in Their Shoes: Can One Person Change the World?* (New York: Simon & Schuster, 2013), 17.

23. Ibid., 19.

24. Data derived from *http://www.buildon.org/what-we-do/*, on June 1, 2015.

Still, there were roadblocks and scary turns along the way to success. Ziolkowski and his colleagues didn't know much about running a nonprofit; they learned by trial and error and by listening to good advice. They encountered cultural and language barriers, and sometimes crime and political turmoil. Ziolkowski and his brother contracted malaria in Malawi, and, as a result of a bicycle accident in the same country, Jim developed a badly infected ankle that almost caused him to lose his foot. Back in the United States, Ziolkowski moved to Harlem so he could better appreciate the lives of the students in the afterschool programs there and have more credibility among them. Along the way, Ziolkowski made some cultural missteps, but gained invaluable insight. His story and that of buildOn illustrate the ethical and social benefits that can result from the virtuous exercise of service.[25]

## Volunteering Develops Virtues

The development of skills is closely connected to the development of virtues. Through the experience of volunteering, with proper training, support, and supervision, a self-reflective volunteer can expect to grow in all five categories of virtue (ch. 2).

- *Virtues of care.* Volunteers are usually motivated to serve because they want to help. Serving expresses and expands their compassion and altruism. Many volunteers deeply connect with the service experience and bond with clients and coworkers, which can be seen in both Klein's and Ziolkowski's stories.

- *Virtues of respect.* Teaching a child to develop sensitivity for the plight of the poor and oppressed and a sense of solidarity with them is not easy, especially when the teaching is only verbal. Volunteering with people who have had few advantages in life helps a young person understand the human face of injustice.

- *Virtues of perceiving and thinking.* Service encourages volunteers to perceive their shared humanity with those they serve. To be most effective, volunteers also need to be able to reason critically about the complex mix of factors faced by the people they help: social injustices, social deficits, cultural obstacles, personal choices, and bad luck.[26] Klein's comments reflect the development in critical thinking that volunteers can experience. She saw how resources for human flourishing are barred to many people through

---

25. Disclosure: The author is a faculty advisor to a college chapter of buildOn and has donated money to buildOn. It was because of his involvement in the organization that he read Ziolkowski's memoir and came to believe that buildOn serves as a good model of service, regardless of the personal connection.

26. For this reason, service learning is a valuable methodology for students. A good resource for students and teachers is Erin Brigham, *See, Judge, Act: Catholic Social Teaching and Service Learning* (Winona, MN: Anselm Academic, 2013).

a complex interaction of personal problems, inefficient systems, and unfair distribution of resources and opportunities. In her position, she learned to navigate these obstacles so she could assist clients.

- *Virtues of acting and relating.* Certain such virtues—courage, temperance, patience, humility, and even humor—are useful in dealing with the frustrations encountered in service, the frustrations about which Klein wrote. With advice and support from fellow volunteers and organizational leaders, volunteers learn to face these challenges. Volunteers may also develop capabilities for speaking in public, advocating for a cause, and negotiating with others inside and outside of the organizations they serve.

- *Virtues of purpose.* For the great majority of volunteers, their service is an expression of their sense of moral purpose. For some, their service is motivated by their religious faith or sense of spirituality. Regardless of how volunteers get involved or what exactly motives them, nearly all regularly find great meaning in service. Personal testimonies, such as those of Ziolkowski and Klein, and the research cited above support the well-known anonymous saying: "You make a living by what you get; you make a life by what you give."

## Charities Flourish because of the People Involved

A volunteer organization benefits greatly from participation. When volunteers are committed to an organization's mission and possess the virtues just described, the organization is more effective. Likewise, donors are essential. Larger volunteer organizations often have paid employees and leaders. With paid staff, the organization can become more professional and expand its services. Typically, the staff includes people with passion and expertise drawn to the nonprofit sector by a sense of personal satisfaction, despite the fact that salaries are generally 10 to 30 percent lower than in the private sector.[27] Obviously, the cause of philanthropy is advanced when a talented, passionate person such as Ziolkowski—who could have made hundreds of thousands of dollars by the time he was thirty years old by working in finance—devotes his talents to a nonprofit organization instead.

Charitable organizations and nonprofits exist because people have needs, and the people helped are typically grateful for the assistance. Nonetheless, such organizations must beware of developing attitudes of paternalism. The virtuous attitude—and the one that makes a charity successful in promoting flourishing—is to view recipients as *partners.* A partnership model means that the organization and its employees and volunteers must begin by listening to the people of the

---

27. Rick Cohen, "Nonprofit Salaries: Achieving Parity with the Private Sector," *Nonprofit Quarterly,* June 21, 2010, *http://nonprofitquarterly.org/2010/06/21/nonprofit-salaries-achieving-parity -with-the-private-sector/.*

community that will be served. It is their needs and interests that should drive a project. The people have direct experience with the challenges they face; moreover, they have skills and insights for addressing those challenges. If service is to be effective, it must grow out of ongoing, respectful dialogue.

BuildOn adopts this attitude when building schools in developing countries. It creates a covenant with the local community. Ziolkowski notes that starting with its third school, in Nepal, buildOn proposed "a true partnership, not charity. To guarantee that we have everyone's support, we asked all the adults in the village to sign the covenant. Because so many adults were illiterate, many signed with a thumbprint. This was done at all the villages thereafter and still happens today."[28] This approach reflects the advice of the twelfth-century Jewish rabbi Moses Maimonides, who famously described eight levels of charity. The highest level "is where one takes the hand of an Israelite and gives him a gift or a loan, or makes a partnership with him, or finds him employment, in order to strengthen him until he need to ask help of no one."[29]

Volunteers and organizational employees often say that they gain more from the service than they give. The client-partners of a volunteer organization share their values, virtues, and life-experience with everyone else in the organization. For example, Ziolkowski devotes a chapter of his memoir to a girl named Raiya Gaddy, a high school sophomore who participates in buildOn in Detroit. Her notable quality is her smile, which bespeaks compassion and hope. Gaddy became deeply depressed after the murder of her brother, but regained her buoyant personality by working with veterans in a buildOn program. "Helping them smile gave me my smile back," she says.[30] For Ziolkowski, Gaddy represents the people who are part of buildOn, whether givers or receivers of service (Gaddy is both). "Raiya uplifted me with her courage and resilience," Ziolkowski says. "She became one of buildOn's most impressive leaders," helping to build a school in Nicaragua and spearheading many programs at home in Detroit.[31]

## Volunteer Groups and Society

Relationship number 2 in the community connections chart is between a group and society (fig. 8.4). Volunteer organizations contribute to society materially and ethically; they also receive assistance from society to enable their contributions.

---

28. Ziolkowski, *Walk in Their Shoes*, 90.

29. Moses Maimonedes, "Laws Concerning Gifts to the Poor: The Book of Seeds," trans. Judah Mandelbaum, in *The Perfect Gift*, ed. Amy A. Kass (Bloomington, IN: Indiana University Press, 2002), 126.

30. Ziolkowski, *Walk in Their Shoes*, 137.

31. Ibid., 148, 147.

## Volunteer Groups and Society

**Figure 8.4.** Community Connections: A Volunteer Group and Society

# Charities Contribute to Society Materially and Ethically

The most evident social impact of a volunteer organization occurs in the community where the volunteer work is done. Volunteerism changes lives by promoting the flourishing and character of the clients, who are thereby empowered to better help their families, social groups, and the local community.[32] A volunteer group contributes to society both materially and ethically, with benefits going to clients and volunteers and rippling out toward other persons and groups. The material benefits include the goods, services, and jobs that nonprofits provide, all of which have economic value. The 1.44 million registered nonprofits reported more than $1.65 trillion in total revenues and $1.57 trillion in total expenses in 2012.[33] The nonprofit sector contributed an estimated $887.3 billion to the U.S. economy in 2012, composing 5.4 percent of the country's gross domestic product.[34] This sector accounts for roughly 9 percent of wages and salaries paid to American workers, while the monetary value of the service rendered by volunteers, if it were paid work, is estimated at $163 billion.[35]

The ethical impact cannot be quantified, but figuratively, it might be expressed with two multiplier effects. First, consider the sense of meaning that a single volunteer experiences and multiply that by 62.6 million American volunteers. Second, consider the benefits of service for a single client and multiply that by two million organizations, each of which annually helps anywhere from a handful to thousands of people.

---

32. The claim made here is that those helped are better able to help others, not that they always will. There is a vast literature in both psychology and game theory exploring factors that promote altruism. It certainly seems that reciprocity—having already been helped by someone— encourages people to help others. See Rodolfo Cortes Barragan and Carol S. Dweck, "Rethinking Natural Altruism: Simple Reciprocal Interactions Trigger Children's Benevolence," *Proceedings of the National Academy of Sciences* 111, no. 48 (December 2, 2014): 17,071–74; and Luis Cabral et al., "Intrinsic and Instrumental Reciprocity: An Experimental Study," *Games and Economic Behavior* 87 (September 2014): 100–121.

33. NCCS, "Quick Facts." This figure includes nonprofit hospitals and private universities, which, although they constitute only 3 percent of organizations, account for more than 60 percent of revenues in this sector (data derived from Urban Institute, *Nonprofit Sector in Brief*, table 2).

34. *Nonprofit Sector in Brief*, 1.

35. NCCS, "Quick Facts" for the figure about wages (9.2 percent in 2010) and *Nonprofit Sector in Brief*, 14, for the monetary value of volunteer work.

Consider, for example, Sheila Simpkins, previously a homeless woman and drug addict arrested more than two hundred times for prostitution and living on the streets of Nashville. A program called Magdalene, run by Episcopal priest Rev. Becca Stevens, helped get her off the streets. Simpkins has since earned her bachelor's degree and plans to get a master's degree in social work. Now married and with two young children, Simpkins says, "I haven't done a lot of things right in my life, but this is one thing I'm going to do right. I'm going to be the world's best mom."[36] The Magdalene program has been life-changing for individuals and impressive in its overall success. Seventy-two percent of the women who enter the two-year residential program complete it, which adds up to more than 150 "graduates" during its first two decades.[37] The number of women positively influenced by this one program, and the rippling effect they subsequently have on their communities, is impressive.

While the ethical contributions of volunteer organizations to society cannot be specifically measured, they are nonetheless real. Millions of people enjoy greater social respect and self-respect thanks to volunteer organizations. People helped by these organizations testify as to how their lives have changed, and they later help others and build social capital. Volunteer groups remind society about values that matter.

## Society Assists Charities Materially and Ethically

Given the benefits of charitable organizations to society, it makes sense for society to help those organizations carry out their work. The two groups with a significant relationship to the philanthropic sector are business and government.

### Business

Businesses of all sizes donate money, goods, services, and employees' time to charities. A solid majority of companies of all sizes donate to charity, but small- and medium-sized companies give proportionately more. Seventy-seven percent of businesses with annual revenues under $250,000 give to charity and 80 percent of businesses earning between $250,000 and $1 million give, while 69 percent of companies earning more than $1 million do.[38] A 2008 survey of small businesses owners found that they give an average of 6 percent of profits to

---

36. Nicholas Kristof, "From the Streets to the 'World's Best Mom,'" *New York Times*, October 12, 2013, *http://www.nytimes.com/2013/10/13/opinion/sunday/kristof-from-the-streets-to-worlds-best -mom.html?_r=0*. The Magdalene program is profiled at greater length in Kristof and WuDunn, *A Path Appears*, 154–61.

37. Kristof and WuDunn, *A Path Appears*, 160.

38. Caroline Preston, "Most Small Companies Make Charitable Donations, Survey Finds," *Prospecting* (blog), *Chronicle of Philanthropy*, November 20, 2008, *https://philanthropy.com/article /Most-Small-Companies-Make/225215*.

charity, while the *Giving in Numbers 2014* survey of large corporations found a median total giving of 1 percent of pre-tax profits.[39]

A major way that many larger businesses facilitate charity is by matching employee donations. Such programs exist at 86 percent of corporations.[40] Businesses also get involved by giving of their employees' time. Larger companies are in a better position to give substantial hours to charity. In the *Giving in Numbers* survey, on average, 31 percent of employees did at least one hour of volunteer service on company time during 2013. Utility companies led in this category, with 42 percent of employees volunteering for at least an hour. Companies reported that company-sponsored days of service, in which a large number of employees serve at various community organizations simultaneously, are their most successful form of service.[41] Companies also donate pro-bono services, offer employees paid release-time to volunteer, and give donations to the organizations at which their employees volunteer.

Businesses often pick out a few specific charities or causes to which they have personal connections and where they believe they can make a greater impact. For instance, a local clothing store might donate clothing so unemployed people have professional outfits for job interviews. A musical instrument store may donate instruments and repair services to schools that cannot afford them or to musicians in developing countries. On the other end of the spectrum, large companies often make sustained contributions to charities by combining many of the activities mentioned.

## Government

Government uses its taxing powers to facilitate charity. The U.S. federal government instituted a corporate income tax in 1909 and a personal income tax in 1913. From the beginning, charitable organizations were exempted from taxation. Since 1917, individuals have been able to deduct the value of their charitable donations from their taxable income. The original rationale for these deductions was to maintain donations to charities at a time when tax rates skyrocketed to pay for America's effort in World War I.[42] The tax breaks have endured to encourage charitable giving. Section 170 of Title 26 of the U.S. Code governs the types of organizations that are tax-exempt and the rules for

---

39. Caroline Preston, "Making a Big Difference," *Chronicle of Philanthropy* 21, no. 1 (October 16, 2008): 1; and Committee Encouraging Corporate Philanthropy (CECP) in association with the Conference Board, *Giving in Numbers: 2014 Edition* (New York: CECP, 2014), 6, *http://cecp.co /measurement/benchmarking-reports/giving-in-numbers.html*.

40. CECP, *Giving in Numbers*, 5.

41. Ibid., 24.

42. For a historical overview of the legislation, see Paul Ansberger et al., "A History of the Tax-Exempt Sector: An SOI Perspective," *Statistics of Income Bulletin* (Winter 2008): 105–35, *http://www.irs.gov/pub/irs-soi/tehistory.pdf*.

tax deductions. For instance, the code provides that individuals can deduct up to 50 percent of their income for charitable donations, while corporations can deduct up to 10 percent.[43]

The federal government's provisions for tax-exempt donations and tax-exempt status are part of the reason that so many nonprofit organizations exist. It is fairly simple for a small charity to maintain an annual registration as a tax-exempt organization by filling out an online form with a few items of basic information. The organizations thus registered are known as 501(c)(3) organizations under the U.S. tax code. A 501(c)(3) must be organized and operated exclusively for purposes that are "charitable, religious, educational, scientific, literary, [or that are directed to] testing for public safety, fostering national or international amateur sports competition, [or] preventing cruelty to children or animals." It must not be organized toward private interests, hence there are no profits for owners or shareholders, and "it may not be an action organization, i.e., it may not attempt to influence legislation as a substantial part of its activities and it may not participate in any campaign activity for or against political candidates."[44]

Government also collaborates with philanthropic organizations. One model involves creating grants and funneling social-welfare monies to charitable organizations. The federal government, through grants and projects from its various social-service agencies, is a major funder of the philanthropic sector. It is fair to say that, without government support, many charities would not be able to serve as many people as they do.[45] Alternatively, the federal government would have to create even more of its own programs, which is unappealing to many taxpayers. In many cases, the government is more efficient and can better address needs by helping the agencies that are already working in communities.

Charitable groups are vital to the health of American civil society—a statement that was true when the Frenchman Alexis de Tocqueville profiled Americans' "art of association" in the 1830s, and that remains true now.[46] Liberals and conservatives alike have voiced support for collaboration between the government and the nonprofit sector. For example, President Barack Obama continued

---

43. 26 U.S. Code § 170, "Charitable, etc., contributions and gifts," Subsection (b)(1)(A) for the rule for individuals and (b)(2)(A) for corporations, *https://www.law.cornell.edu/uscode/text/26/170*.

44. Internal Revenue Service, "Exemption Requirements—501(c)(3) Organizations," *http://www.irs.gov/Charities-&-Non-Profits/Charitable-Organizations/Exemption-Requirements-Section-501(c)(3)-Organizations*, and "Exempt Purposes—Internal Revenue Code Section 501(c)(3)," *http://www.irs.gov/Charities-&-Non-Profits/Charitable-Organizations/Exempt-Purposes-Internal-Revenue-Code-Section-501(c)(3)*.

45. It should be noted that only large charities with sufficient infrastructure and expertise receive a significant amount of government support. The average governmental support for charities is 9.2 percent of their budgets in the form of grants and 23 percent in the form of fees for services (Urban Institute, *Nonprofit Sector in Brief*, figure 2).

46. Alexis de Tocqueville, *Democracy in America*, ed. Richard Heffner (New York: Signet Classic, 2001). See ch. 4.

the initiative created by President George W. Bush in 2001, known as the Office for Faith-Based and Neighborhood Partnerships. Within the Constitutional rules regulating the distinction between church and state, this office has contributed to promoting governmental collaborations with philanthropies both religious and secular.

## Increased Social Capital for All

A final benefit to note in the group-society relationship is this: all citizens, even those not directly volunteering in an organization, benefit from the work of nonprofits. Volunteer organizations make major contributions to social flourishing. While many of the examples here have focused on groups that address basic needs, the scope of volunteer organizations is vast. Museums, libraries, and cultural organizations; nonprofit hospitals and public health organizations; private schools and universities; ecological societies; and groups promoting peace, civic dialogue, and public engagement—all of these organizations add to the social capital that helps individuals live well. Because virtually every person in society takes advantage of the institutions just mentioned, everyone benefits from philanthropy during their lifetime. Payton and Moody say each person has a philanthropic autobiography. Most people can think of specific acts of volunteering and donating, at various times in their lives, and most "have also been on the receiving end of philanthropy—not necessarily direct charity, but philanthropy. The good works of others, past and present, make our lives possible."[47] These authors comment that, if one were to write out this autobiography, the story would be substantial and diverse, including moments of helping and being helped and evidence of how one's character and skills were improved. Participating in volunteer groups also motivates one to be civic-minded and engage in social and political activity as an adult.[48] Charitable volunteerism is thus one of the best and most common ways for citizens to develop social virtues.

# Challenges within Volunteer Groups and Virtuous Responses

Having examined the benefits of organized service for persons, volunteer groups, and society, it is important to consider how people and groups who want to serve virtuously might do so. The case study of buildOn features

---

47. Payton and Moody, *Understanding Philanthropy*, 15.

48. This reflects a finding of Sidney Verba, Kay Lehman Schlozman, and Henry Brady in *Voice and Equality: Civic Voluntarism in American Politics* (Cambridge, MA: Harvard University Press, 1995). Their study fits nicely with the social capital theory of Robert Putnam explained in ch. 4 of this book.

challenges that volunteer groups and their members encounter internally, that is, within the life and work of the organizations and their members. Although not entirely separate from external challenges, internal challenges are mostly under the group's control.

## Internal Challenges

*Getting started.* For an individual who cares about a problem, what is the first step to take? Join an existing group dealing with the same or a similar challenge? Or start one's own activity or group? Fortunately, the challenge is usually an embarrassment of riches versus too few options. There are many groups already working on nearly every social problem. To get involved, all an individual need do is conduct research about the volunteer opportunities in his or her vicinity and try one out. For a group, or for those who want to start a group, the initial challenge is to identify and properly define the problem that needs to be addressed, decide if it can be addressed, and plan the first steps. The would-be leaders must research the needs they want to address and any existing groups devoted to these needs, asking themselves whether their proposed service is necessary. With some two million charities in existence, this is no easy task. Donors with substantial resources face a similar dilemma: give to an existing activity or start a new foundation? Throughout the world of service opportunities, people are challenged to sort out the "what" and "why" questions amid a plethora of options.

*The supply of volunteers.* A new organization has to find volunteers, which is often not difficult; the bigger challenge is retaining them after their excitement wears off. "It is a growing problem," says Robert Grimm Jr., the director of research and policy development at the Corporation for National and Community Service. "There's a high amount of service enthusiasm in a couple of groups, particularly young people and boomers," but once people actually volunteer, "they have an experience that just is not very satisfying."[49] For some volunteers, the problem could lie in their characters, if they have unrealistic expectations or superficial commitment. Yet there are potential problems that organizations need to address, such as these, identified by Grimm: poor planning in the use of volunteers, volunteers feeling that they are assigned to unimportant tasks, and volunteers not being helped to understand the connection between their activities and the mission of the organization. While responses to these problems are under an organization's control, it could be that it will be harder for organizations to find volunteers as time goes on, given recent statistics revealing a gradual decline in Americans' volunteerism.

49. Debra E. Blum, "Volunteers Fail to Return to Many Charities, a New Study Finds," *Chronicle of Philanthropy* 20, no. 20 (August 7, 2008): 11. "Boomers" refers to the American baby boomers, those born 1946–1964.

*Raising money.* New groups need money. Ziolkowski had a big dream when he started Building with Books but didn't know if others would believe in his dream. He and his partners were eager to start building schools, but found the process of writing grants time-consuming. "I envisioned a $100,000 budget, but we were applying for $2,500 here and $5,000 there. I needed a Niagara but could only ask for droplets."[50] Groups also need to keep asking for money. A perennial topic within the media is whether people grow fatigued by fundraising appeals. Since total giving by Americans has increased for four years in a row up to 2013, this may not be the case.[51] But charities need to have an approach that does not annoy current and potential donors. The general public may not understand the necessity of fundraising and what counts as reasonable overhead costs. Even charity watchdog groups have tried to debunk the "overhead myth," which is "the false conception that financial ratios are the sole indicator of nonprofit performance."[52]

*When charities abuse their roles.* While most charities are honorable, fraud nonetheless occurs with distressing frequency.[53] Fraudulent and misguided charities focus excessively on making money: they spend most of their revenues on fundraising costs, pay handsome salaries to their executives, and give little direct aid to those in need. The *Tampa Bay Times* has ranked the nation's fifty worst charities based on ten years of data from tax returns. These fifty organizations, which often have names that mimic reputable charities, on average paid 70.5 percent of their revenues to professional fundraisers ($935 million), kept 26.2 percent for themselves, and gave only 3.3 percent to the people they purport to serve.[54] Fraud and scandals can occur within charities, as within any business. When they do occur, the bad news can undermine the public's confidence in charities, even reputable ones.

*Teleopathy.* Teleopathy (ch. 4) is "sickness" related to the charity's goals. At the extreme, a group can lose touch with its internal passions and become hyper-focused on external rewards. Its goals become such things as exceeding last year's fundraising levels or achieving public recognition. Some charities

---

50. Ziolkowski, *Walk in Their Shoes*, 28.

51. "Americans Gave $335.17 Billion to Charity in 2013; Total Approaches Pre-Recession Peak," Lilly Family School of Philanthropy, June 17, 2014, *https://philanthropy.iupui.edu/news-events/news -item.html?id=127*. On the worry about donor fatigue before the 2007 recession, see Stephanie Strom, "Many Dismissing 'Donor Fatigue' as Myth," *New York Times*, April 30, 2006, *http://www .nytimes.com/2006/04/30/us/30donor.html*.

52. See *http://overheadmyth.com*, sponsored by GuideStar, Charity Navigator, and the Better Business Bureau Wise Giving Alliance.

53. Fortunately, there is no evidence that the organization profiled in the case study, buildOn, fell prey to any of these problems. It has earned a four-star rating from Charity Navigator, which reports that buildOn devotes 86.9 percent of its budget to program costs, 3.2 percent to administrative expenses, and 9.7 percent to fundraising.

54. "America's Worst Charities," *Tampa Bay Times*, updated December 9, 2014, *http://www.tampa bay.com/americas-worst-charities/*. As the website points out, charity-watchdog groups recommend that no more than 35 percent of a charity's revenues go toward fundraising costs.

might even resent the success of other charities and become competitive rather than collaborating for the common good. Less dramatically, most organizations face times of crisis when they become unclear or internally divided about their mission. Leaders sometimes face fear—of failure or even success. Sometimes, volunteers, employees, and leaders get "burned out," especially when engaged in direct, intensive service with clients who have chronic problems. In these ways, an organization can become unbalanced and lose sight of its reason for being.

*Maximizing and assessing effectiveness.* Thomas Tierney and Joel Fleishman, who have been involved in the philanthropic sector as advisors, grant-makers, and academic analysts, identify a fundamental challenge facing philanthropy: it "has no built-in systemic forces to motivate continuous improvement."[55] They continue,

> Unlike business leaders, philanthropists have no market forces with which to contend. There are no competitors fighting to take market share away from them, no customers who will take their money elsewhere if they fail to deliver, no shareholders poised to dump their stock. . . . In this Galapagos Island–like world, where there are no natural predators, philanthropy is inclined to persist, but not to excel.[56]

Tierney and Fleishman believe that situation leaves philanthropists with the obligation to impose excellence on themselves: "If you do not demand excellence of yourself no one else will require it of you."[57] The risk for an organization such as buildOn is that building a school is a feel-good activity that can win the hearts of donors, but maintaining a school and educating effectively are difficult activities and may not be as winsome.

## Responses to Internal Challenges

The responses to internal challenges come from both individuals and groups. In both cases, drawing upon virtues is the core of an ethical response. If individuals and groups want their service to be meaningful and effective, the following, virtue-motivated practices are recommended.

### Individual Practices

The practices of individuals address three internal challenges: getting started, the supply of volunteers, and effectiveness. For individuals, the starting point is to do something—just about anything—to serve. Getting involved

---

55. Thomas J. Tierney and Joel L. Fleishman, *Give Smart: Philanthropy That Gets Results* (New York: Public Affairs, 2011), 5.

56. Ibid.

57. Ibid.

expresses one's virtues of care and purpose. Informal opportunities present themselves every day, such as paying a visit to a housebound neighbor, doing a chore for an elderly neighbor, helping a child with his or her homework, and so on. One can also help with one-time events at an organization to which one already belongs, for example, in a fundraising activity at the school one's child attends, in a food drive at one's church, and so on. For a more sustained impact, one can start volunteering in an organization on a regular basis. People often poorly estimate the time and money they spend on activities. To ensure that one is living up to one's goals for serving and giving, one could keep a log of volunteer experiences and donations. Parents might track their family involvement. These practices help ensure that individuals get started on service, stay involved, and remain a dependable resource for the organizations that depend on them.

Similarly, individuals may make donations to any number of causes. Since many charities exist and most people's resources for giving are limited, it is important to research charities that are effective and spend money well. Websites such as Charity Navigator, GiveWell, and others enable one to do this (see "Recommendations for Further Reading" at the end of the chapter). Some people, such as students and those on fixed incomes, have the time and skills to donate, but not much money. Others have the money but not a lot of time. However, there is a case to be made for people giving both time and money, to the extent they can manage it, because the two activities encourage different virtues. Serving people directly keeps a person aware of personal connections; it strengthens one's emotional intelligence and ability to perceive others' needs. Donating, guided by rational planning, helps one think about impact and causes. Moreover, assessing one's own financial giving lets one take stock of his or her generosity. Comte-Sponville says, "I understand that money isn't everything. But why would we be more generous in nonfinancial or nonquantifiable areas? Why would our hearts be more open than our wallets? The opposite is more likely."[58]

Reflecting critically on one's service is important. Experiences must be interpreted and informed. Short bursts of direct service may leave one naïve or condescending. Discussing service with experienced volunteers at an organization, participating in service-learning programs, and reading about the philanthropic sector help one avoid these pitfalls.

Personal impact is only part of the picture if volunteers care—as they should—about the effectiveness of their serving and giving. Therefore, individuals should research the causes and underlying needs related to the problems that concern them and then support organizations that address these. At the international level, individuals may donate money to proven organizations. For example, Kristof and WuDunn give practical suggestions for getting involved in effective international charity, such as making a donation through Kiva, which provides microloans for social development projects; Givology, which aims to

---

58. Comte-Sponville, *A Small Treatise on the Great Virtues*, 92.

support high-impact education initiatives; or the Against Malaria Foundation, which provides antimalarial bed nets.[59] Sometimes, when a person remains highly involved in an international cause, direct service becomes an option, such as through the school building projects conducted by buildOn in developing countries. International service trips, especially those run by universities and churches, have become increasingly popular. Although these trips can benefit both the volunteers and the communities they visit, care should be exercised that such ventures don't become "feel-good" and paternalistic.[60] Careful forethought and planning can help avoid such pitfalls.

Finally, individuals can promote effective, systemic responses to social problems by participating in advocacy and political activity. From home, one can research a social issue, join an organization that provides information on upcoming legislation related to that issue, write emails and make calls to legislators, and sign petitions. To make a more personal connection, there are local advocacy groups devoted to particular issues that one can join. For example, a person concerned about environmental quality could join a local chapter of the Sierra Club, the Nature Conservancy, 350.org, or the Environmental Defense Fund, and through the chapter, participate in direct service activities such as cleaning up a beach, planting a community garden, or writing emails and making calls about related political legislation. In these ways, individuals can express the virtue of justice.

## Group Practices

The practices of groups can address all six internal challenges, but the focus here will be on three: the supply of volunteers, teleopathy, and effectiveness. By expressing virtues of care in their work with clients and volunteers, organizations address the recruitment and retention of volunteers. Organizations should take care to nurture long-term relationships with donors and volunteers. It is important that charities not overlook nurturing relationships with existing donors, even as they focus on developing new ones.[61] Organizations need to be aware

---

59. Kristof and WuDunn, "Six Steps You Can Take in the Next Six Minutes," in *A Path Appears*, 316–17, and "Four Steps You Can Take in the Next Ten Minutes," in *Half the Sky* (New York: Vintage, 2010), 251–52.

60. A provocative article by one who considered herself guilty of this flaw is by Lauren Kascak, with Sayantani Dasgupta, "#InstagrammingAfrica: The Narcissism of Global Voluntourism," *Sociological Images*, December 29, 2014, *http://thesocietypages.org/socimages/2014/12/29/instragramming africa-the-narcissism-of-global-voluntourism/*. A judicious examination of the benefits and risks of volunteer service trips is by Jenny Morgan, a program officer with the London-based Overseas Development Institute: "Volunteer Tourism: What Are the Benefits for International Development?," *VolunTourist Newsletter*, accessed January 27, 2015, *http://www.voluntourism.org/news-study andresearch62.htm*.

61. Holly Hall, "Charities Show Strides in Keeping Loyal Donors, but Are Too Focused on Short-Term Results, Scholars Say," *Chronicle of Philanthropy*, December 31, 2014, *https://philanthropy .com/article/Charities-Show-Strides-in/152013*.

of generational and cultural trends that influence volunteers. Research suggests that would-be volunteers of the baby boom generation want their volunteering to be "meaningful, something about which they are passionate and on their own schedule."[62] Organizations also need to engage in good practices for training and retaining volunteers. These practices include being specific with volunteers, giving them important information in writing, giving them strategies for doing their work well, providing them a contact person, making good matches between volunteers and clients, showing appreciation, and involving them in evaluating the program.[63] Organizations should offer leadership opportunities to volunteers and develop future leaders of the organization from within their own ranks.

It is vitally important for leaders and managers of charitable organizations to be in touch with what is going on in day-to-day operations and to interact, at least occasionally, with clients. Ziolkowski is a good example of a philanthropic leader who stays deeply connected to the people his organization serves. Even though he has cut back on international travel to school-building sites because of family obligations and the medical needs of his son,[64] he continually meets and interacts with buildOn's American students, as evidenced in his memoir.

An organization can get caught up in maintaining its operations, pleasing donors, and so on, leading to the problem of teleopathy. As a result, an organization needs mechanisms for avoiding complacency and teleopathy. One mechanism is to regularly reexamine the mission statement to ensure it is being followed in the day-to-day operations. The leaders must focus zealously on their purpose and avoid distractions. For example, in the early months of Building with Books, Ziolkowski and his partners wanted to trek around Africa scouting remote locations in which to build schools. To make this travel easier, Ziolkowski proposed to Honda Motor Company that it donate three giant 750cc dirt bikes to their organization, to which Honda agreed. But then Ziolkowski started having doubts. "This wasn't supposed to be *Easy Rider* joins the Peace Corps. The bikes would be a distraction, or worse; if they broke down or if we were pulled over by the authorities, the delay could jeopardize our ability to build the schools." The group decided to turn down the offer. "That decision was a kind of turning point: it said—to the outside world, but also to ourselves—that we were dedicated to our cause more than to our own desire for fun."[65]

Finally, to address the challenge of effectiveness, volunteer organizations need to honestly evaluate themselves and join the growing trend of rigorous program assessment. Ziolkowski has thought about effectiveness and long-term

---

62. Patricia M. Seaman, "Time for My Life Now: Early Boomer Women's Anticipation of Volunteering in Retirement," *The Gerontologist* 52, no. 2 (2012): 245–254, at 245.

63. These ideas were drawn from Jennifer Tingley, "Volunteer Programs: When Good Intentions Aren't Enough," *Educational Leadership* 58, no. 7 (April 2001): 53–55.

64. Ziolkowski, *Walk in Their Shoes*, 209 and ch. 10.

65. Ibid., 35–36.

sustainability in the school-building enterprise. BuildOn's approach is to foster a partnership with the local communities where a school will be built. The process includes requiring the community to set up a project leadership committee with equal numbers of men and women. The covenant that community members sign requires that half of the students in the school be girls. "Once a school is complete, buildOn staff carefully monitor and evaluate its success. If after three years all aspects of the covenant have been continually upheld, and the community's daughters have been educated as well as its sons, buildOn will return to aid in the construction of a second school. This approach incentivizes success, and illustrates to communities the power of teamwork and equality."[66] In its U.S. programs, buildOn reports a 95 percent high school graduation rate for students who participate in its afterschool service programs.[67] Since the high school graduation rates in the cities where buildOn works, such as Detroit and the Bronx, are 60 to 65 percent, and since the U.S. rate is 80 percent overall and 65 to 70 percent for African-American students, buildOn's results are impressive.[68]

## Challenges outside Volunteer Groups and Virtuous Responses

The external challenges to volunteer groups are social, cultural, economic, and political forces that make the jobs of these organizations complex and sometimes controversial. No single organization can directly change these forces, although they can try to advocate for change and work with other institutions on systemic responses.

### External Challenges

*The needs are great.* For organizations working on global poverty, domestic homelessness, unemployment, drug addiction, and the educational achievement gap, the problems are massive and the human needs constant. Moreover, when the economy goes through a recession, problems grow. And while much money is given to charity in the United States, charitable spending has been stuck at

---

66. Information and quotation from *http://www.buildon.org/what-we-do/international-programs/*, where a picture of the covenant is also posted. On community partnerships and gender equity, see also Ziolkowski, *Walk in Their Shoes*, 66–67, 152–64, and 256.

67. As reported in its 2013 audit and 2013 federal tax return (990 form) at *http://www.buildon .org/finances/*.

68. Alexandra Pannoni, "Study: Record High School Graduation Rate on Track for 2020," *U.S. News & World Report*, April 28, 2014, *http://www.usnews.com/education/blogs/high-school-notes /2014/04/28/high-school-graduation-rates-reach-record*; "Detroit Praised for 65 Percent Graduation Rate, Increase Echoed across the State," CBS Detroit, February 13, 2013, *http://detroit.cbslocal .com/2013/02/13/detroit-praised-for-65-percent-graduation-rate-increase-echoed-across-the-state/*. The only factor that would undermine this finding is if buildOn "cherry picked" the most-likely-to-succeed students for its programs, but there is no evidence that it does so.

approximately two percent of gross domestic product for many years.[69] The challenge, then, is that human suffering is great and that suffering is likely to continue indefinitely.

*Large sources of funding can skew priorities.* While wealthy donors can do significant good by giving substantial gifts to charities, large gifts and well-funded charities are accused of wielding an outsized influence, whether intentionally or unintentionally. For example, when Joan Kroc, at her death in October 2003, bequeathed $1.5 billion to the Salvation Army to build community centers, that gift threatened to skew the charity's focus. The amount of money was so significant, the Salvation Army could have gotten sidetracked, spending most of its time building opulent centers that would not fit with its humble image and mission of direct service to the needy. Stern, who tells the story, suggests that Kroc's gift, though well-intentioned, "was not reasonably calculated to make the Salvation Army better at its central functions; it is more likely to leave it stretched and more thinly resourced for the long run."[70] An example of a charity that has, according to some, a disproportionate influence is the Bill and Melinda Gates Foundation. This foundation has done admirable work in the fight against global poverty and disease, and it is promoting more focus on data and results in the philanthropic sector. Yet some philanthropists, activists, and commentators have criticized Bill Gates and the foundation for wielding too much influence in public policy, particularly on the topic of education reform.[71]

*Major philanthropic partners cause or contribute to suffering.* At times, corporate and political officials behave unethically and others suffer as a result. But, more systemically, corporations benefit from a capitalist economy which, whatever its benefits, nevertheless fails to meet human needs. Poverty is an ongoing feature of the global economy, and mounting inequality is a notable feature of the U.S. economy. It is in the interests of corporations to keep their taxes low and have beneficial governmental regulations, so many corporations spend heavily on political campaigns and lobbying. Politicians at all levels of government are likely to give their ear to those who keep their reelection coffers full. Thus the sectors of business and government, because of their power and self-interest, can act in ways that sometimes harm the public good or, at the least, create new problems even as they solve others. Nonprofits are left to pick up the pieces. For example, there are numerous cases where state government officials, under pressure from gun manufacturers and gun-rights groups,

69. Suzanne Perry, "The Stubborn 2% Giving Rate," *Chronicle of Philanthropy*, June 17, 2013, *https://philanthropy.com/article/The-Stubborn-2-Giving-Rate/154691*.

70. Stern, *With Charity for All*, 147.

71. See, for example, Diane Ravitch, "Bill Gates: Selling Bad Advice to the Public Schools," *The Daily Beast,* May 23, 2011, *http://www.thedailybeast.com/articles/2011/05/23/bill-gates-selling-bad-advice-to-the-public-schools.html*.

refrain from passing laws that would make guns safer.[72] Thus the violence that plagues communities saturated with handguns is not sufficiently addressed by these political and business interests. Community groups that work on antiviolence programs and churches that console the victims of violence are doing their part to address the gun violence issue, but these nonprofits are understandably impatient for leadership from the other sectors.

*Public policy.* Can charities partner with businesses and government if they feel the need to criticize them? In fact, there are several policy challenges that can only be summarized briefly here. What links all of them is that the government has many of the same purposes and responsibilities as the philanthropic sector, so their activities must sometimes overlap and sometimes be kept separate. As there is no perfect way to demarcate the roles of government and philanthropy, the following policy questions arise:

- Is it good for the government to collaborate with philanthropies by giving them grants and contracts, or does this channeling of money remove the government from some of its responsibilities for reducing poverty, improving education, and so on?
- When service organizations take public money, are they undermining policy-oriented responses that would create justice more than charity?
- Does the government's granting of funds to religiously affiliated charities improperly support religion with taxpayers' money? Does it encourage or force those organizations to mute their religious identities?[73]
- What kind of organizations should be tax-exempt and how should they be regulated?[74]
- Should tax deductions for individual and corporate donations to charities continue? Should the levels be adjusted, and if so, up or down? Can anything be done to improve the overall level of giving?
- How can government encourage more effective and more responsible charities?

## Responses to External Challenges

The general answer to these challenges is for those who serve and give to become more effective and better networked. Government, business, and the

---

72. For an example, see Nicholas D. Kristof, "Smart Guns Save Lives. So Where Are They?," *New York Times,* January 17, 2015, *http://www.nytimes.com/2015/01/18/opinion/sunday/nicholas-kristof-smart-guns-save-lives-so-where-are-they.html.*

73. A good resource on these and related questions is E. J. Dionne and Ming Hsu Chen, eds., *Sacred Places, Civic Purposes: Should Government Help Faith-Based Charity?* (Washington, DC: Brookings Institution Press, 2001).

74. For a comparison of the types of tax-exempt organizations, see Matt Bernius, "501(c)4 vs 501(c)3 vs 527," *Outside the Beltway* (blog), May 16, 2013, *http://www.outsidethebeltway.com/501c4-vs-501c3-vs-527/.*

philanthropic community can assist through the following initiatives, some of which involve one of these three sectors and some of which involve all three.

## Government: Tax Policies

There are good arguments for maintaining the practice of allowing tax deductions for charitable giving and for making changes that would facilitate additional giving. Some argue that "trying to influence people's decisions by giving them a tax break is pointless" since Americans' giving in the aggregate does not change much throughout time regardless of tax policies.[75] It remains at roughly two percent of gross domestic product. In addition, by eliminating these deductions, government would realize more tax revenue. By contrast, there is evidence that tax policy does facilitate individuals' decisions about whether and how much to give. For instance, donations spike toward the end of the calendar year, because that's the deadline for charitable gifts to be deductible in one's upcoming tax return.[76] In addition, when cash-strapped states have tried to increase their tax revenues by eliminating or cutting charitable deduction credits, charities in these states have seen deductions fall. It is doubtful that these curtailments are cost-effective for state governments, because additional government services often must replace the lost charitable services. Therefore, some states have reversed course and reinstated charitable tax deductions.[77] The Independent Sector, an organization that studies and promotes philanthropy, recommends tax policy be adjusted to incentivize charitable giving by more Americans.[78] The approach could include allowing all charitable contributions to be deducted from an individual's or family's adjusted income and finding a way to allow the deduction for taxpayers who fill out the simple tax form and do not itemize deductions.[79]

A second policy issue is the tax-exempt status of nonprofit organizations. The category of "social welfare organizations" has been expanded in the past decade far beyond its original purpose. Thousands of partisan political organizations have registered as such under section 501(c)(4) of the U.S. tax code, a status

75. This quote and the following supporting points are from Daniel J. Mitchell and Diana Aviv, in "Should We End the Tax Deduction for Charitable Donations?," *Wall Street Journal,* December 16, 2012, *http://www.wsj.com/articles/SB10001424127887324469304578143351470610998.*

76. Ibid. Diane Aviv presents the fact that more than "22% of online charitable donations are made on Dec. 30 and 31 each year."

77. Elaine S. Povich, "Charitable Giving Tied to State Tax Deduction Decisions," *Stateline,* The Pew Charitable Trusts, September 24, 2013, *http://www.pewtrusts.org/en/research-and-analysis/blogs/stateline/2013/09/24/charitable-giving-tied-to-state-tax-deduction-decisions.*

78. Independent Sector, "IS Guiding Principles for Public Policy on Charitable Giving," September 2012, *https://www.independentsector.org/is_guiding_principles_for_public_policy_on_charitable_giving.*

79. Joseph Cordes et al., "Extending the Charitable Deduction to Nonitemizers: Policy Issues and Options," Urban Institute, May 1, 2000, *http://webarchive.urban.org/publications/310338.html.* There was discussion of such proposals among federal policymakers in the early 2000s, but no changes to the tax laws were made at that time, and interest in the issue seems to have faded since then.

that allows them to keep the names of their donors secret.[80] The IRS proposed regulations in late 2013 to tighten the criteria for allowable political activities by 501(c)(4)s, but had to back down under intense criticism—mostly, but not solely, from conservatives.[81] In addition, the IRS does not have the budget or political support to conduct investigations into groups that may be flouting the rules.[82] While no set of regulations will please everyone, there is still need for changes to the current situation to restore the original purpose of the tax code categories: charities and groups that engage in non-electioneering advocacy should be tax-exempt and may keep donors' names private, while groups that engage in partisan activity should not be tax-exempt and should have donor-disclosure rules parallel to the rules for donations to candidates and parties.[83]

## All Three Sectors: Effectiveness and Salaries

The philanthropic community, foundations, and, to a lesser extent, businesses and government, can promote and incentivize best practices for charitable effectiveness. Organizations that advise the philanthropic community have recommended best practices for nonprofits to adopt in areas of governance, finance, and disclosure.[84] Donors, foundations, and governments should direct their grants to charities with established metrics for measuring success.[85] Businesses should work with nonprofits to establish better-organized markets for philanthropic services. Former president Bill Clinton makes this recommendation, giving dozens of business-led examples (such as when Wal-Mart established its Sustainability 360 plan to become 100 percent renewable in its energy usage and create zero waste) and examples of those led by nonprofits and small social-entrepreneurships (such as the fair-trade coffee market).[86]

---

80. Howard Gleckman, "The IRS-Tea Party Scandal: Many Political Groups Should Not Be Tax-Exempt," *Forbes*, May 13, 2013, *http://www.forbes.com/sites/beltway/2013/05/13/irs-was -wrong-to-single-out-tea-parties-but-many-political-groups-should-not-be-tax-exempt/*.

81. "Treasury, IRS Will Issue Proposed Guidance for Tax-Exempt Social Welfare Organizations," IRS, November 26, 2013, *http://www.irs.gov/uac/Newsroom/Treasury,-IRS-Will-Issue -Proposed-Guidance-for-Tax-Exempt-Social-Welfare-Organizations*; Stephanie Condon, "After Controversy, IRS to Revise Rule Changes for Tax-Exempt Political Groups," CBS News, May 23, 2014. *http://www.cbsnews.com/news/controversial-irs-rules-changes-for-tax-exempt-political-groups-on-hold/*.

82. Julie Patel, "IRS Rarely Audits Nonprofits for Politicking," Center for Public Integrity, January 22, 2015, *http://www.publicintegrity.org/2015/01/22/16640/irs-rarely-audits-nonprofits-politicking*.

83. For a contrary point of view, that donors' names should not have to be disclosed, see Ian Tuttle, "Should 501s Be 527s?," *National Review Online*, July 2, 2013, *http://www.nationalreview.com /article/352531/should-501s-be-527s-ian-tuttle*.

84. See the Independent Sector's menu on Governance Resources at *https://www.independent sector.org/principles* and the National Council of Nonprofits' page on Principles and Practices, under "Tools & Resources," at *https://www.councilofnonprofits.org*.

85. Stern, *With Charity for All*, ch. 8.

86. Bill Clinton, *Giving: How Each of Us Can Change the World* (New York: Knopf, 2007), 156–57 on Wal-Mart, 170–71 on coffee, and chs. 10–11 overall.

Donors and charity-watchdog groups must realize that fundraising and competitive salaries are necessary expenses. Unrealistic expectations about low overhead should not be the primary indicator of effectiveness. Nonetheless, the most reputable nonprofits keep their expenses in both categories modest. While the philanthropic community sets a general expectation—"in most cause areas, the most efficient charities spend 75 percent or more of their budget on their programs and services and less than 25 percent on fundraising and administrative fees"[87]—there are some legitimate exceptions. Therefore, those donating to nonprofit organizations should be wary of institutions with high overhead and fundraising costs, while also considering the overall effectiveness of a group as the most important factor.

Since nonprofit-sector work is important for society, it should pay well enough to entice the best employees. Nonprofit-sector jobs at any level tend to pay 10 to 30 percent less than comparable private-sector work. While it is true that nonprofit workers are motivated by more than money, the situation is not fair. "Mission and motivation are laudable," says journalist Rick Cohen, "but substandard incomes are not."[88] Since there are many types of nonprofit employment, there is no single solution to this problem. But business, government, and the nonprofit sector should commit to "a national policy to make every human-service job a good job: one that pays a living wage with good benefits, and includes adequate training, professional status, and the prospect of advancement—a career rather than casual labor."[89] This policy would entail that better-resourced nonprofits, such as hospitals and universities, pay better wages, and that those who fund nonprofits—whether corporations, government agencies, or private donors—provide enough resources to support better salaries.

Recently, much praise has been given to "social entrepreneurship," which is the process of working for social change through socially responsible businesses (for example, Tom's Shoes, which donates a pair of shoes to someone in a developing country for every pair of shoes it sells) and innovative nonprofits (such as buildOn). In developing countries, advances are occurring in local communities when the social entrepreneurship model is applied.[90] Several books explain the possibilities open to anyone for creating a meaningful, successful career as a social entrepreneur.[91] The idea that one can "do well by doing good" is more widely accepted now than it was a few decades ago.

---

87. Charity Navigator, "Top 10 Best Practices of Savvy Donors."

88. Cohen, "Nonprofit Salaries."

89. Robert Kuttner, "Good Jobs for Americans Who Help Americans," *The American Prospect,* May 8, 2008, quoted in Cohen.

90. There are many examples in Kristof and WuDunn, *A Path Appears,* and on the book's website, *http://apathappears.org.*

91. See David Bornstein and Susan Davis, *Social Entrepreneurship: What Everyone Needs to Know* (New York: Oxford University Press, 2010) and Rupert Scofield, *The Social Entrepreneur's Handbook* (New York: McGraw-Hill, 2011).

## All Three Sectors: Collaborations

Collaborative relationships can make service more effective and also benefit each group that participates. An exciting example of collaboration among nonprofits, government, and business is the Pathways in Technology Early College High School, known as P-TECH, "the first school in the nation that connects high school, college, and the world of work through college and industry partnerships."[92] IBM, the New York City Board of Education, and two public colleges collaborate on P-TECH, which is open to all New York City students regardless of past grades and test performance. The school follows a "9-14" model, giving students two year's of college credits by the time they graduate. The computer science curriculum, extracurricular programs, and support structures help students prepare for finishing college and landing jobs in the technology section. In fact, IBM promises that successful graduates will be "first in line" for jobs at the company. P-TECH is just one example of collaboration between the three sectors that could be a model for future initiatives.

## Philanthropies: Keeping Justice in View

Volunteer organizations should work toward justice even if their primary mission is direct service. There are differences between love as a virtue and justice as a social principle, but the two values are connected on a spectrum. An organization that does direct charitable service—such as a soup kitchen or a program for visiting the homebound elderly—falls on the love side of the spectrum. But such charitable service contributes to justice indirectly if the service is done in a way that respects clients and makes some effort to expand their ability to effect change in their own lives. An organization that works for political and social change—such as a workers' rights organization or an environmental policy institute—falls on the justice side of the spectrum. But these organizations can and should operate in a way that expresses love (e.g., compassion, kindness, civility) in their internal and external relationships. Service organizations should always keep in view how their work is oriented to justice, and advocacy organizations should always keep in view the human relationship at the heart of their work. In various ways, the organizations profiled in this chapter hold the two sides of the spectrum together.[93]

The implications of advocating for social change can be tricky for nonprofits. Even when they follow the law, which allows 501(c)(3) organizations to engage in general political advocacy as an educational activity, critics may see

---

92. This information comes from the program's website, *http://www.ptechnyc.org/site/default.aspx?PageID=1*. Technically speaking, there are a few modest admissions priorities—for students from Brooklyn and for students who showed interest in P-Tech by attending an information fair.

93. This portrait of the connections between justice and charity is inspired by Pope Benedict XVI, *Deus Caritas Est* [*God Is Love*], encyclical letter, December 25, 2005, no. 26–29, *http://w2.vatican.va/content/benedict-xvi/en/encyclicals/documents/hf_ben-xvi_enc_20051225_deus-caritas-est.html*.

them as meddling in politics. At the same time, the explosion of groups registered as 501(c)(4)s or as explicitly political 527 groups has saturated the media with partisan rhetoric, making many Americans look askance at political advocacy, except toward the viewpoints with which they already agree. There is also a certain stigma against charity workers raising uncomfortable questions about the causes of and solutions to social problems. Dom Hélder Pessoa Câmara, a Catholic archbishop in Brazil in the 1970s, famously said, "When I give food to the poor, they call me a saint. When I ask why they are poor, they call me a communist."[94] His words illustrate the bind facing volunteer organizations.

Consider the position of a 501(c)(3) organization that provides food to the hungry through food banks. It is not supposed to be "political," yet the problem of hunger can be made better or worse by political policies. If the organization wants to end hunger, it needs to speak about political priorities and programs. What can the organization do? It can create a sibling 501(c)(4) organization that engages in political advocacy or that networks with other advocacy organizations. For instance, Bread for the World Institute, a Christian-inspired 501(c)(3) organization that provides policy analysis about hunger, has a sibling organization, Bread for the World, that lobbies for political policies to reduce and end hunger. Bread for the World is a 501(c)(4) organization that can lobby politicians, because political advocacy is its main mission. Charities should not shy away from educating about the social and political implications of their missions. In fact, they and their related advocacy groups have much to contribute to civic dialogue as they fight to reclaim the public space that has been encroached upon by the explosion of partisan advocacy groups into the nonprofit arena.

## Conclusion

A person who serves others requires a basic level of good character. To even be interested in serving requires compassion. The majority of Americans are interested and involved in service, at least at an informal level. One-quarter of Americans volunteer in organizations and two-thirds donate to charity. Since service builds character and promotes personal and social flourishing, supporters of virtue ethics want to explore ways to expand volunteerism and giving. The challenges facing volunteer groups and their members can be addressed when people act upon their virtues. Likewise, charitable groups can perform their tasks even better by committing to love and justice, adopting the practices recommended by charity watchdog groups, advocating for smart policies, and collaborating smartly. The main ethical obligation of persons and other social

---

94. Quoted in John Dear, *Peace behind Bars: A Peacemaking Priest's Journal from Jail* (New York: Sheed & Ward, 1995), 65.

institutions—businesses and government—is to help nonprofits do their job well and not to create additional problems for them to solve.

Based upon these virtue-oriented guidelines, service can be effective, meaningful, and socially transformative. The case study of Jim Ziolkowski and buildOn has illustrated these three benefits. The overarching question of his memoir is, "Can one person change the world?" Ziolkowski says that the best answer he's heard came from a student in buildOn's program in the South Bronx: "Yes, but not by yourself."[95]

## Questions for Review

1. Approximately what percentage of Americans volunteer in a given year?
2. What are the sources of philanthropic funding?
3. What is meant by these terms describing service groups: *voluntary, nonprofit*, and *mediating*?
4. Describe a capability that volunteering develops in a volunteer, and tell how it is developed. Do the same with a virtue.
5. Describe a virtue that volunteering develops in a volunteer, and tell how it is developed.
6. What are some main ways that businesses facilitate philanthropy?
7. What are some main ways that government facilitates philanthropy?
8. What factors should individuals consider when deciding where to volunteer their time and to which organizations to donate money?
9. What initiatives inside and outside of the philanthropic sector promote the effectiveness of nonprofits?
10. What is the role of nonprofits promoting social justice and the virtue of justice?

## Discussion Questions and Activities

1. Write your philanthropic autobiography. First, reflect on the ways that you have benefitted from the informal service given by others and the ways you informally serve others. Next, take stock of your own volunteerism through philanthropic organizations and of the ways you have benefitted from such organizations—keeping in mind the diversity of these organizations, from churches to schools to museums to hospitals, etc.
2. Examine a volunteer experience in which you got to know a person being assisted by the organization. What capabilities and virtues did the service

---

95. Ziolkowski, *Walk in Their Shoes*, 239.

help that person develop? Discuss a few of these in detail, with examples to illustrate.

3. Based on the data in this chapter, do you believe the business sector does as much as it can to support philanthropy? Construct ethical arguments supporting the positions (a) that the business sector has an intrinsic responsibility to support philanthropy strongly and (b) that philanthropy is not the responsibility of business. Which side of this debate is strongest?

4. Do you see any ethical concerns with the support and cooperation that government gives to charities? For instance, is the government favoring some charities more than others? Is the government entangling itself with religion? By supporting nonprofits in their charitable activities, does the government take money away from programs that would create systemic solutions based on justice?

5. Some have criticized service trips to foreign countries as "voluntourism." What are the ethical arguments in favor of such trips and against them? Which side of the debate do you support, and why?

6. Does it make sense for a young person to pursue a career in the nonprofit sector? What are the downsides and sacrifices? Can one have a "philanthropic career" in a for-profit business setting? Could the philanthropic and business sectors do anything to make philanthropic careers more available and more enticing?

## Recommendations for Further Reading

Bornstein, David, and Susan Davis. *Social Entrepreneurship: What Everyone Needs to Know*. New York: Oxford University Press, 2010.

A readable primer, in a question-and-answer format, on social entrepreneurship, which is the process of working for social change through innovative nonprofits and socially responsible businesses.

Boyle, Greg. *Tattoos on the Heart: The Power of Boundless Compassion*. New York: Free Press, 2010.

An inspiring memoir of a Catholic priest who works for charity and justice with Latino youth and former gang members in East Los Angeles. Together they have started several local businesses called "Homeboy Industries." Boyle focuses on the spiritual purpose that animates his service and how much his character has grown from his relationships with the youth.

Brigham, Erin. *See, Judge, Act: Catholic Social Teaching and Service Learning*. Winona, MN: Anselm Academic, 2013.

A textbook designed for use in service-learning courses with a theological focus. Applies a critical methodology of social analysis and ethical reflection to the types of service-learning experiences students typically encounter.

Kass, Amy A., ed. *Giving Well and Doing Good: Readings for Thoughtful Philanthropists.* Bloomington, IN: Indiana University Press, 2008.

An anthology of short readings to spur reflection on various aspects of philanthropy. Texts include the Bible and other religious sources, philosophy, poetry, short stories, history, and contemporary nonfiction.

Kristof, Nicholas D., and Cheryl WuDunn. *A Path Appears: Transforming Lives, Creating Opportunity.* New York: Knopf, 2014.

Discusses trends in anti-poverty philanthropy and how it is becoming more data-driven, entrepreneurial, and collaborative. Includes a list of many organizations engaged in public health, education, and economic development.

Payton, Robert L., and Michael P. Moody. *Understanding Philanthropy: Its Meaning and Mission.* Bloomington, IN: University of Indiana Press, 2008.

An excellent starting point for the academic study of philanthropy. Describes characteristics of the philanthropic sector and explores the ethical and civic importance of philanthropy.

Ziolkowski, Jim, with James S. Hirsch. *Walk in Their Shoes: Can One Person Change the World?* New York: Simon & Schuster, 2013.

The story of buildOn—a charity that builds schools in developing countries and involves American at-risk youth in service programs—and of its founder, Jim Ziolkowski.

## Websites for news, opinion, and research on philanthropy and social change:

A Path Appears. *http://apathappears.org.*

Charity Navigator. *http://www.charitynavigator.org.*

Chronicle of Philanthropy. *https://philanthropy.com.*

GiveWell. *http://www.givewell.org.*

Lilly Family School of Philanthropy at Indiana University–Purdue University Indianapolis. *https://philanthropy.iupui.edu.*

New Internationalist. *http://newint.org.*

Nonprofit Quarterly. *http://nonprofitquarterly.org.*

Philanthropy Journal. *http://www.philanthropyjournal.org.*

Philanthropy Roundtable. *http://www.philanthropyroundtable.org.*

Sojourners. *https://sojo.net.*

Stanford Social Innovation Review. *http://ssir.org.*

# Index

Note: An f, s or t following a page number indicates a figure, sidebar or table, respectively.